AF323397

Flying Dragons, Flowing Streams

Flying Dragons, Flowing Streams

Music in the Life of San Francisco's Chinese

RONALD RIDDLE

FOREWORD BY
H. M. LAI

CONTRIBUTIONS IN INTERCULTURAL
AND COMPARATIVE STUDIES, NUMBER 7

GREENWOOD PRESS
WESTPORT, CONNECTICUT · LONDON, ENGLAND

Library of Congress Cataloging in Publication Data

Riddle, Ronald.
  Flying Dragons, flowing streams.

  (Contributions in intercultural and comparative
studies, ISSN 0147-1031 ; no. 7)
  Bibliography: p.
  Includes Index.
  `1. Chinese Americans—California—San Francisco—
Music—History and criticism. 2. Music—California—
San Francisco—History and criticism. 3. Music—China—
History and criticism. 4. San Francisco (Calif.)—Social
life and customs. I. Title. II. Series.
ML200.8.S2R5 1983 781-7'2951079461 82-12005
ISBN 0-313-23682-8 (lib. bdg.)

Library of Congress Catalog Card Number: 82-12005
ISBN: 0-313-23682-8
ISSN: 0147-1031

First published in 1983

Greenwood Press
A division of Congressional Information Service, Inc.
88 Post Road West
Westport, Connecticut 06881

Printed in the United States of America

10 9 8 7 6 5 4 3 2 1

Copyright Acknowledgments

Grateful acknowledgment is given for permission to use excerpts

From pp. 141, 215–17, FIFTH CHINESE DAUGHTER by Jade Snow Wong.
Copyright © 1950 by Jade Snow Wong. Reprinted by permission of Harper & Row,
Publishers, Inc., and Curtis Brown, Ltd.

From pp. 223–59, ''Music Clubs and Ensembles in San Francisco's Chinese Community,'' by Ronald Riddle, in EIGHT URBAN MUSICAL CULTURES: TRADI-
TION AND CHANGE, ed. Bruno Nettl (Urbana, University of Illinois Press,
1978). Copyright © 1978 by the Board of Trustees of the University of Illinois.

Every reasonable effort has been made to trace the owners of copyright materials
used in this book, but in some cases this has proven impossible. The publisher will be
glad to receive information leading to more complete acknowledgment in subsequent printings of this book and in the meantime extends its apologies for any
omissions.

TO
MABEL L. QUON

Contents

Foreword

When Chinese pioneers first left their native Pearl River delta region to establish a Chinese American community in California during the mid-nineteenth century, they also brought along a number of elements of Chinese culture. One of these, the music theater, was soon established in the New World, sped somewhat by events in their native Guangdong where, concurrently with the Taiping Rebellion, Cantonese opera actor Li Wenmao had led an armed uprising against the Chinese imperial government in 1854. Because of this involvement, the authorities banned performances of the opera, and it had to lead an underground existence until 1868 when the ban was lifted. Thus, for more than a decade, the repertoire could only be staged publicly abroad where operatic troupes did not have to fear official retribution. The west coast of North America, with a large concentration of Cantonese, was one of these refuges. Here the opera became established and played a prominent role in the Gold Mountain (the Chinese term for California) musical scene.

After the first introduction of the Chinese opera to America, society in China experienced great changes. This was also reflected in its music. For example, during the first part of the twentieth century, a form of chamber music, now known as Guangdong music, developed from the music used to accompany Cantonese opera performances. Western instruments such as the violin and saxophone were introduced into Cantonese musical ensembles. Chinese musical compositions began to adopt some Western techniques. Arrangements of classical and folk instrumental orchestral compositions, as well as popular songs and music, also became popular. In parallel to these developments, the Cantonese opera, which during the nineteenth century was very similar to the Peking opera in style, evolved into one which has strong regional characteristics and uses vernacular Cantonese. All these changes in the mother country were reflected in the music and music theater activities among the Chinese of America, although changes in the New World usually lagged behind the mother country by a few years, and when introduced, were selectively accepted and adapted to local conditions.

Being a small ethnic minority in Western society, Chinese Americans were also greatly influenced by the Western musical tradition. During the nineteenth century, the chief instigators of these changes were the Protestant missionaries with their church hymnals. With increasing Americanization during the first part of the twentieth century, many, especially the younger generation, forsook the music traditions of their immigrant forebears for the popular and symphonic music, brass bands, and dance orchestras of the West.

Thus both the Chinese and Western traditions played significant roles in shaping the course of development of Chinese American musical life. For the most part, these two musical cultures coexisted side by side in the Chinese American community.

In the past, there has been little or no scholarly study of this interesting sector of Chinese American culture. Hence Dr. Riddle's research is a pioneer effort. His work presents insights which have been gained through personal experiences and observations, and provides rare opportunities for the reader to glimpse the Chinese American musical world. It is also a timely study, since Chinese American society is now undergoing rapid changes and cultural institutions existing today may disappear or may exist in the future only in greatly modified forms. For these reasons, Dr. Riddle's study is a meaningful analysis of the historical development and current status of Chinese American musical life which should be of interest to musicologists, to students of Chinese American history and society, and to general readers interested in the development of a fascinating facet of one of the components making up the mosaic of America's multi-ethnic, pluralistic society.

H.M. Lai

Preface

What follows is a social history. It offers a beginning toward understanding the musical culture of America's Chinese, through an examination of the musical life of their oldest and largest community. It is only in recent years that the musics of American urban minority groups have engaged the research attention of ethnomusicologists. Investigation in this area has been antedated by a half century of research on the music and musicians of one specific urban musical culture, that of black Americans, particularly as regards jazz. But other minority groups in cities have had to wait until the 1960s, for the most part, for scholarly attention to their music and its role. Even today the material that has seen print consists of only a handful of articles, plus several song collections, mainly of European folk musics in American cities.[1]

There is no question as to the usefulness of such literature, scant as it is, in the understanding of American music as a whole; but it provides little in the way of a precedent or model for the investigation of the musical culture of America's urban Chinese. These quiet dwellers in cities-within-cities, virtually walled off from the rest of American society in past decades, have inhabited this soil in sizable numbers since the 1850s—thus long predating the large-scale immigration of other minority groups whose musical retentions and syncretisms have been more extensively studied.

Despite their long history on these shores, the Chinese are only recent arrivals with respect to the perceivable effect that American urban life has had on their musical culture. The apparent paradox of long-time settlement and short-time musical change among the Chinese is explained in part by the profound differences between Western and Far Eastern conceptions of music and the barriers to stylistic interpenetration that result from highly disparate notions of melody, texture, rhythm, and tone color. But this is only part of the story, and perhaps a smaller part. What has made America's Chinese unique among all immigrant groups of large population has been this group's tendency, until recent years, to regard its American experience as temporary—as a sojourn rather than a settlement. Thus few cultural developments have taken place other than those that have been carried over from the homeland. In an all-male society of laboring sojourners, there is no passing of culture traits from generation to generation on American soil, simply because there *is* no "generation to generation," only arrivals and departures. Exceptions exist to this disjunctive pattern—and certainly it does not hold true in the present day—but generational discontinuity has kept America's Chinese music in a corner by itself throughout most of its history. I have accordingly emphasized this feature of Chinatown's music in my introductory and concluding chapters, and it is naturally intrinsic elsewhere in the study as well.

I should like to express my gratitude to a number of people who have given me inspiration and help in the preparation of this study.

The encouragement and useful suggestions of Bruno Nettl have been invaluable every step of the way. Two other University of Illinois faculty members have offered helpful insights to me: musicologist Alexander L. Ringer and anthropologist Lawrence W. Crissmann. Charles Hamm of Dartmouth College was the first to whom I mentioned the idea of this project, and I have enjoyed his support and sympathy from the beginning.

Much of the historical research in this study was carried out in the libraries of the University of California, Berkeley. I am particularly grateful for help from the staffs of the Bancroft Library and the university's Newspaper Library. Other assistance was genially given at the California State Library in Sacramento. At the San Francisco Public Library I have benefited from the kind and expert suggestions of Gladys Hansen, Special Collections Librarian. I also wish to acknowledge the assistance of Patricia Bryant, reference librarian of my own institution, New College of the University of South Florida. Maria Russin Ivancin, my research assistant at New College, gave invaluable help as the manuscript neared completion.

Much of the information in this study comes from field work in San Francisco's present-day Chinese community. Literally hundreds of individuals have aided me in this search. My largest debt and warmest thanks are to Mabel L. Quon, of the Nam Chung Musical Society, who, over many years, has provided valuable information and has helped open many doors to me for further field research. It is to her that this book is dedicated. She has also read portions of this study and given numerous useful suggestions. Others who have read and generously offered comments on parts of the manuscript have been Him Mark Lai, Lim Lai, and James P. Wong.

Among the informants who have graciously responded to my questions have been: William Au, Bruce Bartholomew, Therese Bartholomew, Mary Chan, Joyce Cheng, Larry Cheung, Sherlyn Chew, Thomas Chinn, Lambert Choy, Anthony Dong, Chung Fong, Herbert Fong, Harry Ho, David Huang, Kenneth Joe, Munwu Chau King, S. T. Kwan, Marks Lamm, Benjamin Lau, C. C. Lee, Ning Lee, Ting Lee, David Ming-yueh Liang, Lawrence P. L. Liu, Reno Liu (Gil Yiu-nui), Wilma Pang, C. Y. Peng, Yim T. Quan, Thomas Tong, Betty Wong, Ernest Wong, Shirley Wong, Sidney Wong, Victor Wong, William D. Y. Wu, Winston Wu, Mina E. Yee, Richard Yee, and Samuel Yuen. I am deeply grateful for the kindness of these and the many others not listed. Whatever merits lie in this study's coverage of recent history are largely the result of their help. For deficiencies and misinterpretations, however, I claim full responsibility.

Special thanks are due my editor, Ann Pescatello, who has helpfully stimulated both my thinking and my pace of activity as the study grew into book form.

Lastly, my deep appreciation goes to Anna and Maynard Briggs, my parents, who have been unfailingly helpful and encouraging throughout this project.

A note on romanization: Transliterations into English will be found in several varieties. For Cantonese proper names, I have simply used the existing spellings which have found currency among Chinese in the United States. I have used the Wade-Giles romanization for words in the Northern (Mandarin) dialect. Though the Wade-Giles system is rapidly being superseded by the pīnyīn system of transliteration, I have retained the former system both because of its continuing wide acceptance and because it appears with some frequency in the quoted sources in historical parts of the book, and I should like to maintain a fairly consistent romanization of at least Mandarin—though no entirely consistent method of romanizing Cantonese has ever been successfully adopted.

NOTE

1. Samuel G. Armistead and Joseph H. Silverman, "Hispanic Balladry among the Sephardic Jews of the West Coast," *Western Folklore* 19 (1960), pp. 229-44; Stephen Erdely, "Folksinging of the American Hungarians in Cleveland," *Ethnomusicology* 8 (1964), pp. 14-27; Jacob A. Evanson, "Folk Songs of an Industrial City" [dealing with the music of Slovaks in Pittsburgh], in George Korson, ed., *Pennsylvania Songs and Legends* (Philadelphia, University of Pennsylvania Press, 1949); Bruno Nettl, "Preliminary Remarks on Urban Folk Music in Detroit," *Western Folklore* 16 (1957), pp. 37-42; Harriet Pawlowska, *Merrily We Sing, 105 Polish Folk Songs* (Detroit, Wayne State University Press, 1961); Shulamith Rybak, "Puerto Rican Children's Songs in New York," *Midwest Folklore* 8 (1958), pp. 5-20. The progress of urban ethnomusicology in general can be seen in the contributions to the recent volume, *Eight Urban Musical Cultures*, ed. Bruno Nettl (Urbana, University of Illinois Press, 1978).

Flying Dragons, Flowing Streams

Introduction

THE SETTING

Virtually since its founding, San Francisco has contained a large and significant community of Chinese. Today's Chinatown—whose core comprises about fifteen square blocks in the heart of the city—is a unique ethnic enclave among cities of the Western world. It is the largest concentrated settlement of Chinese outside of Asia, and it has occupied the same geographical location since the first Chinese sojourners were attracted by the discovery of gold in California in 1848.

Once described by Kipling as "a corner of Canton," San Francisco's Chinatown, like most communities of overseas Chinese, is populated almost entirely by immigrants from the southern province of Kwangtung or their descendants; and their dialects and life-patterns reflect strongly those of the province's hundreds of villages or of the capital—Canton—itself. The circumstance for the original surge of Chinese immigration in the 1840s and 1850s was a fortuitous combination of disaster and revolution at home combined with the spectacular attraction of riches to be mined in the golden hills beyond the sea.

Southern China was ripe for diaspora. The urge to emigrate was motivated in large part by social tumult and economic uncertainties

in the homeland. The ruling Manchu dynasty had decayed and declined, and by the middle of the nineteenth century had become notably corrupt and unjust in its administration. The popular unrest
that resulted from misgovernment was exacerbated by an ever-di-
minishing availability of land, owing to population increases, and a
devastating cycle of flood, famine, and drought. The economy was
racked by inflation, stemming from the Opium War; and native
handicraft industries suffered severely from the growing importation of Western goods. The T'ai-ping Rebellion of 1851–1864
brought havoc to all China; and Kwangtung endured a decade of
related uprisings in the Pearl River Delta region instigated by the
Triad Societies and a dozen years of warfare between Cantonese
and Hakka elements, starting in 1856.[1] For thousands of men in the
area of the Pearl River Delta, economic dislocations and distress
left little choice but to seek work outside of China and to support
their families from abroad for extended periods. Many took passage to Southeast Asia, Australia, South America, and the West In-
dies.

When news of California's gold discovery reached Canton in
1848, America became a prime destination. From the ports of Canton, Hong Kong, and Macao, an ever-increasing stream of job
seekers from the small farms and villages of Kwangtung boarded
ships for San Francisco. Over 500 men left Hong Kong on forty-
four vessels in 1850. By the end of the following year it was estimated that there were twenty-five thousand Chinese in California engaged in mining or manual labor.[2] Their numbers would continue
to increase throughout the nineteenth century, to a peak in 1890 of
some 107,488 Chinese officially accounted for in America, most of
them on the West Coast, after which a forty-year decline would result from U.S. legislation excluding Chinese immigration. From
1882, when the First Exclusion Law was passed, until Exclusion Repeal in 1943, immigration from China was negligible. But from the
1940s to the present day, new waves of immigration have re-infused
American Chinese communities with first-generation Chinese.[3]

Chinese immigration in the nineteenth century was of a special
character. The new population was almost totally male, and its individuals had no intention of settling permanently outside of
China.

Of the Chinese who came to California at least one-half were married and expected not merely to make their personal fortune but to support a family at home. . . . At this period there was so strong a sentiment in China against any respectable woman leaving home even with her husband that very few went to America. . . . The few who went to California were for the most part . . . women of the working class or women of disreputable character.[4]

Initially, a lack of women was by no means limited to the Chinese community, as the general population of San Francisco and the Gold Rush country was preponderantly male in the 1840s and 1850s, when the sojourning mentality was the rule rather than the exception. However, while San Francisco's sex ratio gradually became normalized among the white community, Chinatown continued throughout the nineteenth century and well into the twentieth to exist as a man's society, its sparse female population generally consisting of either the wives of affluent merchants or young women imported for prostitution and entertainment.

By 1890 there were nearly twenty-seven Chinese men for every Chinese woman in the United States. In the twentieth century this disparity declined only slowly, largely through the birth of Chinese females in this country, as immigration of women was exceedingly rare (almost nonexistent between 1924 and 1943, when even Chinese wives of American citizens were excluded from entry).[5] As late as 1930 the male majority was nearly four to one. Only with the admission of women through the War Brides Act of 1945 and subsequent legislation to liberalize immigration has Chinese society moved toward sexual parity, though men still significantly outnumber women,[6] and a large "bachelor society" continues to exist today among elderly men in Chinatown who never married or were unable to return to families and children in China.[7]

The lack of Chinese women and the immigrants' penchant for return to their homeland has made for a distinctive generational discontinuity in Chinatown. Prior to recent decades, the bulk of the Chinese population considered California as only a temporary home. Even those who stayed for long periods or for life often continued to maintain their families in China, returning to them only for brief visits. Gradually, many Chinese did choose to settle here permanently with families, and very few of today's American Chinese envision a retirement to the homeland. Yet it took eighty years for a significant second generation to emerge in Chinatown; and even today, one finds that most San Francisco Chinese are first or second generation, despite the existence of a Chinese community here for over a century and a quarter.

The first Chinese in California are said to have landed in San Francisco on 2 February 1848—two men and a woman brought by the merchant Charles V. Gillespie. While this date, cited by H. H. Bancroft,[8] lacks convincing documentation, one may note an editorial in the San Francisco *Star* several months later which mentions the presence of "two or three 'celestials' in San Francisco who found ready employment."[9] Soon thereafter, immigration began on a mass scale. In the decade of 1849–1859 an average of 7,100 Chinese disembarked each year and an average of 2,660 returned to China,[10] making for a substantial turnover but a burgeoning growth nonetheless, with the Chinese population in California reaching the number of 22,385—or 19 percent of the state's total population—in 1860.[11]

The attitude of other Californians toward the Chinese in the 1850s was essentially favorable:

In the first few years the Chinaman was welcomed, praised, and considered almost indispensable; for in those days race antipathy was subordinated to industrial necessity, and in a heterogeneous community where every Caucasian expected to be a miner or a speculator, the reticent, industrious, adaptable Chinese could find room and something more than toleration.[12]

The generally friendly attitude toward the new arrivals can be noted in an announcement in the daily *Alta California* of 12 May 1852 that

Quite a large number of the Celestials have arrived among us of late, enticed thither by the golden romance that has filled the world. Scarcely a ship arrives that does not bring an increase to this worthy integer of our population. The China boys will yet vote at the same polls, study at the same schools and bow at the same altar as our own countrymen.

As general laborers, carpenters, and cooks, the Chinese were highly valued. Their willingness to do domestic chores and other

jobs scorned by the white man curried much favor in a society lacking women and an established laboring class. As miners they were
unaggressive and noncompetitive with the whites, often devoting
their energies to claims already abandoned and achieving modest
successes by dint of patience and long hard work. Further, they
were respected for their quiet dignity and general tendency to mind
their own business and stay out of trouble. "In light of the fifty
years of intolerance that followed," comments Mary Coolidge,

the cordiality with which the Chinese were welcomed by the first pioneers is
almost incredible. It finds explanation in the necessities and contradictions
of the time. In San Francisco the services of the Chinese were indispensable
to decent living, and there were few other immigrants who would conde-
scend to menial services or even to manual labor. The city itself had not yet
become the prey of politicians and of so-called labor parties; and . . . the
predatory hoodlum had not yet been evolved.[13]

Even in this "honeymoon" period of the 1850s, however, early
winds of race antipathy and political Know-Nothingism were felt
by the Chinese, and discriminatory taxes and regulations were leveled against them.[14] In the 1860s, anti-Chinese feelings increased
among many elements of society—particularly among miners and
kindred laborers who saw the Chinese as an economic threat—as
did the flow of bills restricting and taxing Chinese. Yet the full
force of anti-Chinese sentiment was not to be felt until the 1870s.
The end of the preceding decade saw the completion of the transcontinental railroad—thus throwing many thousands of Chinese laborers out of work—and the petering out of mining resources. Unemployment mounted among Californians, and the economic
slump was aggravated by a flow of new settlers from America's
Eastern Seaboard, seeking to escape the economic depression on
that coast. Chinese became increasingly subject to verbal and physical abuse on the streets and in the countryside, as white miners, laborers, and farmers alike rallied to the political cry "The Chinese
Must Go!" Now vilified for his alien demeanor and dress, his "pa-
ganism," and a variety of fantasized immoral, unsanitary, and
treacherous ways, the hard-working Chinese became essentially a
victim of his virtues. The very attributes of industriousness, frugality, and self restraint that had been admired by the welcomers of

the 1850s became a collective thorn in the side of the white unemployed. A decade of outrages and violence against the Chinese was climaxed by the passage of the federal Exclusion Act of 1882, which would effectively cut off Chinese immigration for more than sixty years to come.

The remaining years of the nineteenth century were to see a precipitous decline in America's Chinese population, as returnees to China were not replaced. The era also saw a dispersal of Chinese from California to other states in which job opportunities and a less antagonistic racial climate were to be found.

San Francisco's once-bustling Chinese community diminished in population in the 1890s, and the neighborhood was virtually wiped out by the earthquake and fire of 1906. Rebuilt only a few years later on the same site, Chinatown continued as a tourist attraction and supported a relatively small Chinese community which continued to decline in population until the 1930s, when a small increase in numbers finally began to be felt—the belated emergence of a second-generation population. In general, the sealing off of Chinatown from further immigration in the twentieth century served to bring about a gradual Americanization of many of its citizens,[15] particularly among the American-born, though restrictive covenants and various legal constraints served to keep most Chinese confined to residence in the ghetto, whatever degree of success and prosperity they might otherwise achieve.

With the repeal of Exclusion Laws in 1943 and subsequent liberalizations in immigration policies, the Chinese population of the United States shot up from 77,504 in 1950 and reached 481,583 in the 1970 Census.[16] San Francisco's Chinese population rose correspondingly in this period from 17,782 in 1940 to around 80,000 in 1975.[17] About half of today's San Francisco Chinese live in areas outside of Chinatown itself, as families have grown more affluent and barriers to residential neighborhoods have been lifted. The enclave of Chinatown remains the first home for immigrants, and the large majority of its population is foreign born, though the figure is about 50 percent for San Francisco's Chinese community as a whole.

Throughout its history, Chinatown, like other overseas Chinese communities, has had an "extraterritorial" quality that has set it

off from other ethnic neighborhoods and the city as a whole. From
its earliest years, the Chinese community—through an elaborate
web of interconnecting organizations[18]—has managed to settle its
own affairs and handle its own problems. Cantonese[19] remains the
prevailing spoken language, and the community's social, cultural,
and gastronomic needs are largely met within its borders. Without
the new influx of immigrants after 1943, San Francisco's Chinatown might well have become a thing of the past, as has been the
pattern in such western cities as Butte, Boise, and Denver.[20] Such
was predicted by sociologist Rose Hum Lee in 1949, before substantial change had been brought about by the new immigration.
Betty Lee Sung asks:

Does the demolition or relocation of these Chinatowns [Honolulu, Philadelphia, Pittsburgh, Los Angeles] confirm Professor Lee's assertion that
Chinatowns will soon be relegated to the pages of history? The answer
would be yes if no large influx of new arrivals replaced the earlier generations who have outgrown the transitional stage. However, [from 1957 to
1967] over 40,000 Chinese have entered the country. These new immigrants
must run the course of their own process of accommodation. They are re-
placing the former inhabitants of Chinatown and revitalizing it. . . .[21]

There is certainly no demise in sight for San Francisco's thriving
and lively Chinatown. The generational discontinuity that resulted
from earlier immigrants' eventual return to their homeland has
now ceased. Chinatown continues to be the first stop for the South
China immigrant, but eventual financial success fulfills the aspira-
tion to move not back to China (with rare exceptions) but simply
out of the inner city itself, typically to San Francisco's suburban-
esque outlying residential neighborhoods—especially the Richmond and Sunset districts, a few blocks closer to China perhaps,
but more significantly a quiet and verdant retreat toward the ocean
and away from the noise, sprawl, and increasing street crime that
characterize today's Chinatown.

Chinatown's present community has a population density that is
exceeded only by areas of Manhattan Island. Its ostensible prosperity hides an "invisible" poverty that is astonishing: 41 percent of its
population falls below the poverty level by federal standards, and it
is plagued by severe problems of health and housing.[22] Many of

these problems are a reflection of Chinatown's population of elderly bachelors and of its recent immigrants; both groups are typically poor, shabbily housed, and in need of health care. In recent years, federally aided programs to improve housing, health, and education in Chinatown have helped to meet these problems and have altered somewhat the traditional pattern of self-sufficiency within the community.

A salient feature of today's Chinatown is its abundance of young people, as over 50 percent of the community's population is twenty-one years of age or under.[23] Since the early 1960s, a dramatic upsurge has been seen in juvenile delinquency. The activities of teenage gangs in crimes of violence is seen as a direct result of the frustrations suffered by youths who are brought here from Hong Kong while in their teens. Past the age limit for English-language instruction in the public schools, the youthful immigrants are thus hobbled from finding jobs or furthering their education. The startling rise in criminal activity in the Chinatown since the 1960s has considerably changed the neighborhood's traditional image of an area free of juvenile crime, in which young people exhibited the results of family discipline and respect for authority.[24]

It is among the young that another feature of today's Chinatown is most strongly exhibited: an increasing interest in the cultural and political values of the People's Republic of China. Numerous young people's groups involve themselves in the study of Mainland China movements, bringing about a change in the conservative and Kuomintang-oriented climate that pervaded Chinatown in past decades. Since Richard Nixon's visit to Peking in 1970 and the subsequent American rapprochement with the People's Republic, even Chinatown's older citizens have taken a renewed interest in their ancestral homeland, and not a few have made visits to the People's Republic to seek out relatives and to see the results of changes in China since 1949.[25]

CHINATOWN'S MUSICAL CULTURE

Though a variety of musics and musical activities has characterized San Francisco's Chinese community over the past 130 years, two large areas of activity have predominated: the Chinese theater—synonymous throughout this book with professional Cantonese opera—and amateur music clubs and ensembles. The professional theater was the prime source of musical life in the nineteenth century. In subsequent years it has undergone a gradual decline, finally ceasing as a full-time institution in the mid-1940s and reappearing only for brief periods in the years since. Music clubs and amateur ensembles began their growth early in the present century, with the founding of the Cathay Club in 1911, and have become the focus of Chinatown's musical life, particularly over the past thirty years. The history of San Francisco's Chinese theater and the rise and present-day activities of clubs and amateur musicians accordingly dominate the study to follow.

It may be noted that no significant professional class of musicians has ever emerged from Chinatown's milieu, though occasional individuals have become noted for their musical ability. While music has been part of the community's life from the beginning, full-time careers in that area have never been seriously cultivated. Virtually the only career musicians of consequence in Chinatown have been the performers in the Chinese theater, who (with rare exceptions) have always been only temporary residents, as their lives are inherently peripatetic, and San Francisco is only one of many way-stations in their theatrical itinerary. In general, the lack of interest in music as a career field (as well as its seemingly ironic popularity as an amateur pursuit) may be seen to stem in part from the somewhat ambivalent traditional Chinese attitude toward music: on the one hand, the activity is regarded as a noble and elevating pursuit, contributing to the harmony of the state and worthy of a gentleman's cultivation, along with poetry, calligraphy, and other artistic pastimes. On the other hand, music as a profession is anathema to the traditional Chinese way of life. Professional musicians have been classed with such transient folk as actors, foot-soldiers, beggars, prostitutes, and others who inhabit a rank of traditional Chinese society that is so low as to be virtually outside the pale.

Together with this general distaste for music as a career field is the fact that Chinatown, as previously pointed out, is still largely a first- and second-generation community, and career employment in the arts is not characteristically sought by the early generations of an upwardly mobile immigrant community. Young Chinese—

with their parents' blessing—typically aspire to the professions, particularly medicine and engineering (law, with its demands for fluency in English, is a less frequent choice), with their promise of good income combined with relative independence from the employment whims of the prevailing white culture.

Essentially, music and music-drama are to be enjoyed as recreation, whether passively (at the theater) or actively (at the music club), and as a traditional accompaniment to rites of passage and holiday celebrations. As such, it contributes much to the cultural life of the Chinese community but never becomes an overriding concern. To outside observers, the community might seem scarcely to have a musical culture at all, as overt musical activity is only sporadically in evidence. But it is characteristic of Chinatown to keep its music-making pretty much to itself and not to take it too seriously. Earning a living, getting an education, and simply surviving are, after all, far greater concerns in a society whose members still find themselves somewhat short of first-class citizenship. Along the way, one finds time for singing and playing in any case; and music flourishes behind the doors of club rooms and cellars and sometimes in the theater or at the picnic ground. It is the very elusiveness of music in Chinatown that has accounted in part for its attraction to the present writer, though its beauty far overshadows the challenge it poses for scholarly detective work. I have sought to make the phenomenon less elusive through description and an exploration of its functions, from the early 1850s to the present day. In the following pages I hope to give some illumination to an aspect of the cultural life of America's Chinese that has seldom been emphasized and which has gone almost entirely neglected in the literature on music in America.

NOTES

1. The Triad Societies were secret anti-Manchu groups and the ancestors of the tongs in American Chinese communities. See Barbara E. Ward, "Chinese Secret Societies," in *Secret Societies*, ed. Norman MacKenzie (London, Aldus Books, 1967), pp. 174–203.

2. Mary Roberts Coolidge, *Chinese Immigration* (New York, Henry Holt, 1909), p. 17.

3. U.S. Census Bureau figure, quoted in Thomas W. Chinn, H. Mark Lai, and Philip P. Choy, eds. *A History of the Chinese in California: A Syllabus* (San Francisco, Chinese Historical Society of America, 1969), p. 19.

4. Coolidge, p. 20.

5. William L. Tung, *The Chinese in America, 1820–1973* (Dobbs Ferry, N.Y., Oceana, 1974), p. 27.

6. The ratio stood at 129.8 in California in 1967. Betty Lee Sung, *Mountain of Gold: The Story of the Chinese in America* (New York, Macmillan, 1967), p. 116.

7. Figures on ratios from Sung, pp. 116–17. Chinatown's present "bachelor society" is described in Victor G. Nee and Brett de Bary Nee, *Longtime Californ': A Documentary Study of an American Chinatown* (New York, Pantheon, 1972), pp. 13–122.

8. *History of California*, 6 vols. (San Francisco, History Co., 1884–90), vol. 6, p. 83.

9. 1 April 1848. Other accounts, some semi-legendary, date the earliest Chinese arrivals on the West Coast as early as A.D. 499. See G. F. Hudson, *Europe and China* (London, 1931), p. 301; Fang Hao, *History of Communication Between China and the West (Chung Hsi Chiao-tung Shih* (in Chinese), 3 vols. (Taipei, 1955), vol. 3, pp. 262–63; Homer H. Dubs and Robert S. Smith, "Chinese in Mexico City in 1635," *Far Eastern Quarterly* 1 (1942), pp. 387–89.

10. The years 1852 and 1854 together account for almost half of the total arrivals of 71,137—the number fluctuating between 3,000 and 6,000 in the other years. Figures derived from statistics in O. Gibson, *The Chinese in America* (Cincinnati, 1877), pp. 19–20, and Elmer C. Sandmeyer, *The Anti-Chinese Movement in California* (Urbana, University of Illinois Press, 1939), pp. 19–20. See also Ellen Rawson Wood, "California and the Chinese: The First Decade" (M.A. thesis, University of California, Berkeley, 1961), p. 16.

11. Wood, p. 17.

12. Coolidge, p. 21.

13. Ibid, p. 25.

14. Such as the 1853 "foreign miners' tax" of $4.00 a month which in large effect was a tax on the Chinese, who paid 85 percent of this revenue. The tax was later declared unconstitutional, but the money was never refunded. Coolidge, pp. 33–36.

15. See, e.g., "Flappers of Chinatown," *New York Times Magazine*, 27 May 1923, p. 12; Frank J. Taylor, "San Francisco's New Chinese City," *Travel* 52 (March 1929), pp. 18–21, 54.

16. 1940 and 1950 figures from the 1962 *World Almanac*; 1970 figure from United States Bureau of the Census (1970 Census of Population, Subject Reports), *Japanese, Chinese, and Filipinos in the United States* (1973), p. 60. The earlier two figures do not include Alaska and Hawaii.

17. 1940 figure from Lim P. Lee, Albert Lim, and H.K. Wong, co-chairmen, *Report of the San Francisco Chinese Community Citizens' Survey and Fact Finding Committee*, abridged ed. (San Francisco, H. J. Carle, 1969), p. 6. 1975 figure is my own estimate. Cf. Nee and Nee, p. xxii.

18. See below, pp. 191–93.

19. The word is used loosely to encompass several different but related dialects from Kwangtung province, the most widespread in San Francisco being Toishanese, the main tongue of the Chinese in the United States. See Sung, p. 19.

20. In 1940 Rose Hum Lee found twenty-eight cities with some area called Chinatown. (*The Chinese in the United States of America*, Hong Kong, Hong Kong University Press, 1960, pp. 65–66.) By 1966, Peter Sih, in another survey, could find only sixteen. (Sung, p. 144.)

21. Sung, p. 145.

22. Nee and Nee, p. xxii.

23. Lee, Lim, and Wong, p. 134.

24. See below, p. 221.

25. See, for example, Shirley Sun, "Chinatown: The East Wind is Blowing," *California Living* (San Francisco *Chronicle* magazine section), 8 May 1973, pp. 10–12.

Part I

THE NINETEENTH CENTURY

1

Chinese Theater: The Early Years (1852–1869)

Circumstances were favorable in several respects for the arrival of the first Chinese theatrical company in San Francisco in 1852. The Chinese population of California had swelled in a few years to an estimated twenty-five thousand.[1] Although the majority of Chinese worked in the mines to the north, the city's resident contingent of Chinese was constantly augmented by others newly arriving, awaiting departure, or visiting from the Gold Rush hinterlands. Beyond the bustling fan-tan tables of Chinatown's gambling houses, there was little organized entertainment available for the Chinese prior to the importation of Cantonese opera.

Interest in the arrival of Chinese theater was not confined to the Chinese quarter, however. The Gold Rush had transformed San Francisco from little more than a village to a thriving city of some forty-two thousand by 1852,[2] and entertainment was in great demand. Preceded by circus performances and amateur entertainments, the first professional company of Western drama had arrived in San Francisco from Australia in 1850, and the city experienced its first full-length Western opera the following year.[3] In 1852, as during decades to come, the Chinese opera theater was to find much patronage from curious and entertainment-starved occidentals as well as the Chinese.

On the night of 18 October 1852, San Francisco saw its first Chinese opera, presented by the Hong Took Tong ("Associated Theatrical Benefit Society"), a company that had recently arrived from Canton with 123 performers.[4] Brought to America by Chinese impresarios, the company was financed by a group of merchants in Canton, who reportedly advanced some two thousand pounds for passage money and expenses. Members of the troupe were also shareholders in the venture.[5] The company gave performances for five months, opening at the American Theater for a week's run, then performing continuously at a theater of their own construction from December till March of the following year.

For their opening-night program, the Hong Took Tong advertised "the beautiful spectacle of THE EIGHT GENII offering their congratulations to the High Ruler Yuk Hwang, on his Birthday." Parts 2 and 3 bore the lengthy titles, "Too Tsia made High Minister by the six States" and "Parting at the Bridge of Parkew of Kwan Wanchang and Tsow Tsow," the whole show to be concluded with "THE DEFEATED REVENGE." Tickets were initially priced at six dollars for a private box, four dollars for dress circle and parquette, and respectively three and two dollars for the pit and gallery.[6] Prices were dropped after only two nights, however, which suggests that the novelty was beginning to wear thin. A mere dollar would now admit the patron to dress circle, pit, or gallery. Other changes bolstered the price-cutting effort to bring in more non-Chinese customers. Advertisements ceased to stress the drama itself, noting rather that the show featured "feats of skill, vaulting, tumbling and dramatic performance, which we hope will prove to our friends and the public generally the most novel and interesting entertainment of the season." Further, performances would now open with a play by "the American company," as for instance a presentation of "MY NEIGHBOR'S WIFE" to preface the Hong Took Tong's third night.

The company's opening performance had drawn a full house, including a reviewer from the daily *Alta California*, who found much of interest to comment upon. The altered stage set-up was itself novel to behold. The wings had been removed, as these have no place in traditional Chinese drama; and the orchestra sat right on the stage, rather than in the pit. These dozen or so musicians lined the rear of the stage, "accompanying the whole performance through with their peculiar strains, and regaling themselves in the interval with their pipes and cigars." Since the dialogue itself was unintelligible, "the American portion of the audience had to enjoy themselves in imagining what was going on, and in admiring the stage properties and the costumes . . . some of which were really splendid." Visually, the show was an unquestioned success, as spectators watched with awe the "very agile and dextrous 'ground and lofty tumbling' " which enlivened the incomprehensible plot. On the whole, the *Alta* reviewer found the exhibition to be "a great novelty" and "well worth seeing."[7]

Another reporter found that the "ladies" in the company were "altogether the best specimens we have yet been favored with."[8] Ladies they were not, however, but specially trained male actors, as the Chinese stage—like the Elizabethan—was for men only. The beguiled reporter's delight is certainly understandable, in any case, since women—or even facsimiles thereof—were still a scarce and much-treasured sight in this raw new city of sweat, stubble, and gold dust.

The Hong Took Tong had brought with them the prefabricated framework for a new Chinese theater.[9] After their appearances at the American, the company proceeded to erect their new building on Dupont Street (the present Grant Avenue, Chinatown's main street).[10] The finished theater was "a curious pagoda-looking edifice . . . painted, outside and in, in an extraordinary manner" and large enough to seat at least a thousand.[11] The new house opened its doors on the morning of 23 December 1852 and seldom closed them for the rest of the winter. Programs ran seven days a week, morning and night.[12]

The occidental crowd delighted in the juggling, mock battles, and acrobatic feats that pervaded the operatic performances. The plots and declamation, however, continued to occasion only bewilderment. A visiting Scotsman noted that the dramatic performances themselves were kept short, mercifully so since they were "quite unintelligible to outside barbarians," but there was much to admire in the "extraordinary gorgeous dresses" of the actors. The music, by contrast, provided only discomfort: ". . . the incessant noise they made with gongs and kettledrums was so discordant and deafening that a few minutes at a time was as long as any one could stay in the place." Most praiseworthy were the exhibitions of dare-devil expertise:

The most exciting part . . . was when one man, and decidedly a man of some little nerve, made a spread eagle of himself and stood up against a door, while half-a-dozen others, at a distance of fifteen or twenty feet, pelted the door with sharp-pointed bowie-knives, putting a knife into every square inch of the door, but never touching the man. It was very pleasant to see.[13]

In late March the Hong Took Tong announced the end of its season and prepared for a tour. The building was sold at auction, and the troupe headed by steamer to New York. Disaster was to follow. The Eastern Seaboard lacked San Francisco's taste for the avant-garde, and the troupe flopped spectacularly in New York and New Jersey. Out of money and out of work, the performers languished for a time in a New York alms house and finally had to rely on charity for funds to return to China.[14]

In San Francisco, meanwhile, the ill-fated company's former theater-building was converted into a receiving station for Chinese immigrant laborers. These newcomers provided much unsolicited music for the neighborhood as well, evoking much displeasure among nearby residents, and they were unwitting pioneers in what was to become a venerable tradition of nude entertainment in San Francisco. The newspapers recorded indignant offense taken by neighbors as the immigrants took their baths in the yard, quite openly and in large numbers. Regarded as a noisy and malodorous crowd, the transients enlivened their surroundings considerably, as had the theatrical troupe that preceded them. One letter writer complained that "many a time and oft night is made hideous by their discordant revels."[15]

From the time of the Hong Took Tong's first performances, there was to be more or less continuous Chinese touring musical drama in San Francisco throughout the rest of the century. There was clearly an intense need and a profitable market for this most popular of entertainments among the Chinese. In the virtually all-male society of "Little China," as the neighborhood was called in its earliest days, the theater had no real rivals, save gambling and prostitution, for the recreation of the immigrants, restricted as they were to their sealed-off neighborhood. Besides being welcome fare for the captive audience of Chinese, moreover, the theater was a colorful and important attraction to tourists and residents alike.

Not until 1868 was another building to be erected specifically for Chinese theater in San Francisco. But there was much dramatic activity in the meantime, as the touring Chinese companies made use of occidental playhouses and various makeshift quarters. The possibility exists that a second Chinese theatrical group began operations in Chinatown even while the Hong Took Tong was still performing in its Dupont Street theater. The authors of the 1855 *Annals of San Francisco* state that "another Chinese theater" was opened in 1853, though the *Annals* may well be simply misdating the Hong Took Tong's opening performance on Dupont Street.[16] Miska Hauser, the Hungarian violin virtuoso who visited San Francisco in 1853, attended the Chinese theater on two occasions, but his comments in a letter shed little light: ". . . I saw eighty actors in glittering and expensive costumes running aimlessly about, fighting, pummeling, and shooting. That is all I can say to describe the Chinese play."[17]

In the fall of 1855 a Western playhouse metamorphosed into the Shanghai Theater, suitably decked out for Chinese opera.[18] The new enterprise survived well into the following year and attracted the attention of reporters from both the *Chronicle* and the *Alta*. The *Chronicle* writer marvels at the skill of the actors who impersonated women, stating that "those who play the female characters resemble females so much, even to their small feet and fine, long tapering fingers, that it is only on undoubted authority that we can be induced to believe it."[19] Both reporters are surprised by the bareness of the stage, the *Alta* observer noting that "there was no scenery, no drop curtain, no wings, or flies, nor any of the paraphernalia usually seen in a theatre." The same reporter's description of the music foreshadows many a tortured journalistic account to appear in the decades to come:

. . . in the rear [center stage], seated upon stools were several ordinarily apparelled "Johns," who were twanging away on some instruments, whence issued a series of discordant sounds, compared to which the mingled midnight music of forty cats, and half a dozen hand organs and hurdy-gurdies, whould have been delicious.[20]

Early Chinese theatrical troupes also staged successful runs to the north of San Francisco. Sacramento in 1855 was bemused to find a Chinese puppet show in its midst. During the celebrations of the Chinese New Year, Americans wandered into a Chinese gambling house to observe costumed "busts stuck upon sticks . . . between three and four feet in length" and to listen to the music of a Chinese orchestra, which played behind a calico screen.[21] The puppet show met with unexpected popularity.

Farther north, in Calaveras County, Chinese miners and their American colleagues were treated to a long run of a Chinese theatrical company of some thirty actors and musicians. That such excursions by troupes from San Francisco were most carefully planned can be seen in the following account:

The theatre is a frame building, one hundred feet long by forty-five wide, and thirty feet high. It is covered with canvas. It cost $1,500. All the scenery, fixtures and stage-furniture were constructed by native artisans [that is, by the Chinese themselves]. The chairs are especially of singular construction, built more with a view to their adaption for other use than for seats. The stage floor was carpeted and had no foot-lights, but the wings, on both sides of the stage, were ornamented with three large lights, burning *Chinese Oil*, on the bonfire principle, from earthen vases, suspended on iron cranes. . . . The musicians, nine in number, were in position behind the stage, close up to the drop-curtain, so that the actors were between the audience and the music. The music seems to be a series of soft, *whining* tones, varying between bad, worse and intolerable. Some of the musicians play on several instruments, and others on two instruments at the same time. The drop-curtain, side-wings and other scenery were stationary, and ornamented with tinsel, inscriptions, and other ensignia, illustrating the character of the play and announcing the *great success* of the company.[22]

Performers from southern China were well prepared for such complex ventures, having become accustomed to a nomadic life of one-night appearances in the villages and towns of Kwangtung.[23]

In December 1856 a reporter from the *Bulletin* wrote an extended review of the Chinese troupe which had moved into San Francisco's converted Adelphi Theater. Here we find one of the first attempts by a Western writer to tell objectively and sympathetically what precisely was going on. In his long description of the historical drama, the writer attempts to explain the functional duties of supernumeraries whose constant visibility has often puzzled Western viewers: "The servants, dressed as we ordinarily see Chinamen in the streets, walk about upon the stage among the richly dressed actors, as they are playing, and hand a cup of tea to this one and a sword to that one, as the directions of the play require." The stage is continually open, remarks the writer, and without a curtain. There are no wings—only two doors, one for entrance, one for departure. The seemingly incongruous bareness of stage and the resultant need for elaborate pantomime occasion much comment:

If the actor wishes to represent that he goes into a house and slams the door in another's face, a servant [one of those conventionally clad stagehands] hands him a chair; the actor takes it into the middle of the stage and slams it down on its side near the other actor's feet. The slamming actor then stands on one side of the chair, and the spectators are called upon to imagine that he is on the inside of a house. If it is wished to represent the crossing of a bridge, two tables are placed three or four feet apart and a board laid from one to the other. The actor then mounts a chair to one of the tables, walks over the board or bridge, and descends by a chair. If an actor wishes to represent himself as riding on horseback, he goes through the pantomime of mounting an imaginary steed, and uses the whip at a terrible rate on an imaginary rump behind him.

Unlike most of his journalistic colleagues—who were inclined to cackle and snort at such goings-on—this reporter acknowledges a degree of cultural relativity in taste: "It will be seen at once that in the course of a play, a great many scenes occur which are exceedingly ridiculous in our eyes; but the Chinese look on them as perfect and unapproachable." But the music is another story:

The Chinese orchestra . . . keeps up an interminable humming, banging, scraping, and screeching of Chinese fiddles, pipes, cymbals and gongs. The horrid din accompanies the speeches, sometimes louder and sometimes lower, and hardly ceases from the moment the play begins until it closes.[24]

Chinese music as such would continue to get a bad press throughout the century. Another veritable leitmotiv among Victorian-age reviewers is the expression of moral offense felt at the sight of the

Chinese practice of representing the birth of a baby during the course of an opera scene. An early example of such consternation is seen in a reporter's account of a scene during an opera presented to a mining-town audience to the north of San Francisco in 1857. The reviewer of the Placer *Press* was generally laudatory, but he is shocked to find that the Chinese "were not of a rigid school of morality." Truly extraordinary to the reviewer was "the birth of a young celestial upon the stage, the uproar and confusion upon which is immense." (The scene had earlier shocked San Francisco viewers at the Adelphi.) Such evidence of reprehensible morality the reviewer attributes, however, to the Chinese exposure to *Western* ways:

The Chinese degenerate rapidly when they mix with the outsiders. They have witnessed *Camille*, *The Duke's Wager*, and other plays of the like character, and in order, we suppose, to show that they could "do a thing or two," have rather run the thing into the ground.[25]

In the spring of the following year the same troupe leased a building on Dupont Street and held forth nightly between seven and eleven. An observer in the *Bulletin* noted,

Persons passing in that neighborhood . . . will be likely to hear a horrible medley of sounds from gongs, rattling bones, banjoes, fiddles, drums and screaming voices, which it may be necessary to state, is Chinese operatic music and singing.

A proper Chinese stage had been set up, and the usual disposition of orchestra and players was arranged.

On one side of the stage are the orchestra, smoking and drumming away at their instruments; and at the other a lot of stage instruments in the shape of huge swords, battle axes, flags, tables, chairs and whatever else may be needed in the course of the play. There are no shifting scenes and no drop curtain; but the audience is called upon to imagine the "scene" by large signs in Chinese characters, which are changed with each change of scene.

The reporter noted that the players "never make blunders in their parts, and never forget or hesitate over a word."[26]

On 5 March 1860 the *Bulletin* reported a "celebrated company of Chinese actors" in town, performing nightly at the Union Theater. The *Bulletin*'s account is one of the earliest in which the writer attempts to use the actual names of Chinese musical instruments:

The instruments of music were two gee-heens, one sam-leen, (stringed instruments,) one see-oo, (wind instrument,) one koo-law, one law, one soo-law, and two other varieties of gongs, and one implement of unknown name, which struck in one part, gives out a chuck, and at the other, emitted the inspiriting music of the *bones* of Ethiopian minstrelsy. Of course, several of the performers varied their instruments as plaintive or warlike music was in demand.

The writer probably referred respectively to two hu-ch'ins; a san-hsien; a so-na; one each of large, medium-size, and small gongs, together with "two other varieties" (cymbals, perhaps); and the tan-p'i-ku used in conjunction with the pan, the latter suggesting the bone clappers indigenous to American minstrel theater.

Here, as is the convention with Chinese-opera audiences today, the spectators were a relaxed and chatty group.

The audience, composed almost exclusively of Chinese, never applaud, but sit it out with decorum, lighting their cigars at the foot-lights, and resting their feet with shoes kicked off, on the benches. The front seats in the dress circle are given up entirely to the women, and no man does so improper a thing as to approach them or in any manner address them. They smoke their cheroots, eat melon seeds and comfits, and when the scene grows tiresome gabble without restraint.[27]

Two months later, a widely heralded theatrical company of five arrived from Hong Kong "*en route* for Paris, where they are engaged to appear before the Imperial Court of Louis Napoleon, and who have repeatedly performed before the Emperor of China and the Grand Dignitaries of Pekin."[28] The troupe was invited to perform for three nights in San Francisco, with a resident Chinese-theater company on hand to support the luminous quintet just arrived. In a perfunctory review, the *Bulletin*'s reporter pooh-poohed the press-release ballyhoo about the "new" stars:

We have seen every one of [these] principal actors in Dupont street, and, time and time again, the very piece played by them last night, and the old silk dresses, with all their spots and diffused dirt. The Ah Wing, Ah Kung, Ah Chun, Ah Ping and Ah Wye, are only the Smith, Brown, Robinson & Co. of the old troupe, that has amused the Johns of San Francisco and the mines for many years.

The reporter may not have understood the somewhat rotating nature of actors' lives in the Chinese community—that actors did indeed alternate engagements in China and the United States, as no theatrical group intended to seek permanent residence on these shores. In any event, the writer conceded that: "However old or new actors—humbug or no—the performance altogether is very curious to American eyes and ears." It was noted that the actors had acquired a new habit—of acknowledging applause with a deep and affected bow. As each actor went through this Western rite, "it appeared as if he were often laughing in his sleeve at the 'outside barbarians,' and 'gagging' the piece."[29]

Despite the transient nature of the individual troupes, the Chinese theater had become an entrenched part of the San Francisco scene by the 1860s. A ready audience was assured. Every tenth person in California in 1860 was Chinese; and by the end of that decade there were sixty-three thousand Chinese in the United States, 99 percent of whom were on the West Coast. The Chinese population of California was now widely dispersed to areas where mining, railroad building, and farm labor provided a livelihood. San Francisco County in 1870 contained but 12,030 Chinese of the state's total of 49,277; but the population of the city was rotatively increased by Chinese laborers returning for a few days in the city and by temporary groups of newly arrived Chinese just off the boat.[30] An idea of the type of individual seen in the Chinese community can be gained from a journalist's account of a ship debarkation in the late 1860s:

. . . a living stream of the blue coated men of Asia, bearing long bamboo poles across their shoulders, from which depend packages of bedding, matting, clothing, and things of which we know neither the names nor the uses, pours down the plank. . . . They appear to be of an average age of twenty-five years . . . and though somewhat less in stature than Caucasians, healthy, active and able-bodied to a man. As they come down upon the wharf, they separate into messes or gangs of ten, twenty, or thirty each, being recognized through some to us incomprehensible free-masonry system of signs by the agents of the Six Companies as they come, are assigned places on the long broad shedded wharf [to await inspection by the customs officers].[31]

This ship discharged 1,272 Chinese.

The new arrivals found toleration and even welcome in these early years of the state. While prejudice and abuse were not unknown, the mood of the 1860s was relatively benign with regard to the newcomers. The Chinese were considered by many to be indispensable and were praised for their industry and efficiency.

The editor of the Pacific News remarked upon their industry, quietness, cheerfulness and cleanliness of their personal habits. Whatever the white man scorned to do, the Chinaman took up; whatever the white man did, the Chinese could learn to do; he was a gap-filler, doing what no one else would do, or what remained undone, adapting himself to the white man's tasks, and slipping away, unprotestingly, to other tasks when the white man wanted his job.[32]

San Francisco in the 1860s was a city of increasing wealth and cultural sophistication. The archetypal forty-niner—unshorn, rough and ready, with pick in hand—had given way to the urbane boulevardier who dwelled in plush drawing rooms and traveled in style by carriage. San Francisco's new prosperity was reflected in its growing attraction as a spot to visit, where the tourist could find comfortable accommodations and good service as well as colorful scenery and adventure in a mild and Italianate climate. Accounts of the sights and sounds of the city began reaching the rest of the world through books and magazine articles. High priority on any visitor's list of sightseeing attractions was Chinatown. And—as in subsequent decades—no trip to Chinatown was complete without a visit to the Chinese theater. Typically the visitor's reaction was one of stunned fascination. One found delight in colorful costumes and acrobatics, bewilderment in arcane plots and inexplicable stage conventions. As for music—a long and arduous search through such accounts has disclosed none that is favorable, though a few border on objectivity. Humor and mock horror lighten many written-down reactions, but it is plain that to the Western listener the music was experienced only as a whelming and relentless irritation to the ears.

The writer Artemus Ward visited the Chinese theater in 1863 and wrote some unexceptional observations on it, dealing mainly with the apparent great length of the plays. Whether San Francisco's most notable literary figures of the time—Bret Harte and Mark Twain—ever visited the Chinese theater is not known; at any rate, they wrote nothing on the matter that has been discovered.[33] A less celebrated visitor, William Henry Brewer, tackled the subject at some length in 1863. Brewer, a member of a geological survey expedition to California, wrote home to describe his visit to a Chinese theater. He regretted his inability to describe the action accurately:

Words would entirely fail. Whether it was opera, tragedy or comedy or a mixture of the three, I have no idea—I think it was perhaps a mixture—but it was all comical enough, and yet intensely interesting because of its extreme singularity, so very unlike anything I have ever seen before.

Brewer describes the playhouse as "a rather poor building" in which members of the lower classes huddled under a low ceiling, some of them smoking opium, or so it seemed. Against the wall on one side of the stage was an "idol" with a lamp burning in front of it. "A stage extends entirely across one side, raised about three feet above the floor, covered with mats, and without drop curtain in front or side scenes." Fancy Chinese curtains enclosed two doors at opposite ends of the rear wall which led to rooms backstage. What engaged Brewer's attention most vividly, however, was the orchestra, consisting of five or six players, of whom he wrote:

One holds a small metallic instrument, a sort of cross between a small gong and flat bell; another has several blocks, of different sizes and shapes, upon which he beats with two sticks, making a *noise* but surely not *music*; another beats a drum, looking and sounding like a half-barrel tub covered with leather. A large gong hangs beside him, which he pounds in the "terrific" portions of the play. Another plays most of the time on a stringed instrument, in principle somewhat like a fiddle with two strings, but entirely unlike a fiddle, or anything else describable, in both shape and sounds.[34]

Brewer's "cross between a small gong and a flat bell" might well have been a T'ang-lo, a small, flat, hand-held gong about ten centimeters in diameter.[35] The "several blocks" were presumably of the mu-yü or single-block pan variety, the "half-barrel tub" a T'ang-ku, and the stringed instrument a hu-ch'in. His further description suggests a san-hsien (or possibly a p'ip'a) and a so-na, all of which add up to an ensemble that would be right at home in present-day Peking opera:

In the noisy parts of the play he beats a pair of huge cymbals—about as musical as would be the clashing together of two pieces of sheet iron. Another plays on a guitar-like instrument, or, by way of variety, lays this down and blows a sort of shrill clarinet.

There is "system" in this music, he says, but neither melody nor harmony. And it could not be expressed in Western notation. The orchestra both accompanies and plays interludes on its own. Some of the interludes he describes as "awful":

Imagine a room in which one man is mending pots, another filing a saw, another hammering boards, another beating a gong, and two boys trying to tune fiddles, and you will have some idea of some of their grand efforts in the music line.

Like most non-Chinese observers, Brewer was in total ignorance of the plot or the meaning of the dialogue. Though he found the acting in general to be "comical," he could not fathom its import: ". . . I could only tell which part was considered funny and which pathetic by watching the effect on the audience; it could never be perceived from the play itself."[36]

More thoroughly enthusiastic was the report of James Rusling, whose travels through San Francisco in the mid-1860s brought him to the Cantonese opera. He found the costumes rich, the pantomime excellent, the humor irresistible, and the love passages "a good reproduction of the grand passion." (The music, however, was "hideous.") He sat surrounded by "two or three hundred Chinese . . . mainly males, listening to a play that required eighty weeks or months—our informants were not certain which."[37]

Another writer of the time had a more severe judgment:

The appointments of their stage were of the rudest kind, the acting, whether of tragedy or comedy, equally farcical in foreign eyes, the singing nasal, the orchestra deafening with lamentable monotones from gongs reeds, stringed instruments, and anvils of hard wood.[38]

Throughout the mid-1860s, there was at least one theater operating full time in Chinatown.[39] It was not until the summer of 1867, however, that construction began on the first building to be erected specifically for Chinese theater since the Hong Took Tong's prefabricated edifice of 1852. The new theater, located on Jackson Street above Kearney, opened the following January. It was named the "Hing Chuen Yuen" ("Prosperous Complete Origin") and was said to have cost its backers a pretty penny ($20,000 according to one account; twice that according to another).[40] The new building contained, in addition to the theater itself, a dormitory, dining rooms, and other facilities for performers and other personnel of the troupe. Situated at the end of a long passageway flanked by Chinese bazaars, the building is described by the *Alta* as being "quite plain and unpretentious on the outside."[41]

The theatre proper [continues the *Alta*] is in the rear, and quite disconnected from the front building. It is arranged in every particular like an American temple of the drama, having a pit or parquette, dress circle and galleries, and is lighted with gas throughout. The orchestra occupy an alcove in the rear of the stage—not in front of it, as with us—and the actors make their entrances and exits by side doors, or openings, hung with the costliest bullion-embroidered silk curtains, no drop curtain being used.[42]

A few days prior to its opening, the new theater underwent a formal dedication "to the gods supposed to preside over the Celestial drama." A reporter described the ceremonies:

Incense was burned profusely; the leading characters of the historic drama, in gorgeous costume, were on the stage; smoke was blown against the four walls, representing the four quarters of the globe, from whence intelligence is invoked, and other ceremonies which cannot be described in the English language were performed, the whole closing with the beheading of a cock and a grand display of fireworks and a *feu de joi*, which consumed half a ton of fire-crackers, more or less.[43]

Having satisfied the demands of these traditions, the theater's trustees now turned to the modern world and arranged for a grand banquet to precede the opening-night production. Invitations were sent out to members of the press, the entire legal bench, and prominent members of the bar, the state legislature, and the city's Board of Supervisors. Also invited were foreign consuls, various merchants, and representatives of the army and navy. All in all, about a hundred of the city's dignitaries were present on the night of 27 January at the Hang Heong Low Restaurant on Dupont Street. The dinner was to be memorable by any standard. It consisted of seven courses, each comprising about twenty dishes—a grand total of perhaps 140 separate dishes, "exclusive of the sweetmeats in great profusion which were on the tables at the outset, and fruits of all kinds not obtainable in the markets." Claret, champagne, brandy, and Chinese liquors were served with every course. At each table sat a Chinese host who also served as interpreter. In the best Chinese tradition, toasts and expressions of gratitude and goodwill were rendered ceremoniously back and forth between hosts and guests as all assembled proceeded from course to course. Ivory chopsticks were available to all, but tables were set with Western cutlery as well. "Pointed and pithy" speeches were offered by distinguished guests and responded to by the hosts, as all savored the bird's-nest soup, water chestnuts, chicken tidbits fried in batter, and a host of other Chinese delicacies. At nine o'clock, after four hours of this gastronomic Armageddon, the guests adjourned to the theater—leaving the last three courses unserved.

The festive air of good feeling carried over to the theatrical event of the evening. "The Company is a new one," said the *Alta* reporter, "fresh from China, and the costumes are elaborate and costly almost beyond description."[44] The opening-night offering was a historical drama, one in which the whole stage was at times crowded with performers. Also crowded was the house itself, whose attendance was well in excess of the theater's planned capacity of some fifteen hundred.[45] The audience's response was in marked contrast to the reactions that earlier Chinese theatricals had evoked from uncomprehending San Francisco audiences. The *Alta* reported that "the best feeling" appeared to exist in the audience, and "the rounds of applause were frequent and prolonged."[46]

After some sixteen years of experience with the Chinese drama, San Francisco was now the home of the first permanently established Chinese theater in the United States. The Hing Chuen Yuen was to become known for many years as the "Royal Chinese Theatre" and would serve as a focus of attention for visitors from all over the world.

The opening of the new theater was not without negative incident, however. Actors from the Globe Theatre formed a sort of picket line, which was dispersed by police.[47] Another disturbance resulted from the moral objections of a Chinese washermen's association to the theater's decision to set aside a portion of the dress circle for unaccompanied women. Two nights after the opening, the outraged laundrymen assembled in such numbers as to block the sidewalks and even the street itself in front of the theater. Every woman entering the theater was jostled and hooted at. A collision with the police soon followed, and the crowd was broken up, with arrests made for obscene language and the possession of deadly weapons. Despite the police action and subsequent convictions, however, a crowd assembled again the next day as an audience was arriving for a matinee performance. The police assembled as well, however, and the afternoon passed without incident.[48]

Chinese theater was by no means to become a monopoly of the Hing Chuen Yuen, however. The drama was to prosper on various stages in San Francisco and throughout the state, attended by out-of-towners and locals alike, who found the entertainment diverting and "really meritorious in those exhibitions that [were] understood."[49] In the year after the Hing Chuen Yuen's opening, three Chinese theaters were doing business concurrently in San Francisco.[50]

Such rivalry notwithstanding, the Hing Chuen Yuen was destined to remain for some years as the leading playhouse of the Chinese. A visit to this "Royal Chinese" theater was to become de rigueur for travelers to San Francisco, and their published accounts would celebrate its exotic attractions for some decades to come.

NOTES

1. Mary Roberts Coolidge, *Chinese Immigration* (New York, Henry Holt and Co., 1909), p. 498.

2. Gladys Hansen, ed., *San Francisco: The Bay and Its Cities* (New York, Hastings House, 1973), p. 30.

3. Concerning the Australian troupe, see ibid., pp. 133–34. Bellini's *La Sonnambula*, presented in February 1851, was San Francisco's first Western opera. Edward M. Gagey, *The San Francisco Stage: A History* (New York, Columbia University Press, 1950), p. 32.

4. It was not San Francisco's very first professional Chinese entertainment. A company of Chinese jugglers had preceded them by a few days in the same theater, thence leaving for New Orleans and other points east. There is no evidence that music had a part in their performance. See Lois Rodecape, "Celestial Drama in the Golden Hills: Chinese Theatre in California, 1849–1869," *California Historical Society Quarterly* 23 (1944), pp. 100–01.

5. San Francisco *Alta California*, 20 October 1852. (Hereafter cited as *Alta*.)

6. *Alta*, 16 October 1852.

7. *Alta*, 20 October 1852.

8. Rodecape, p. 102.

9. *Alta*, 20 October 1852. Prefabricated houses from China were quite common in the San Francisco of Gold Rush days. The units were generally shipped from Canton and erected by Chinese laborers at any location specified, thus providing quick and convenient quarters for sojourning miners and others in haste. See, e.g., Etienne Derbec, *A French Journalist in the California Gold Rush: The Letters of Etienne Derbec*, ed. A. P. Nasatir (Georgetown, Calif., Talisman, 1964), p. 90; John Frost, *History of the State of California* (Auburn, N.Y., Derby and Miller, 1850), p. 55; Ludvig Verner Helms, *Pioneering in the Far East* . . . (London, W.H. Allen, 1882), p. 85.

10. Near what is now Union Street. *Herald*, 22 December 1852.

11. J.D. Borthwick, *3 Years in California* (Edinburgh, William Blackford, 1857; reprint ed., Oakland, Calif., Biobooks, 1948), p. 62 in the 1948 edition. See also *Herald*, 22 December 1852; *Alta*, 25 December 1852.

12. Rodecape, p. 102.

13. Borthwick, pp. 62–63.

14. *Alta*, 1 April 1853; *Herald*, 27 March 1853; New York *Times*, 18 May 1853; *Herald*, 27 November 1853, 11 January 1854. See also George C[linton] D[ensmore] Odell, *Annals of the New York Stage*, 15 vols. (New York, Columbia University Press, 1927–49), vol. 6, pp. 242, 270–71, 275.

15. *Herald*, 22 April 1855; see also *Alta*, 30 August 1854.

16. Frank Soulé, John H. Gihon, and James Nisbet, *The Annals of San Francisco* . . . (New York, D. Appleton, 1855), p. 384.

17. Miska Hauser, *Letters of Miska Hauser, 1853*, ed. Cornel Lengyel (New York, AMS, 1972), p. 41.

18. San Francisco *Chronicle*, 13 December 1855.

19. *Chronicle*, 24 April 1856.

20. Ibid.

21. Sacramento *Union*, 17 February 1855. Public puppet shows, with music, had been staged by Chinese in San Francisco as early as the summer of 1853. See G.R. MacMinn, *Theater of the Golden Era of California* (Caldwell, Idaho, Caxton, 1941), pp. 493–95.

22. San Francisco *Bulletin*, 6 October 1856.

23. See below, pp. 86–87.

24. *Bulletin*, 6 December 1856.

25. *Bulletin*, 12 May 1857, verbatim from the Placer (Calif.) *Press*. Portrayals of birth on stage would continue to shock and astonish Western spectators throughout the century. See below, p. 144.

26. *Bulletin*, 26 March 1858.

27. *Bulletin*, 5 March 1860. Emphasis in original, together with parenthetical interpolations and punctuation thereof.

28. *Alta*, 14 May 1860.

29. *Bulletin*, 17 May 1860.

30. U.S. Census figures cited in Coolidge, pp. 501, 503.

31. "From the Orient Direct," *Atlantic Monthly* 24 (1869), pp. 542–48, quoted in Chinn, Lai, and Choy, who provide the bracketed information as well, p. 16.

32. Coolidge, p. 22.

33. Charles Farrar Browne, ed., *Artemus Ward, His Travels* (London, Chatto and Windus, 1890), pp. 198–99.

34. William Henry Brewer, *Up and Down California in 1860-1864* (New Haven, Yale University Press, 1930), pp. 366–67. Emphasis in original.

35. See Tsai-ping Liang, *Chinese Musical Instruments & Pictures* (Taipei, Chinese Classical Music Association, 1970), p. 21.

36. Brewer, p. 367.

37. James Rusling, *The Great West and Pacific Coast* (New York, Sheldon, 1877), p. 308.

38. Franklin Tuthill, *The History of California* (San Francisco, H.H. Bancroft, 1866), p. 374.

39. Daniel Cleaveland notes that there was one in 1867, two in 1868. Letter to J. Ross Browne, 27 July 1868, in G.K. Fitch Papers, Bancroft Library, University of California, Berkeley.

40. Henry G. Langley, compiler, *The San Francisco City Directory* (San Francisco, Langley, 1863-68, 1868-69), p. 15. Sporadic reports of "new" Chinese theaters between these dates appear to describe various conversions of preexisting buildings.

41. *Alta*, 28 January 1868. Or in Langley's words, "gloomy and uninviting." (*Directory*, 1868-69, p. 15.)

42. *Alta*, 28 January 1868.

43. *Alta*, 24 January 1868.

44. *Alta*, 28 January 1868.

45. Figure given by the theater's manager in 1876. *Alta*, 11 January 1876.

46. *Alta*, 28 January 1868.

47. *Bulletin*, 30 January 1868.

48. *Alta*, 31 January 1868.

49. *Alta*, 19, 23, 24, and 25 September 1869.

50. Augustus W. Loomis, "Holiday in the Chinese Quarter," *Overland Monthly* 2 (1869), p. 144.

2

Chinese Theater: Years of Prosperity (1870–1889)

As San Francisco moved into the 1870s, anti-Chinese feelings increased dramatically as a series of economic adversities ravaged the city and state. The decade would bring two economic depressions (1873 and 1877) together with a severe decline in mining and railroad building. Out-of-work Californians became increasingly embittered toward the Chinese—heathen rivals for the fewer and fewer jobs to be had. Smoldering intolerance would be fanned into flame in the later 1870s by the oratory of Dennis Kearney, who rallied his followers with the slogan, ''The Chinese Must Go!'' A crescendo of persecutive legislation developed within the state. Such official xenophobia was to find its way to Washington and culminate in the Exclusion Act of 1882. The act would ban virtually all Chinese immigration for some fifty years to come.

Troubles for the Chinese in the 1870s were presaged by the completion of the transcontinental railroad in 1869. On 10 May, the golden spike was hammered at Promontory Point, Utah, amidst salvos of manifest-destiny oratory and national self-congratulation. After the cheers and fireworks died away, however, the West found itself confronted with a multitude of out-of-work laborers—some twenty-five thousand of them, many of them Chinese. Some railroad building would continue in California and neighboring states, but it was clear that the boom was over. The decline in mining yields was scarcely less precipitous. By 1873 the gold mines were virtually depleted. The mid-1870s also saw the exhaustion of the Comstock Lode, whose trove of silver, quartz, and copper had enriched the western economy for twenty years. Mining stocks in the Comstock's yields were held by rich and poor alike, but it was the poor who faced real catastrophe when the bottom dropped out of the market in 1876. After having weathered the depression of 1873, San Francisco was again plunged into the financial doldrums in 1877. The time was ripe for demagoguery and scapegoat hunting. The newspapers were full of what was now virulently discussed as "The Chinese Question." A wave of persecution and violence swept over the Chinese community, as social agitation led to legislation to deprive the Chinese of what few rights they had to start with in the land they had envisioned as "The Golden Mountain."

An increasingly negative image of the Chinese was developing in the minds of Americans. Earlier, there had been appreciation and downright admiration of the Chinese for their work habits, frugality, and peaceable demeanor. But as the economy worsened, the image of the Chinese (as reflected in the press and political oratory of the day) evolved more and more to considerations of alleged immorality and conspiratorial economic threat. Though John Chinaman was not a drinker, he smoked opium—exposing innocent whites to the odious habit. He dwelt in filthy and malodorous hovels. Local folklore had it that his eating habits were unspeakable (it was widely believed that rats were a favorite item of his diet) and that he was a carrier of diseases to which he himself was immune. His women—enslaved slatterns; and he was even alleged to have a lascivious eye for the dainty maidens of *white* mining-town society as well. Worse—and presumably at the root of the prejudice—he and his compatriots were mere sojourners, opportunists here to bleed the economy while whites went without work. John bought no real estate, benefited no banks. His money scarcely circulated, as the bulk of it was sent right back to China. His gambling houses, opium dens, and brothels were touted as menaces to all right-thinking Americans, who were ever in danger of being lured from their own gentle pastimes and centers of culture.

As scapegoats, the Chinese were ideal. Their large numbers, physical differences, and alien modes of dress and behavior made them an all-too-visible target for the outlet of economic frustration. As jobs became scarcer on railroads and in the mines, the Chinese turned to farm-laboring, to domestic service, and to menial chores in factories, often taking jobs that were scorned by whites, many of whom still clung to dreams of gold and overnight prosperity. But even the most lowly of jobs was a job nonetheless, and the sight of a gainfully employed Chinese aroused envy and hatred among the languishing victims of a deflated economy. In general, as Betty Lee Sung has observed, the metamorphosis was quite a thing to behold:

. . . whereas the Chinese had been praised for their industry, their honesty, their thrift, and their peaceful ways, they were now charged with being debased and servile coolies, clannish, dangerous, deceitful, and vicious.[1]

While the Chinese theater would continue and even flourish during these hard times, the theatrical houses themselves were the frequent scenes of real-life violence and tragedy during the 1870s. Time and again, riots and mayhem would interrupt the operatic plots as the Chinese themselves gave vent to irritations in these tense years, loosing their frustrations in their only large-scale gathering places.

In a sense, the banquet and grand opening of the Hing Chuen Yuen in 1868, described in the previous chapter, signaled the end of a period of at least tolerably good relations between the Chinese and their white neighbors. The shared warmth and merriness of that integrated audience reflected a mood that was not destined to continue in the decade to come. Indeed, the whole idea of a racially mixed audience was soon seen to be only the white man's prerogative. In the following year, two Chinese merchants accepted an invitation to attend a San Francisco theater outside of Chinatown, and their presence nearly precipitated a riot. Only the arrival of a large force of police served to quell the pandemonium that resulted from the sight of Chinese faces in a white theater.[2] That such Chinese incursions were rare is indicated by the San Francisco *Post*'s reaction to Chinese visitors to an American opera house in 1877. On 8 October, two Chinese men and a Chinese woman were observed to occupy a box at a performance of *Mignon*. "It was an unprecedented spectacle," reported the *Post*, and it "gave rise to a good deal of comment among the fashionable audience in attendance, much of which was of a decidedly hostile character."

Pigtails and shaven heads were evidently not an agreeable concomitant of a visit to the opera. In the adjoining box sat three ladies and two gentlemen, whose social standing may be inferred from the fact that Generals Sherman and McDowell called upon them during the evening and had a pleasant chat. The contrast between the occupants of the two boxes was so striking as to cause general remark. Is it possible that these Mongols were paid by leaders of the pro-Chinese sentiment in our midst in order to demonstrate that the Chinese are adopting our customs and seeking to assimilate with us socially?[3]

The disturbances that plagued the Chinese theaters during the 1870s were sometimes the result of white interference, but many upsets involved the Chinese alone. An affray on the night of 8 May 1870 at the Jackson Street theater developed between westernized and other Chinese: "It appears that hostile feelings exist on the part of some Celestials . . . against those . . . who have become so far Americanized as to have their queues cut off, and wear our dress." Several of these Americanized patrons were attacked with a hatchet:

One of the victims had the side of his head cut open, in addition to receiving a fearful wound across the back. Another received two blows on the top of his head, inflicting frightful cuts. The injured men fell to the floor senseless, the blood streaming from them in torrents, and for a time they were hardly able to recognize any of their friends who were soon at hand. The desperate assailant . . . attempted to make his escape. . . . but was captured . . . and . . . booked for assault to murder.[4]

White policemen were a ubiquitous sight at the Chinese theaters. Often these were "special officers," not members of the regular police department but hired by the Chinese themselves to help keep order. The policeman who captured the hatchet-wielder in the above account was such an officer.[5]

However, as the decade wore on, interference by the city's official police force in the affairs of the theater became frequent. In

October 1876 a raid on "the old Chinese theater on Jackson street" was occasioned by the management's indifference to a one A.M. closing rule. After having been "warned over and over again" that prosecution would follow further refusal, the management was surprised by a police raid at one o'clock sharp on the morning of 25 October. In spite of the presence of a squad of patrolmen, however, the proprietors did not close the theater—or rather were prevented from doing so by indignant members of the audience, who demolished benches and raised general hell. The ensuing panic and confusion were described as "terrific." Police arrested two of the proprietors, seven actors (including the "leading lady"), and some twenty bench-smashers from the audience.[6]

Less than a week later, the same theater was the scene of a catastrophe occasioned by neither law nor vengeance. The single word "Fire!" caused a stampede of some two thousand spectators. Nineteen were killed, most of them crushed to death under the exit doors themselves, which were wrenched from their hinges by the panic-stricken crowd.[7]

It appears that the cry of fire raised by a Chinaman, though unnecessary, was not unfounded. Some small article actually caught fire in a box near the stage, and was the cause of the fatal alarm. The fire was extinguished with a bucket of water. Two white men—a special officer and an expressman—barely escaped with their lives.

According to newspaper reports, the play itself continued uninterrupted by the panic. The actors and musicians did not cease until a police officer ordered them off the stage.

It required the most determined efforts of the police to force the crowd, struggling for exit, back into the Theatre, to allow a chance for carrying away the dead and wounded from the door-way. But for this, a large number must have been tramped [sic] to death. It took a strong force of officers to keep back the crowds that soon congregated and blockaded the street.[8]

The scene in front of the theater was ghastly, as

. . . the dead and dying lay on the street and sidewalks, the dying groaning and struggling, and the stream of chattering and appalled Chinamen poured out, hopping over bodies like crossing a drift of logs.[9]

(Incredibly, during the very height of the excitement, "a white man distinguished himself by passing along the sidewalk on the outskirts of the crowd, and pommeling every Chinaman he could get a lick at.") When the bodies were removed to an undertaker's establishment, crowds thronged to see the sight. Though the spectators were generally quiet, the *Alta* reporter overheard mutterings of bigotry even in the immediate wake of the disaster:

"Is any white man killed?" asked a man, for there was a rumor to that effect. "No—no white man hurt." "Good," was the reply, "it don't matter about these," making a significant movement with his foot toward the dead Chinese.[10]

The early summer of 1877 brought an incident that rocked the theatrical world of San Francisco's Chinatown. The rivalry between the Royal Chinese Theater and its opposite number—the playhouse across the street known to occidentals as the "Oriental Academy of Music"—erupted into lawsuits, imprisonments, and violence over the disposition of a theatrical troupe that had been in town for about a year. In June of the previous year, a company of nine actors had arrived for a year's engagement at the Royal Chinese Theater. The contract had been drawn up in China, with provisions that the starting actor was to receive $800 for the year's work, another actor to receive $600, the "leading lady" actor $400, and varying amounts for others, down to $50 for the lowest of the group. Toward the end of their contractual term, the troupe made plans to move across the street to accept a lucrative offer from the Luk Suhn Fung Company, managers of the Oriental Academy of Music. There was a heated disagreement with the Royal Chinese management, however, regarding the precise night of the contract's termination. When negotiation failed, the Royal Chinese managers drove the recalcitrant actors into an upstairs room of the theater and imprisoned them there for thirteen days. Upon regaining their freedom, the group immediately went to work across the street and filed suit for $1,200 against the Royal Chinese management for their incarceration. Simultaneously, their new employers commenced an action to recover from the same management $5,000 for having detained the actors from their new employment.

Excitement over the matter was intense in Chinatown. The prevailing sentiment was reported to be in favor of the oppressed nine.

On the Saturday following the actors' opening night, an attempt was made to blow their new theater sky-high

with a deposit of from 10 to 12 pounds of powder so tamped and arranged that it would on its explosion that night, have blown Messrs. Luk Suhn Fung Company's Academy of Music and their talented histrionic celebrities and their patrons even further from China than they are at present.[11]

Apparent countermeasures followed. A Chinese woman who was a friend of the Royal Chinese management was murdered by an unknown assailant who was believed to be a hired desperado of the academy company; and an attempt was made on the life of another woman under the same circumstances. "To the Eastern reader," stated the *Chronicle*, "all this would seem like the wildest kind of hyperbole, but everything stated is an actual fact, for which actions have been commenced in the civil and criminal courts."

The Chinese theater seemed to have no end of legal problems. In September 1878, a group of over a hundred property owners and residents within the considerable hearing distance of the theater protested about the house's audibility in a petition to the Board of Supervisors.

The petition . . . sets forth that owing to new improvements in the theater, in the matter of additional windows, therein, increased volume is given to the execrable noises that are part of the performance, and the din is so loud and frequent that the district . . . is nightly disturbed far into the small hours of the morning.[12]

Denied was the petitioners' request that the theater be required to close at ten P.M.; but a subsequent legal action ordered a one A.M. closing time.[13]

The theater's owners were not eager to comply. Within two weeks a riot broke out when police attempted to enforce the closing-time order. The *Call* reported that:

Last Saturday night, a benefit was given at the Chinese theatre on Church alley, near Washington street, and it was announced that the show would run until two o'clock in the morning. About eighteen hundred Chinamen attended the performance, and everything went very well until one o'clock in the morning, when Officer Brown walked into the theatre and attempted to enforce the ordinance which requires that theatres shall close at one o'clock in the morning. The officer rapped on the back of a bench, and exclaimed in stentorian voice, that "the Chinese must go," but the Chinese would not budge. He then went behind the scenes and drove the actors and musicians from the stage. As he did this, the audience raised the cry of "Tah Kive Lah," which means "strike him." Some of the audience made for the stage, probably with the intention of striking the officer, but the arrival of reinforcements and the exhibition of firearms caused the advancing party to retreat. The audience, or rather the major portion thereof, then took to tearing up the benches and everything movable in the premises, destroying the same. They also hurled missiles at the officers on the stage, and then tore down the doors, which they used as battering rams to demolish the box office.[14]

Within two weeks another sort of disturbance followed. This time the dispute was reportedly between the Chinese themselves. The Royal Chinese Theater's supremacy was challenged by a new theater, which made its debut with a fresh troupe from China. The new house's opening night was punctuated with noisy heckling from a number of Royal Chinese loyalists in attendance. On 20 October the new theater erupted with a full-scale riot, involving some three thousand spectators. Near closing time, Ah Kid, an actor from the rival troupe, had arisen from his seat and begun pelting the actors on stage with apple cores and cigar butts.[15] Others quickly joined him, and a free-for-all was soon in effect. Police joined the fray:

Officer Avan was the only police officer present, but he clutched Ah Kid and began dragging him out. No sooner had he reached the sidewalk than the man broke away and ran back into the theater, and began smashing windows and chairs. Avan fought his way through the crowd and again arrested Ah Kid, and, by the aid of a citizen, took him and Ah Fong, a Chinaman who had struck him, down to the City Prison. A tremendous crowd of Chinese collected in the street, and had to be clubbed by Captain Short and a squad of police before they dispersed.[16]

The indefatigable Ah Kid was charged with malicious mischief and assault, Ah Fong with battery and obstructing the sidewalk. Shortly after the arrests, a crowd of some three thousand Chinese collected in the street outside the theater. They were dispersed by club-wielding policemen, as was a similar gathering later in the day. One account of these disturbances questions whether the theatrical rivalry was the direct cause. An inquisitive *Chronicle* reporter was told that the rioting was due not so much to inter-theater strife as to the spontaneous anger of spectators who had come to hear a new star who had been imported from China under a contract of $7,000 a year. The star had appeared temperamental and glum at his performances. The spectators, who had been charged an unusually high rate for his appearances, were supposedly incensed at being bilked and responded accordingly.[17] Chinatown's ever-disputing tongs may also have had a hand in the disorders. The ostensible rivalry fight might well have reflected deeper problems between factions in the community—not to speak of the emotional toll that racial prejudice and economic blight were taking. The Chinese were constrained to respond to the city's hostile racial climate only in such indirect and compensatory fashion.

A year and a half later, the theater was again in the news for non-operatic reasons. Arson was attempted at a new theater on Washington Street, according to the *Bulletin*.

A dastardly attempt was made last night to burn the Chinese Theatre, No. 816 Washington street. The performance was in full blast at the time, and it is estimated that fully three thousand persons were in, when the audience were startled by a can of lighted phosphorous which was dropped through a skylight on the stage. Simultaneously five similar boxes were ignited in different portions of the building. A general stampede of the frightened spectators took place, and in their efforts to escape, they scrambled over each other towards the doors. Several police officers were promptly on hand, and by great exertion, succeeded in clearing the theatre without serious injury to any one [sic], but they did not succeed in arresting the incendiaries, nor have been able to discover any clue to their identification. The flames were then speedily extinguished, but not till several hundred dollars damage had been done. It is suspected that the incendiary attempt was prompted by Chinese interested in a rival theatre on Jackson street. A bitter war of rivalry has existed between the two Companies since the Washington street Theatre was opened six months ago, and several attempts have been made to break up the performance in the latter establishment.[18]

   Several months later, both theaters were raided without warning, in what proved to be a futile search for weapons carried by the Chinese.

   In accordance with orders from the Chief of Police Crowley, a detachment of some 100 officers of Captain Douglass' watch reported at the central station at 11:30 o'clock last night. Fifty of them, commanded by Captain Douglass, proceeded to the Chinese theater on Jackson street, and the other half headed by Sergeant Harmon went to the second theater on Washington street. As soon as the officers entered the respective theaters, all means of exit were guarded, and officers rushed forward to hold the stage. Both theaters were crowded to the utmost, the throng being so dense that the actors were inconvenienced, as many of the audience at each were standing upon the stage. The performances ended abruptly, and the audience being driven out, each one as he was about to leave was searched to obtain such weapons as might be concealed on the person.

   The search yielded no concealed weapons, though the account notes that eight pistols were found under benches or in the street, together with several dirk knives, a few silver spoons and forks, and a slingshot.

Not a weapon was found on any person. . . . Some seventy heathens were taken to the prison and there searched. Nothing being found on them they were allowed to go. . . . Chief of Police Crowley states that these raids will be continued, and that their object is to deprive the Chinese, as far as possible, of the murderous weapons which they carry.

However: "The paucity of armed men at the two theaters was a circumstance that was noted by everyone."[19]

   The existence of theaters in Chinatown had begun to be noted in Langley's *San Francisco City Directory* in 1863. In subsequent years, Langley's and the rival *Bishop's Directory* (from 1876) provided a rough indication of the theatrical situation, though a number of discrepancies in the listings of both directories suggests that facts were not always checked thoroughly. In any case, the directories and other sources indicate that there were probably at least two theaters in operation in the Chinatown of the early 1870s.

Finding the theater was no problem to the tourist, according to one source, who notes that the traveler need only listen for the sounds of gongs and cymbals. The same observer, writing in 1871, records that the admission charge is a quarter of a dollar, but adds that "as a rule the Chinese are disinclined to admit foreigners into their theater."[20]

One foreigner who did attain entrance was Charles Nordhoff, who was impressed in general by the cleanliness and decorum of the Chinese. He describes the theater (probably the Royal China) as being "like the lowest of our own, the place of recreation for the vilest class." Yet Nordhoff, with his wife and children, encountered "not a rude or disrespectful word or gesture" in the crowd that filled "the long alleyway which leads to the door." He added: "I can't say that I would have ventured into a place of the same kind, or out of it, in New York without anxiety."

Further, "there never was a more interested or decorous audience in a theatre" than that which watched the "interminable play." To Nordhoff's evident surprise neither the men nor the women. ". . . not a cat-call, not a noise of any kind disturbed the harmony; not a curious look even toward our private box, where sat ladies and children, who must have been objects of curiosity to them."

"How the musicians themselves endure it I don't know," he said. But while describing the music itself as being "ear-piercing" and "like a multitude of insane bagpipes," he admired the players' metrical accuracy, commenting that this "wonderful" orchestra "kept better time than many orchestras I have heard in opera houses."

The first part of the play we saw was what we should call an opera. That is to say, the dialogue was sung to the accompaniment of music. The "music" was ear-piercing, shrill, loud, and to our ears only a horrible discord. But there was evidently a method in it; the leader, whose instrument consisted of two ivory sticks, with which he beat very audible time on a block of iron, had his shirt-sleeved orchestra under full control; and the singers of course, as unnatural as the playing; and when the chief personage of the piece, a high mandarin, dressed gorgeously, and with peacock feathers a yard long sticking out of his crown, attempted a quaver or trill, we all in our box burst into uncontrollable laughter.

The orchestra consisted of fiddles and percussion instruments—"cymbals, small gongs, and various other atrocious devices" constituting the typical instrumentation. One item noted in Nordhoff's detailed account that had not been previously mentioned with regard to Chinese theaters is "at one side, in the screen . . . a square hole, at which you see the nose and eyes of the stage manager occasionally, directing." Thus this particular company was not without its "prompter's box" of a sort.

Nordhoff's criticism, in its fashion, is balanced:

Every thing [sic] is cheap, squalid, and, to our eyes, disreputable. But the players, who came on in the cheap magnificence of players everywhere, were in earnest apparently, and shrieked, and gesticulated, and sang, with what seemed to me the careful and studied precision of men doing their best.

Like many an occidental spectator, Nordhoff felt that the Chinese theater was probably "the strangest sight San Francisco had to show."[21]

Performances lasted until two A.M., according to Nordhoff. On special occasions morning and afternoon performances were added. Mary Cone writes in 1876 that:

The Chinese theatres are in full blast all through the holidays. The doors are opened at seven o'clock in the morning, and the play begins soon after. An intermission at noon gives time for dinner; after which the play is resumed, and with the exception of a couple of hours—from five to seven o'clock in the evening—it is continued until eleven.[22]

Another observer reported in 1875 that the theater was in action from seven in the evening until three the next morning.[23]

Incidental notes on the backstage life at a Chinese theater were recorded by a visiting actress of the occidental stage in March 1875:

. . . I was received with high honor at their theatre, and taken behind the scenes. What a sight! They had one small department to serve as wardrobe room, green-room and dressing-room. The place was crowded with men, no females act, you know, the men taking female parts. . . . A number of actors were changing their costumes, and the cool indifference, not to say gravity, with which they stripped themselves to the bare brown skin in my presence, was startling. I had some difficulty in finding a nook I could fix my eyes on without being shocked. While I stood looking about me, so as to avoid male chemise in the abstract, one almond-eyed gentleman approached, and smiling, asked, "You-ee act-ee?"

I nodded in the affirmative, whereupon he shook his little brown hand from out his long, flowing sleeve and extended it to me with a genuine American grasp. The manager then remarked:

"Ell muchee *big* act-ee."

And every actor present, more or less dressed, nodded and smiled, and I nodded and smiled back again.

I then visited the kitchen, for, *mon ami*, the Chinese actors live in the theatre, and their sleeping dens—pah, I sicken as I think of them. The leading man receives $700 gold a year and his *rice*.[24]

The amused accounts by Chinatown's tourists contrast grimly with the growing tide of anti-Chinese feeling of the mid-1870s that pervaded San Francisco and California in general. To add to other economic problems of the area, the Panic of 1873 sent a fresh influx of non-Chinese sojourners from east of the Rockies, thus swelling a labor market that was already suffering from the blows dealt by the decline of mining and railroad building. Newcomers to California were confronted with Chinese-labor competition at every turn. Even buying land became increasingly difficult, and the difficulty was laid to the Chinese. The aspiring owner of a small farm found that the land was possessed in huge parcels by opportunists who were developing it cheaply with teams of workers—all too visibly from China. Rumbles of discontent among white workingmen grew to indignant outcries against the heathen competition. In the decade ahead, politicians would learn to harness the workingmen's discontent to their own uses. At first simply yielding to workers' demands for an anti-Chinese position, office seekers quickly learned the value of taking the initiative and orchestrating such feelings for the furtherance of their own political careers.

Political opportunism reached explosive proportions as events conspired to plunge California's economy into further doldrums and to bring upon it the most severe period of anti-Chinese agitation. By 1875 the state had begun to inch its way back toward the prosperity that had preceded the economic downturn of 1873. But the respite was short-lived. A series of blows racked the economy in

1876: the winter brought a severe drought, causing the death of thousands of cattle; and the output of the mines decreased by a full third. From the farms and the mines, masses of unemployed men joined the already swollen ranks of job seekers in San Francisco. The restless unemployed were attracted to mass meetings at which orating office seekers villified the cheap-labor Chinese and presented dire visions of rapacious hordes to follow in the sea lanes from Canton. And the resentment seethed in the minds of the out-of-work thousands in the streets of San Francisco.

In the following winter, the Comstock Lode's drastic fall in production sent stock values plummeting. Formerly wealthy speculators suddenly found themselves penniless and in the same boat with the hapless small-time investor. The continued downturn of the economy intensified the frustration and fury of men who had seen their dreams dashed by economic catastrophe. The Chinese suffered much of the brunt of this anger. Increasingly, individual Chinese were assaulted on the streets. On the night of 24 July 1877 a gang of several hundred men rioted against the Chinese, abusing men and women alike and wrecking and burning laundry houses. Though the National Guard was called in, the rioting and vandalizing continued for three days. For several months to come, no Chinese was safe on San Francisco's streets.

Within two months of this rioting, the Workingmen's party was formally organized; the scene was set for coordinated anti-Chinese agitation, and legislation would follow to make life even more miserable for the Chinese. Throughout the late 1870s, racial violence increased along with the growing political clout of the anti-Chinese movement. In 1877 five tenant farmers were murdered for hiring Chinese (the murderer later confessing to having followed orders from the Workingmen's party). The following year saw the entire Chinese population of Truckee rounded up like cattle and driven from town. Violence against the Chinese was daily newspaper fare, together with reports of a steady round of municipal and state legislative acts restricting the Chinese—acts that were regularly declared unconstitutional by the courts at varying levels. Finally the forces of Kearneyism were able to go beyond the state level and have Chinese-exclusion legislation considered in Washington. The cry of ''The Chinese Must Go!'' was now voiced beyond the borders of

California. After the first anti-Chinese immigration bill was passed by Congress but vetoed by Rutherford P. Hayes in 1880, forces united to set the stage for eventual passage of exclusion legislation. A growing number of businessmen and political conservatives rallied with the Democratic party in pressing for exclusion. In the wake of the Garfield assassination and America's attendant fears about domestic tranquillity, the Exclusion Act of 1882 was signed into law by President Arthur, having gained the support of many diverse elements in American life—among them organized labor, Southern congressmen who lumped California's racial problems with their own, and of course a solid bloc of legislators from the western states.

The 1882 bill was only the first in a wave of exclusion and restrictive legislation that would effectively sentence most Chinese to menial work, prevent the uniting of families from abroad, and, for all intents and purposes, perpetuate for the Chinese a society virtually without women through much of the first half of the twentieth century.

The passage of the exclusion law served only to deepen and intensify racial hatred. Anti-Chinese outrages spread throughout the West. Twenty-eight Chinese strikebreakers were massacred in Rock Springs, Wyoming, in 1885. Chinese were driven bodily out of Seattle and Tacoma. Whole industries once manned mainly by Chinese virtually disappeared from San Francisco—cigars, shoes, woolens. Another economic crisis in 1893 brought wholesale unemployment again to California, and anti-Chinese rioting in the Sacramento Valley brought about a condition "approximating civil war."[25] Terrorism and violence flamed throughout California's rural areas, and whole populations of Chinese were driven from towns at gunpoint.

The conflagration finally had its intended demographic effect: For the first time, California saw a drop in its Chinese population, in the 1890s, as Chinese who could afford to returned to China and many others fled to the less turbulent East Coast and other areas of the United States. San Francisco's Chinatown would continue to be the center of Chinese life and culture in North America into the twentieth century, but its residents now faced a future of severely curtailed horizons. In effect, the ghetto walls were raised even higher. The lives of the Chinese would increasingly revolve around the institutions that prevailed within the few blocks in which a Chinese could feel relatively safe, both in San Francisco and in other American Chinatowns. The monotony of the daily routine was not to be tempered by family life or the hope of it. Gambling, prostitution, and the opium pipe offered some short-lived respite to the daily grind (and also supported a community of racketeers within the community). Beyond this was the Chinese theater, which could bring a measure of escape to the spectator and could stir memories of a former home and way of life.

During the late 1870s and 1880s, Chinatown's theatrical activities reached a peak. Though the passing years were cruel to the Chinese population, the theater itself seems to have come into its golden era. Now that a ready audience was assured for actors and impresarios, the theater became a solid and indispensable part of the Chinatown scene. Two new theater buildings were erected in the late 1870s, and the activities of actors and musicians were the object of much attention both in and out of the theater.

The year 1877 even saw, apparently for the first time, the institutionalization of instruction on Chinese instruments, supposedly to provide musicians for the Chinese opera from among Chinatown's own residents. The "organization of a mammoth Chinese orchestra" was announced by a *Chronicle* reporter, who visited a recently established "conservatory of music," founded by a "Professor Lee Tom." The professor's work in "instructing the Chinese youth in the diabolism of heathen music" was to be for the purpose of training young men for the Chinese opera "and to fit them as well to beguile their leisure hours with the softening influence of music."

The instruments employed in its preparation are simple and few in number, embracing the Chinese fiddle, the zung-fu or devil's banjo, the tabor and the tom-tom. The latter is peculiarly simple in its construction, resembling nothing else than a brass skillet bereft of the handle, and which is beaten upon the bottom with sticks.

The bulk of the article is written for laughter rather than enlightenment. However, the few bits of information one can gather from it are of interest with respect to music teaching, composition, and performance. The assembled instruments are essentially those of the opera orchestra: hu-ch'in, san-hsien, and such percussion instruments as the "leader's drum" (tan p'i-ku) and "gongs"—though the latter term may have included cymbals in this case. Additionally, the reporter speaks of "the bass," without further description. No wind instruments are mentioned. At the "grand quarterly rehearsal" to which the reporter was admitted, the instrumentalists all played together for the first time. The reporter attempts at one point to explain principles of Chinese music in a few sentences:

It is governed by no rules of time whatever, but is simply adapted to the narrative or drama which it accompanies, or the varying depths of emotion which it is intended to express. Neither do the different parts in an orchestra bear any relation to each other, further than to unite in swelling the uproar as the spirit of the drama suggests. As an illustration, the gongs and tom-toms are manipulated the more vigorously at thrilling positions, or in accord with the increased energy of the actors. The music is therefore extempore with the musicians individually.

Yet in the rehearsal itself—or in that small part that the reporter heard—the music is apparently not accompanimental. (The programmic picturizations are presumably of the reporter's fancy, not the composer's.) The "professor" conducts the group (with a baton) in the playing of an original work:

. . . some little difficulty was experienced at the outset in procuring a simultaneous jangle of the fiddles and banjos. This trouble having been overcome as far as practicable, the Professor gave the signal for striking up a grand historic anthem composed by himself. . . . The fiddles and banjos first struck in with a wild, voluptuous swell, that suddenly broke off in a mad staccato on the fortissimo grade. . . . Presently the Professor signaled the bass to turn itself loose, in expression of a passage of the narrative where the devil flies away with a junk load of Chinese pirates. The bass was equal to the occasion. . . . The swell of the tom-toms was simply terrific. . . . Then it was that Professor Lee Tom arose in the midst of the tumult with his magic wand, conscious of the majesty of a monstrous musician. After the execution of this impressive passage, Nang Bung, a promising young heathen . . . executed a solo on a gong in expression of a love ditty.[26]

The references to a "narrative" and a "love ditty" might suggest that either singing was taking place or the orchestra was being trained for accompaniment work. The quoted passage lacks precise information, but it does have the virtue (rare in such accounts) of attempting to describe Chinese music with respect to the actual instruments being played (though it contains the now-shopworn similes of catfights and the like, omitted in these excerpts). Despite its faults—and assuming an attempt at veracity—the account does mention some remarkable items that have not turned up in previous descriptions: Western-style conducting, systematic teaching of Chinese music, and an original composition by a Chinatown composer. And if indeed such teaching and rehearsal were largely for the purpose of training for the Chinese opera, such activities point up how solidly established the theater had become in the community, to the extent that the existence of a local corps of opera-trained musicians was reckoned desirable.

Optimism about the Chinese drama's future in Chinatown prompted a veritable boom in theater building in the late 1870s: first the "Look Sun Fung" ("Peacock") theater of 1877, on Washington at Church Alley; then in 1879 the theater that would become known as the "Grand," in the same block, opposite Waverly Place.[27]

The first of these new structures—the "Peacock"—was built at a cost of about $16,000. Described as a "substantial brick" building, the new theater measured 42 by 108 feet, with a 32-foot ceiling. Its capacity was fifteen hundred persons, with a standing-room-only leeway of another five hundred. The "modern-style" interior included a gallery and hanging gallery, and private boxes. Some of the boxes were for Chinese, some for whites. A separate gallery for Chinese females was reached by an outside stairway. An interesting feature of the new building was a ventilating system comprising four octagonal ventilators, each twelve feet in diameter and twelve feet high (reaching from the ceiling to the roof). Also between the ceiling and the roof were seventy-five rooms, surrounding the ventilator shafts, which served as living quarters for the acting company. These are described as being "unusually roomy and well ventilated for Chinese quarters."[28] Above the thirty-two-foot-deep stage was a "joss temple"; underneath were the property rooms. High

over the stage on the back wall—beneath the temple—was a window through which tumblers could leap to the stage. Curiously,
this elaborate new theater seems destined to have had a short life as
a Chinese-opera house, as within a few years there is no mention of
it in lists and descriptions of Chinese theaters. (To judge from a detailed Chinatown map appearing in 1885, the building was apparently converted into a clothing factory.[29])

The Peacock theater was still in operation in 1879, however,
when the *Chronicle* announced still another theater building near-
ing completion, also on Washington Street, a stone's throw from
the 1877 building. The newer theater came about as a result of a
consolidation of the existing three Chinese theaters. As the *Chronicle* explains it,

> . . . for some considerable time past [the Chinese] have contributed to the
> support of three theatres in Chinatown—the Yew Hin Look or Royal Chi-
> nese Theatre, on the north side of Jackson street, between Kearny and Du-
> pont streets, the Quan San Yoke or Gem of Mount Quan, on the south side
> of Jackson street in the same block, and the Look Sun Fung or Peacock,
> on Washington street, between Dupont and Stockton. As the competition
> between these rival places of amusement became sharper and keener, it was
> found that the profits were exceeded by the expenses, so that finally a con-
> solidation was effected and the three theaters came under the control of the
> Wing Ti Ping, or "The Company of Eternal Peace."

However, a number of actors were thrown out of work by the consolidation. These actors persuaded a group of wealthy merchants to
form a joint stock company and commence building still another
theater.

Built on a slightly larger scale than the neighboring Look Sun
Fung ("Peacock"), the new theater was a three-story brick building
ninety-two feet deep with a fifty-two-foot frontage and a thirty-
five-foot ceiling. Built with a large main gallery in the center and
two hanging side galleries, the new structure had a capacity of
twenty-five hundred spectators, somewhat more than could be ac-
commodated by its nearby rival. As with the neighboring theater,
the third story was used for lodgings for actors and other theatrical
personnel. The building's cost was said to be around $15,000.[30]

The continued existence of a Caucasian audience for Chinese
drama is attested to by the "fashionable house" that attended a

three-day run of Cantonese opera and acrobatics that was booked into the American Theater in November 1878 by an ambitious American impresario. The company was advertised as "enroute from Canton to Paris,"[31] but the troupe apparently stayed on in San Francisco or returned there, since it gave its name (Quan San Yoke or "Gem of Mount Quan") to the Chinese theater on the south side of Jackson Street.[32] The program was printed in English, and its contents were probably adapted to Western tastes, but it is nonetheless interesting as a reflection of the sort of program current in Chinese theaters:

GRAND OPERA HOUSE

Mission Street, between Third and Fourth

FREDERICK W. BERT . . . . Manager
Madam Marie Duret . . . . Directress of Amusements

I m m e n s e   H i t ! !

Enthusiastic Applause and Universal Praise
Awarded to the Great
QUAN SAN YOK

Dramatic, Acrobatic and Gymnastic Company,
from the Imperial Theatre, Canton (China),
comprising the largest and most Wonderful
Company of first-class male and female
Artists that ever left
THE FLOWERY KINGDOM

Who, notwithstanding the immense favor with
which their first performance in America
was received, must terminate their
engagement with the

SATURDAY MATINEE,

As they proceed on their way to Paris on Sunday.

A COMPLETE CHANGE OF BILL! The performance
will commence with a Tragedy, entitled

Y A N G   K Y E   S U M ;
Or, The Assassin of the Emperor

Distribution of Characters:

Emperor	Tong Sing
Yang Kye (the Assassin)	Kioong Chan Lung
Empress	Long Tai
Princess Tee Lee	Sun Chay
Minister of State	Leey Kin
Minister of War	Tai Kay
Minister of Foreign Affairs	Ah Lum
Minister of Finance	Chion Sing

Assisted by the Full Company. In their play they
will display their GORGEOUS WARDROBE, more
magnificent than ever before seen out
of China. To be followed by

FAIRY CHILD . . . . POI CHOY

The performance will conclude
with the most startling
Acrobatic and Gymnastic Acts
EVER SEEN, by
SING LEE LO, AH TOK, LOI SAM, TONG KEE, SAM KEE,
and a Full Company of Artists
Including the Marvelous Revolving Living Pyramid!![33]

It was perhaps predictable that the company should bill itself as "acrobatic and gymnastic" as well as dramatic and to give much emphasis to the acrobatic portions. It is as clear today as it was then that the first-time Western observer is likely to take immediate delight in the players' gymnastic dexterity while being typically bemused at best by the music and histrionics. The advertising presents perhaps a lesson learned. In the advertising for the pioneering Hong Took Tong in 1852, the orchestra was mentioned, but not the acrobatics. In the latter-day performance, it is the other way around, reflecting the impresario's prediction of the relative drawing power of various aspects of the company. An intriguing note in the 1878 program announces "first-class Male and *Female* Artists" (emphasis added). If indeed the company did feature actual female performers (rather than impersonators), this must mark the first mention in America of such an innovation. One may well doubt that actual females were so employed, however, as such additions were not commonly made until well into the twentieth century, whether in China or abroad (though we shall see occasional exceptions toward the very end of the nineteenth century).

The Chinese theaters, with their stage facilities, commodious interiors, and flexibility of arrangements (such as movable benches) served a number of functions besides housing the drama, as they were Chinatown's largest public halls and could serve as auditoriums or settings for banquets. We find, for instance, the Look Sung Fung ("Peacock") theater housing the eighth-anniversary celebration of the Methodist Chinese Mission School on the night of 7 June 1878. Much occidental music was heard that night, and the *Alta* reporter remarked that "the musical part of the programme, especially to those who were only accustomed to the nasal twangs and bagpipe notes of the ordinary Chinamen, demonstrated clearly the fact that with proper training, this race possesses voices of melody and power." The capacity audience was seen to show "appreciative delight" at tenor and baritone solos of hymns by Chinese students.[34]

The *Chronicle* of 2 October 1879 noted that the Royal Chinese Theater was converted into a banquet hall for "one of the most select affairs that has ever taken place in this country in Chinese social circles, the event being a grand banquet . . . given by the Chinese Consul-General, Chen Shu Tong, in honor of his fifty-first birthday." Some eight hundred Chinese merchants brought their families. Also accepting invitations, with their families, were a number of Americans, including a naval commodore, an ex-census commissioner, a professor at Hastings Law College, the Chinese Consul, and a representative of the Interior Department. The theater was elegantly transformed:

The seats of the dress circle and balcony of the theater were overlaid with level floors, and handsomely furnished with black walnut dining-tables, elegantly carved chairs and stools of the same material covered with costly and beautiful silk materials. The balcony was devoted exclusively to the ladies, they being partly hidden by a strip of gauze covering the whole front. On the left of the stage, overhead, hung fourteen large scrolls, fourteen inches in width by about eight feet in length, containing in Chinese characters the past life of the Consul, relating his virtues and good deeds, one of which was his private subscription of over $60,000 in behalf of the starving sufferers of the recent famine in China. These scrolls were presented to the Consul by his admiring friends in his native country. Hanging indiscriminately overhead were numerous silken banners upon which were artistically wrought needlework inscriptions and pictures, all of which were presented to the Consul by his friends of this city.

Throughout the day and evening, the celebrants were entertained by the Royal Chinese Theater Company giving "a dramatic rendition of Chinese court life."[35]

The orchestra and singers from the Royal Chinese Company were much in demand for such occasions. Two years earlier, the members of the troupe had held forth at a banquet given by the three hundred Chinese employees of the Lewis Brothers, importers of leaf tobacco. This time the setting was the Hung Fer Low restaurant, at 713 Dupont Street.

With generous disregard of expense the whole numerous orchestra of the Yu Henn Choy Royal Chinese Theater of Jackson street had been engaged to lend to the festive occasion the concordance of sweet sounds. The royal band occupied seats about the middle of the saloon, and its music fell with particularly thrilling effect upon untutored ears, combining, as it did, much of the substantial resonance of a boiler-making shop with the decisive clatter of a night watchman's rattle and the airy and illusive notes of a Washoe canary. When the "tenor" of the troupe, with aristocratic fingernails full two inches in length, strained the muscles of his swelling neck and shot his shrill falsetto into the riot of sound, and when each of the scores of well-dressed, intelligent-looking Chinamen who thronged the floor intoned the long drawn guttarals of his eager conversation, it is safe to say that Wagner's seven days turmoil of opera at Bayreuth was comparatively nowhere.

It would appear that the theater had plenty of reserves on hand, as performances continued meanwhile at the Jackson Street theater.

The preliminary part of the dinner required from 5 o'clock till 6, when the white men sauntered down to Kearney street, and the rank and file of the hosts went over to see into what century the current tragedy at the Royal Chinese Theater had progressed. But the more luxurious of the Asiatics stretched themselves on the carpeted dais of each little alcove of the surrounding walls, and with heads resting on the crimson-covered box cush-

ion, and with the tray of opium-smoking materials by them and the stem of
the lit pipe in their mouths, abandoned themselves to such mystic dreams as
might be inspired by the "lascivious pleasings" and dulcet, boiler-riveting
symphonies of a Chinese brass and string band.[36]

At the end of the decade, consolidation rather than innovation
and growth began to characterize the theatrical scene. For the duration, limits to the profitability of expansion in the Chinese theater
had been found. By early 1879 the managers of the three full-time
theaters in Chinatown found that there was insufficient patronage
to meet the expenses of production. (Chinatown's theaters were not
alone in this respect, as places of amusement were suffering reduced business throughout San Francisco.) As a simple solution to
the problem, the managers first took an obvious step—cutting salaries. Many actors, however, refused to work at the lower rates.
Holdouts who insisted, eighty-two of them, were paid full salary—and then discharged, whereupon they sailed back to China.
Salary cutting proved to be no solution to long-term economic
problems, however. The firing of the eighty-two had the immediate
effect of leaving all three theaters short-handed. Business dropped
off. The next step for the three managers was to pool their resources, banding together to form a joint company that would
mount the same production successively in all three theaters. The
plan of consolidation required firing still more actors, however,
this time between one and two hundred of them. The previously ter-
minated actors had accepted their fate with relative equanimity, but
the newly fired group responded with anger and threats, declaring
that they would not allow the consolidation to work: if they were
not rehired, they would stop any attempts at performance. The
theater managers were unyielding. Finally, confrontations between
actors and employers brought in the police. The trouble started on
20 March when the new policy was to take effect with the first performance by the new consolidated company.

About 6 o'clock in the evening a dispute arose between a former star and
the manager who had discharged him, and the star made the manager see a
thousand stars besides himself by several well-directed blows. Another star
indulged in the same manner with another manager, and Chinatown be-

came alive with rumors. The rushing of about 300 Chinamen down Jackson
street, through Kearny and up Washington, to witness a rumored fight, attracted the attention of the outside world. For an hour Washington street,
between Dupont and Kearny, was alive with the heathen, the point of interest being the store of Chee Kung Tong, where the energetic efforts to clear
the sidewalks were unavailing. When the time came for opening the theaters, two were found closed, the third, on Jackson street being open. About
this time a large crowd of Chinamen gathered to witness the promised row;
but the discharged actors, probably owing to the presence of special policemen, had not attempted to interfere with the performance up to a late
hour.[37]

Eventually, the ousted players found at least a short-term solution in persuading wealthy Chinese merchants to erect a new theater so that the out-of-work actors could compete with the consolidated company. (The latter had now been named Wing Ti
Ping—the Company of Eternal Peace.)[38]
In time, the attractions of the new theater vindicated the ag-
grieved actors. Their success was perhaps confirmed by an attempt
at arson on the new establishment, six months after opening
night—an act suspected to be the work of the now-disgruntled former employers.
The new theater would not be without labor problems of its own,
however. In the following January (1881), the new Grand Chinese
Theater's manager filed a complaint in Superior Court asking for
an injunction that would forbid ten of his actors to work at any theater but his own:

. . . Lee You alleges that in July, 1879, a Chinese theatrical combination or
company, including the defendants, was organized in this city for the purpose of producing and presenting on the stage various Chinese plays. The
above defendants, all being actors, entered into a further agreement with
the plaintiff that if he would furnish money sufficient to erect and fix up
the present "Grand Chinese Theater" they would pledge themselves to him
as a theatrical company for a term of six years, and would constitute him
the manager until such time as the money advanced by him would be fully
refunded, together with interest thereon. Lee You complains that the defendants, contrary to the said agreement, intend to transfer their allegiance
to another Chinese theater, and that he will be greatly injured, thereby, as a
programme for the Chinese holidays has already been arranged, and can-

not be carried out unless they remain with him and fulfill their engagements. The Celestial manager is especially anxious to secure the services of defendants now, as this is the most auspicious season of the whole year for the Chinese theaters.[39]

In the late 1870s and especially in the 1880s San Francisco's Chinese theaters increasingly received national and even international attention through accounts in books written by travelers and through numerous magazine articles. San Francisco was now eminently accessible by either sea or rail. Writers of the colorful sights of the city invariably included Chinatown as one of the most fascinating places to visit. And within Chinatown no institution was more bizarre and entertaining to the occidental visitor than the Chinese theater.

Through reading the various articles and portions of books devoted to San Francisco's Chinese theater in the late 1870s and the 1880s, one can piece together a fairly coherent picture of the dramatic techniques, the stage conventions, the behavior of the Chinese audience, and a number of other aspects that gives us something of a mosaic portrait of the theater during this period. We must draw our accounts largely from writers who brought no previous experience to bear with the medium. Their descriptions are predictably naive and ethnocentric. Essentially, such reports are aimed at capturing on paper the strangeness of the Chinatown ambience rather than describing and assessing in analytical fashion. Only the use of a time machine would ever allow for a truly accurate picture of the musical and dramatic practices of that time and place. Failing that, we can only read and compare the reports of largely bewildered outsiders who attempted to convey their impressions to the outside world.

Against the backdrop of a turbulent society in which anti-Chinese feelings and the effects of the Exclusion Law made life increasingly difficult for San Francisco's Chinese, the Chinese theater appears to have been a remarkably stable enterprise, notwithstanding the occasional storm and stress among the acting companies and theaters themselves. In reading over the various articles and chapters that deal with the attraction through the 1880s, one is struck with the relative lack of change during this period. It would appear that the Chinese theater had reached a high plateau of success in the community. Hundreds of actors were employed at never less than two full-time theaters. The period of ironic prosperity—amidst depression and xenophobia—was not destined to last: By the early 1890s the full effects of the Exclusion Laws would be felt, population would decline in Chinatown, and the theater would see a drop in fortunes followed by total devastation—in the earthquake and fire of 1906. In these scattered accounts of the 1870s and 1880s we read of a time in which Chinese theater flourished in a manner never to be equaled in this country.

Two theaters dominate throughout the 1880s, one of Washington (across from Waverly Place) and one on the south side of Jackson, between Dupont and Kearny. The fate of the other buildings intended for Chinese drama is not known. Such buildings would seem to have been readily convertible to factories, in view of their spacious interiors. On the other hand, the living quarters, kitchen facilities, and other domestic amenities could well have made these structures appropriate for conversion to lodging houses for the Chinese. In any event, the era of theater construction as such was over. Not until the 1920s would new buildings be erected solely for the purpose of housing the Chinese theater.

None of the authors we survey during this period remarks on any appreciable difference between one theater and another other than size and location. The theater buildings are in any case unpretentious structures inside and out. The Royal China appears to have been especially unprepossessing, with its exterior "in nowise remarkable, and, in fact . . . ugly, dingy, and Anglo-Saxon looking."[40] The appearance of the other theater was at least interesting:

The front of the new Chinese theater on Washington street resembles the gable end of a Pennsylvania Dutch barn. It is three stories in height, and has the architectural finish of a country variety store. In the front, on a level with the sidewalk, is a small room shut off with glass doors and windows. Here sit several delicate-featured Chinese repairing watches and jewelry, while about the window, where massive gold rings and ornaments for the hair are displayed, several sight-seers are always gathered, flattening their noses against the panes. . . . To the left of the shop is the main entrance, over which is a sign in gilt letters, "Grand Theater," with four hieroglyphics a foot tall, which express the same thing in more florid style.[41]

Throughout the 1870s and 1880s the admission price for occidentals was consistently fifty cents. The Chinese paid a lower rate, generally a quarter; and rates for Chinese customers got lower as the evening wore on. The Chinese were also privileged to receive a return check enabling them to come and go. One observer was surprised that his money was taken by an American at the entrance, since the theater was owned and managed exclusively by Chinese.

A Chinese money-taker, you may say, would have answered the purpose quite as well; but it is worth while noticing that the number of Chinamen in San Francisco who can talk even "pigeon" [sic] English is, considering the vastness of their aggregate, surprisingly small.[42]

Uninitiated spectators tended to dwell on what was *not* in a Chinese theater as much as what was:

The stage is a mere platform; there are no foot-lights, the only illumination being that from two small gasaliers. There are no curtains, no scenery, flies, or wings; no proscenium, or properties other than a table, two chairs, fans, and weapons. The scene is indicated in the primitive way by displaying a board on which is written "forest," "room," and so on. This is put in front of the actors, and the imagination of the spectators does the rest.[43]

Seating in the main part of the theater was on benches without backs. Boxes along the side of the room extended right into the stage area on both sides. Non-Chinese visitors were especially intrigued by the box that was set aside for women, who in no cases mingled with the men in the theater.

The stage, bare of properties save perhaps a table and a few chairs, was entered not from the side, as there were no wings. Rather, two doors against the rear wall served for entrance and exit, stage-right for the former, stage-left for the latter. Actors thus entered direct from the green room. Two gas jets lit the stage, with "a few scattered jets here and there in the house only serving to make darkness visible. There was no such thing as a chandelier."[44]

In center stage were the musicians, usually six or seven, who
perched on stools against the wall, typically separated from the actors by a table.

Both at the rear of the stage and at other locations throughout
the house were representations of the "joss" and the household
gods. "Nothing bears such distinct testimony to the importance of
the theater in China as this idea, firmly fixed in the Chinese mind,
that the gods take pleasure in dramatic performances as well as [the
Chinese] themselves."[45]

On a central pillar was the "post office"—a bulletin board of
sorts where messages were left for patrons. This was an institution
that was to see long life, as the bulletin-board message service was
still in effect as late as 1936. It was noted in that year that the service "is today still offered in the form of brush-scrawled Chinese
characters on white papers which are impaled on a nail at the right
of the proscenium arch in cases of emergency calls."[46]

The name of the company currently in residence appeared on the
wall above the stage. "The theatres are named as ours are," noted
Catherine Dall, "and beside that they take annually the name of
the troop [sic] that opens the performance of the year." Mrs. Dall
recorded that the current (1880) troupe was known as "Kom Quai
Yuen," which was translated for her as "The Gold Cinnamon Garden."[47] A year later, George Sala made note of a similarly placed
"placard on which, in gaily spangled Roman letters . . . was written up the words . . . 'Quai min Yuen'," which a companion
translated for him as "pleasure, or amusement combined with instruction."[48] These were not the only signs to be seen in the theater,
however. Inscriptions in Chinese were hung against the wall in red,
blue, and purple paper.[49]

The Chinese theater is rich in sign literature, and signs of all descriptions
exist, suited to all needs and addressed to all intelligences: "The utterances
of God are blessings to men"; "Glory to the spirit forever"; "The people
with a loud voice praise him for his blessing." Then, not a foot away perhaps: "Ladies and gentlemen must be separated and treat each other with
proper respect"; "Go up and down peaceably"; "Harmony is the best policy."

A large sign overlooking the pit or orchestra section of seating pro-
claimed "The seats are full of gentlemen." Signs in the dressing

rooms reminded actors that they "must not come up in this dirty place [the make-up room] with their costumes on" and that "people who wash their faces should not spill water on the floor." Within the green room were posted the bills from a local restaurant for the amounts due for lunches on matinee days. Other signs exhorted actors to "Let the voice be clear and the music loud," "Let the gymnasts excel themselves," and "Let man have the spirit of the dragon and of the horse." On entering the stage, the actor was enjoined to enter in good spirits; on leaving he was reminded to "go and change your costume." On stage, various signs invited good luck. In the musician's alcove was the written wish that: "When the performance begins there will be good luck to all," and nearby were expressed such hopes as "May your happiness be great" and "May you receive what your heart desires."[50] As earlier noted, more functional signs were brought to the front of the stage from time to time to announce the time or whereabouts of a given scene.

The theater was constructed as somewhat of an indoor amphitheater. Back from the stage, the floor rose by regular graduations, and at the rear of the room two flights of stairs led to a balcony. On a level with the balcony and running the full length of the room were two narrow galleries—the private boxes, including that reserved for women.

The Chinese men wore their hats in the theater, presenting a uniformly black vista from above. George Fitch remarked at this sight, noting that the scene was relieved by only four white hats—"huge, umbragious, cream-colored *sombreros*" of visiting Mexicans. The benches were crowded with Chinese. "Packed is the proper word," says Fitch, "for they are sitting on low benches, and each bench accommodates as many persons as the seats of a horse-car when the rush for home and dinner has set in."[51]

The audience was remarkably undemonstrative by Western standards. Rarely did any direct response to actions on the stage interrupt the low conversation that went on continuously among the spectators. An amusing episode might evoke smiles, but "the most perfect stillness reigned throughout the house." Only the most extraordinarily affecting scene would bring forth an audible response. Mrs. Dall recalls that at one point "a low murmur of approbation ran through the house, and the actors threw themselves on their faces and touched their foreheads to the floor in acknowledgment."[52]

Vendors circulated quietly among the crowd, offering fruits, nuts, sugarcane, and other edibles. Cigars and cigarettes beclouded the air, both in the audience and on stage (as the musicians, who worked constantly and without off-stage breaks, smoked in the midst of the performance); and one account states that members of the audience drink "saki" during the show.[53]

Women were always in attendance, segregated in their special gallery box. According to Mrs. Dall, "In the afternoon loose women are admitted. In the evening, only those who are 'kept'."[54] Sala noted the presence of "between forty and fifty females and perhaps half as many children." The more aristocratic were accompanied by their female servants. Many of the women smoked during the performance, either cigarettes or small, ornamented reed pipes. Sala added that "at intervals between their smoking they munched . . . and now and again they relieved the lugubrious taciturnity of the auditory by a brief but shrill giggle."[55] George Fitch reported that the women's bright dresses "furnish the only relief to the prevailing somberness," though Theodor Kirchhoff describes them, on the contrary, as plainly dressed, so as not to attract attention.[56] (The divergent accounts could perhaps be explained by Mrs. Dall's distinction between the "loose" women in the afternoon and the "kept" ones at night.)

Theater personnel and spectators were frequently seated on both sides of the stage itself. One writer, having visited the green room during a performance, emerged on stage and stood in the very center of it, observing the musicians. Yet, he notes, "our presence there did not seem in the least to disconcert the spectators, who . . . were attending to the play with open-mouthed interest. . . ."[57] G.B. Densmore noted that "actors and attachees sit at either side of the stage, smoking or eating candy, and, at times, crossing the stage while the play is going on."[58] Sala reported that:

On either side of the performers on the stage there sat, stood, lounged, or loafed about a group of Chinamen, smoking and munching, even as their *confrères* in the parquette did. They would cross the stage from time to time in the most unconcerned manner, threading their way through the ranks of actors, of whom there might be as many as thirty on the stage at a time, and who, on their part, took not the slightest notice of these interlopers, who must have been in some way connected with the house, since every now and then they disappeared through the doors in the rearward wall, returning after a time to resume their loafing and lounging-places of vantage on the stage. Who were these hangers-on, cool as so many cucumbers, and yellow as so many bananas? . . . they could scarcely be gentlemen amateurs, for they wore the same jerkins and trousers of dark serge, and the same low-crowned black hats, as did the twelve hundred silent Chinamen in the pit.[59]

Edwin Booth wrote that he and his party had mingled with the actors on stage even as the play was in progress.[60]

Of further puzzlement to Sala was the occasional descent of one of the "hangers-on," by way of a short flight of steps on either side of the stage, "into a vacant area which should have been the orchestra. But no spectator from the body of the house—none that I saw, at least—ever presumed to ascend the steps leading to the stage."[61] He never solved the problem of the hangers-on, who were probably simply members of the company not performing in that particular play or scene.

An elderly musician in San Francisco's Chinatown related to the present writer how white tourists were sometimes brought by a guide into the theater by way of a basement entrance, from which they would wend their way through various passages, finally climbing stairs and emerging on the stage itself, where they would be seated for the performance. It was because of such underground meanderings, according to this informant, that the persistent myth developed about Chinatown's alleged maze of underground tunnels which were supposedly in use up until the 1906 earthquake.

Kirchhoff and his party were given just such a labyrinthine routing to the stage. They were led through "a maze of narrow, low, poorly lighted passages," traversing the kitchen and green room, and finally ended up on the stage itself. They had plenty of company:

A large number of Chinese stand to the right and left of the stage and very politely make room for us in the right row. As everyone has kept on his hat, we take the privilege of keeping ours on too.

As the stage guests smoked cigars nonchalantly, their guide (a city detective) explained the drama in a loud voice; and the accommodating Chinese took no observable offense even at the laughter and jokes of the stage-sitting spectators, who even took the liberty of touching the actors' costumes from time to time. However, the actors did show evident annoyance at the presence of women in the Kirchhoff party and seemed to avoid conspicuously coming in contact with them.[62]

The taboo against women on the stage was evidently not total, however. A translated playbill cited by McDowell in 1884 contains the following notice:

THE DRAGON AND PEACOCK JUNK!!!
BEAUTIFUL LANTERNS OF DIVERS COLORS!!!
GORGEOUS COSTUMES!!!
Special Notice.—Four genuine girls will draw the junk.

McDowell further notes that:

It is easy to see from the pretentious advertisement that the Chinese have no real objection to the appearance of women on the stage, and it is the lack of intelligence of the women rather than the sense of propriety of the audience that keeps them off. Indeed, there is already one Chinese actress in San Francisco, who, whenever she appears is received with acclamation. She is attached to the Jackson street theater, and, it is safe to say, earns a much larger salary than if she were a man.

Such mentions of Chinese actresses in the late nineteenth century, though few and far between, are nonetheless of special interest, as later writers would assume that women were barred entirely from the stage until well after the 1911 Revolution in China and that the female star of Cantonese opera was a phenomenon only of the 1920s and succeeding years. It would appear from the accounts of McDowell and others that there was ample precedent some forty years earlier for the striking box-office appeal that Chinese actresses would command in the third decade of the twentieth century.

The living conditions, salaries, and social status of actors are subjects for frequent comment by occidental observers in the 1880s. As has been noted, provisions for room and board are invar-

iably included in the theater buildings. The theater, in fact, provided a world for the actor that was nearly self-sufficient.
McDowell describes the Chinese theater in the morning as *en
déshabillé*:

Everyone is sound asleep; the actors in their comfortable sleeping rooms
over the stage; the supernumeraries and petty comedians on some trunk in
the dressing-room, or, more frequently, on the floor.

The visitor at this hour went unhindered: "It is supposed that you
have some business or you would not have come."

Leaving the boxes on your right, and finding your way with difficulty along
a dark and narrow passage-way, you open a little door at the end, and find
yourself presently in the actor's hotel, an intricate rookery of rooms and
corridors where the helpless and luxurious histrion is lodged, fed, shaved,
and dressed. For everything necessary to his existence the actor finds within
the four walls of the theater.[63]

Meals were furnished to the whole company backstage, and the
kitchen and serving areas were much remarked upon in visitors' accounts. Richard Reinhardt in 1877 describes a supper enjoyed by
actors and acrobats in the dressing room of the Royal China Theater:

. . . a spread of roast pig, rice, tea, and Chinese sweetmeats, ranged on a
great, clumsy table of black teak, with smoking joss sticks and red and yellow candles burning around and great globe lanterns swinging overhead.
Downstairs, in a dark, bricked kitchen, others of the dramatic corps take
turns at cooking mysterious native messes amid dense, greasy vapors and
smells even more uncanny than those which salute our noses above.[64]

In the following year, another observer notes that during the hours
of performance "there is a cold collation spread in the dressing-
room of the theatre, of which each actor will partake, without ceremony, at that time of night when he feels most able to do justice to
it."[65] The delights of eating were thus very much a part of life in the
theater, enjoyed by troupers and audience alike. While much of the
food partaken backstage was apparently prepared in the theater's
kitchen, some of it appears to have been catered by local restau-

rants. McDowell notes the posting of bills in the green room from a local restaurant for lunches on matinee days, when cooking chores for the company were presumably suspended.

Thus were the necessities provided for within the four walls. The more affluent actors had servants in their retinue, and some even brought their wives with them. Others married while on tour. So self-enclosed was life in the theater that the betrothed actor did not have to leave the building even to get married—his intended bride would be brought to *him*:

The bridegroom sends a carriage for the bride. When she arrives they worship their ancestors together. Then she presents him with a cup of tea or Chinese whisky, as if to say, "I am your humble servant." After which follows a curious ceremony. The bride, attired in a red skirt of flowing silk, and a gorgeous head-dress on her head, proceeds to pay her respects to every Joss in the theater; as there are thirty or more Josses in every conceivable situation, in niches at every turn of the underground and winding passage-ways, this journey leads her far. Having propitiated the infernal deities, she takes leave of her bridesmaids, is domiciled, and passes under the dominion of her husband.[66]

A family life of sorts was thus available to certain of the actors, though children were apparently lacking as yet from the theatrical domicile. In general, the life of the actor impressed outside observers as a type of captivity, as summed up in the following reporter's words:

His life is passed in two small rooms, having a probable area of about 140 square feet. He has a wife to share his captivity, but this rich man sleeps upon a strip of matting spread upon a shelf.[67]

For figures on the income of Chinese actors, theatrical observers had to rely on information from their Chinese informants. Here one finds considerable variance, with emphasis placed on the highest salaries. In 1876, an annual salary range from $50 to $800 had been reported.[68] A conservative estimate in 1880 is considerably higher: "Chinese actors get from $250 to $1,800 a year salary, with an allowance of opium, rice and tea. Each actor is also furnished with a room and the necessary furniture."[69] Four years later, a range from $200 to $7,000 is given by McDowell, an exceptionally careful investigator in such matters.[70] If the $7,000 figure is accurate, it applied to only one or two actors at most—the stars whose names were a strong box-office attraction. Fitch, in 1882, mentions a $10,000 salary for a leading man from Peking.[71] However in the same year a story on "A Chinese Christening" in the *Call* mentions that one guest—"the greatest impersonator of Chinese female character," and presumably in the highest salary category—was under contract at an annual salary of $6,000.[72] In 1886 one British reporter cited £1,400 and £1,800 (equivalent then to $6,720 and $8,640) as the salaries of two highly paid actors in San Francisco.[73] An anonymous reporter for *Harper's* noted in 1883:

It is not commonly known . . . that there is a national patronage of the drama in China . . . and that actors receive generous salaries, ranging from $1000 to $4000—sums equal to at least three times those amounts here [San Francisco] . . . and an actor who plays the leading female part will receive about $3500.[74]

Loo Chin Goon, described by the New York *Times* as "the most famous and popular actor that ever delighted a Chinese audience in San Francisco," was reported in 1883 to have been earning $5,000 a year.[75]

Salaries of the companies' musicians, however, do not engage journalistic attention. Indeed, their lives go unchronicled in general, beyond a scattering of comments (typically facetious) about their sounds, appearance, and behavior onstage.

That the social status of an actor in traditional China was low is cited by some writers as a reason for the voluntary isolation and reclusive lives reportedly led by actors in the San Francisco companies. In the words of one reporter: "Though they receive very large salaries they are social outcasts, and rarely go into the streets."[76] It may be doubted, however, whether social position as such determined such lack of circulation, especially in the San Francisco milieu, in which actors were simply sojourners among other sojourners. A more plausible explanation of the actors' voluntary confinement might lie in the fortress-like self-sufficiency of the theater's quarters, together with the prodigious working hours put in by theatrical troupers.

The amount of exertion required of the leading actor [for instance] is amazing. He plays seven days in the week, and the performance each day lasts from six to eight hours. The theater is open at two o'clock every day, and short farces and comedies are given during the afternoon to audiences largely made up of women and children. At seven o'clock begins the regular evening performance, which does not end until midnight. Frequently the same actors appear in both performances.[77]

It is evident that working, eating, and sleeping must therefore consume most of the actor's time, and it would seem little wonder that he was seldom seen outside the theater, in McDowell's words, "except for an occasional dinner at the restaurant or a walk through the streets in the afternoon."[78]

Not mentioned by McDowell, however, was perhaps the single most time-consuming activity of all, excepting actual performance: the learning of new parts. The repertoire demands of the San Francisco Chinese theater were quite different from those of the home territory. In southern China the members of an acting company spent the majority of their time touring, in contrast to the more settled existence of their counterparts in the San Francisco theater. Hence, the actor in China might need to be equipped with only a limited number of parts to perform, as a frequent change of location would allow for much repetition of a given play. In San Francisco, by contrast, actors needed to be continuously at work in learning new material.

It is interesting to note in this regard that new plays were mounted with no rehearsal whatever, in the Western sense of the word. Players learned their parts individually, never to interact with others on the stage until the first public performance. Only the most complex of stage interaction might need some pre-staging, but even where complexity of interaction was anticipated, the course of action was more likely to be that of talking matters over in the green room while attending to makeup and costumes rather than staging an actual cast rehearsal.[79]

As for the actors' social status within the San Francisco Chinese community, it is difficult to draw conclusions from published materials, as Chinese social life was not of interest to the prevailing English-language press. Only on rare occasions—such as a social event involving exceptionally colorful feature-story possibilities—did a newspaper article give some hint as to social stratification among the Chinese. One such exception is a long and detailed account of a Chinese christening and elaborate banquet printed in the *Call* in 1882. The event was hosted by a merchant who had been in business for thirty years in San Francisco. Some 290 Chinese and 20 Caucasians had been invited for the occasion. The more notable guests, singled out for mention by the newspaper, were "Sam Yuen, General Manager of the Yee Quan Ying, or Grand Theatre, Lee Yung, one of the proprietors of that theatre, Yung Hong Gee, President of the Sam Yup Company, Chow Hung, the old, and Chow Pong Lai, new Inspector of that Company, and Yun Sing, called Ty Kah Sing (Hightoned), the greatest impersonator of Chinese female character, and who is under engagement at an annual salary of $6,000." At the feast following the christening ceremony, the infant, clothed in ceremonial regalia, was brought out and exhibited to the guests.

Around his neck was suspended a heavy gold chain, on which hung a peculiarly shaped figure of gold, which the father gave the company to understand is a representation of a warrior seated astride of a lion. This he said was a gift from the members of the company of the grand Chinese theatre, and that if worn by the babe as a charm would render him strong and valiant.[80]

The presence of persons associated with the theater, together with the child's gift from the theatrical company, might suggest a special relationship of the host with the theater (a patron or investor, perhaps). That members of the theater's management were present is of course unexceptional in this mercantile gathering, as they were businessmen, too. However, the invitation to the actor would certainly suggest that the latter was far from being a social outcast. One might speculate that the actor's high salary served to mitigate whatever stigma his profession gave him. In any case, from this account one can infer that at least star-category actors were accorded some status in Chinatown society. Those lower on the salary scale (and presumably musicians and other supporting individuals) were perhaps more certainly regarded as being traditionally among the lowly.

It is interesting to note the inferences drawn by several writers with respect to the actor's traditional low standing in Chinese society. Some regard this low status as an element that hampers the improvement of Chinese dramatic art in general. Benjamin Lloyd in 1876 first gives lip service to a culturally relative viewpoint, then downgrades the work of actors:

Viewing it from an American standpoint, the Chinese drama is in a very crude state; but perhaps an intelligent Chinaman would pronounce the same criticism on the art as presented on our own stages, and in the absence of a disinterested third person to judge which opinion is correct, we must be content to leave the question of superiority unsettled. The profession of actor (there are no Chinese actresses) is not considered very reputable by the Chinese; and as a consequence, there is very little rivalry and not much improvement among the Chinese dramatic artists.[81]

Hubert Howe Bancroft similarly declared that "the degraded position of actors has tended to oppose advancement in the histrionic art . . ." but cites another possibility for this alleged retardation as owing to the "undemonstrative nature of the [Chinese] people," who provide a bland and unreactive audience and thus fail to stimulate the performers to greatness.[82] Neither of these speculations holds water, however. With respect to rivalry—it was not only existent in the Chinese theater, it was rampant. And as regards audience reaction and the actors' responses to it, Bancroft sees the matter purely through Western eyes and assumes that a lack of applause or undivided attention connotes a negative reaction to the performance, or an apathetic one at best. Both the nonrivalry and nonstimulus arguments are put forth to explain the alleged lack of improvement and advancement in the Chinese theater. Thus we have two erroneous observations put forth to explicate a condition that neither observer could know existed at all, as neither Lloyd nor Bancroft was privy to the workings of the Chinese theater or knowledgeable as to its history.

The actors' traditional low status had still another implication for McDowell, who stresses the advantages for San Francisco's theaters of actors' chronic indebtedness, a condition that supposedly results from this profession's low rung on the social ladder:

. . . [The actor] occupies in China the lowest place in the scale of caste. He is incapacitated from holding any position of trust or emolument under the government, and this rule applies with all its rigor to his sons and grandsons as well. Nothing but the most desperate fortunes and the extremely large profit accruing would ever tempt a Chinese subject to embrace a profession at once so unlucky and so proscribed. Legally debarred from all other pursuits, with a political curse resting on their lives and those of their children, Chinese actors have little incentive to save, and as a consequence we find that they are almost always in debt. From this has resulted the paradoxical fact that the best company is to be seen in San Francisco, so very many Chinese actors having been obliged to leave their own country on account of business complications. An actor who in China would act the *rôle* of first general, must in San Francisco be content with an engagement as second, and sometimes third general; a first comedian, that of second comedian; and so on through the whole cast.

A sojourn in America simply meant increased revenue:

In China there are but comparatively few stationary theaters, and the majority of the actors belong to strolling companies that depend in the main on the support of some wealthy nobleman who commands the play. Even in the large cities the pit is free, and the revenues are derived entirely from the galleries.

The galleries, in turn, were divided into three ranks:

First rank, teak chairs with high backs $1.50
Second rank, bamboo chairs without backs 80
Third rank, for the first hour 25
       for the second hour 20
       for the third hour 15
       for the fourth hour 10
       for the fifth hour and each succeeding hour 05

In San Francisco, by contrast, matters were much simpler. There were no free admissions; and with the exception of box seats, only one rank existed, the price (according to McDowell) being fixed on the basis of the lowest-paying rank in China. "The same decreasing scale is observed, however, so that a Chinaman pays five cents an hour for his theatrical amusement." (In addition, of course, return checks were given to all Chinese; thus ". . . on leaving the Chinese theater any evening a large number of poor devils who cannot afford to pay the admission price can be seen shadowing the door of the theater and soliciting the return checks of their more fortunate brethren.")[83]

Though musicians were not the object of any special curiosity regarding matters of salary, status, or living conditions, there is no dearth of description of their activities onstage. From a number of published accounts of the San Francisco Chinese theater in the 1880s and the years immediately preceding and following, one can get a fairly consistent picture of the role and activities of the orchestra. In the majority of accounts, a total of seven musicians is mentioned (the lowest number given being "four to six."[84]) The orchestra was situated against the back wall of center stage, facing the audience. A table often separated the musicians from the actors, serving also as "a convenient block for decapitating an enemy after a ferocious combat." The instrumentation would not be out of place in the traditional *Peking* opera, as heard in the present day: hu-ch'in, erh-hu, san-hsien, and (especially for military scenes), so-na, and various percussion such as gongs, cymbals, and the leader's tan-p'i-ku. Fitch conveys a general picture of the orchestra's busy role in the following, though he typifies certain Western misconceptions (that, for instance, the "leader" is the fiddle player, who plays a "one string" instrument):

The musicians, seven in number, are placed along the back of the stage, facing the audience. In the middle is the leader, a tall, gaunt Chinese, who plays a diminutive fiddle with one string. This string is composed of many strands of horse-hair, and over it is drawn a bow similar material. The sound produced is as shrill and ear-piercing as the high notes of a bagpipe. The leader is usually the sole accompanist to a mournful chant. When the sad and sentimental "business" is on, he devotes himself to this instrument. When the action begins, he drops his fiddle and seizes a pair of cymbals as big as a wash-tub, and brings them together with a crash which shakes the theatrical firmament. Next to him sits a melancholy-looking man, who pounds mechanically a brazen gong, pendent by a wire cord and on a level with his head. Beyond him one musician beats a disk of burnished brass with a small metal drumstick, while another sits astride of a small hobby-horse and plays a tattoo upon its head of polished wood. On the other side of the leader are three men who "pick" diminutive banjos, and alternate this discord with performances on a species of horn. The latter produces the only sound that, to English ears, bears the remotest kinship to melody. The devoted musicians remain through the entire performance of six hours, unbroken by a single "wait," and for the greater part of the time they work like galley-slaves. The speeches are delivered to slow music; all the combats, counter-marching, and pantomime which fill out their interminable dramas have their musical accompaniments. The stormy tirades of rival potentates are emphasized by the clash of cymbals and the clangor of gongs, while in mortal combat the entire band aids in spurring on the warriors to deeds of valor.[85]

Fitch's impression was clearly garnered through watching a military play. That the musicians "work like galley-slaves" the better part of the time was apparently true of some plays, however, and not others. Another account finds the orchestra in relative repose—"mainly considerate and silent."[86] But still another complains that "judging from the unceasing din they make, they are paid for the quantity instead of the quality of music produced."[87]

The actual instruments must be inferred from the attempts by various observers to describe them in terms derived from their own experience. (Illustrations sometimes accompanying a reporter's text are of course useful as a correlative check.) I have interpreted (or translated) the following examples:

Hu-ch'in[88]

. . . two Chinese fiddles, neither of them in the slightest tune.[89]

. . . the one-stringed fiddle is held like a violoncello, and is a most painful instrument.[90]

The violin is a small, heavy tamborine, with a long neck, upon which two strings cross one another, holding between them, below the crossing, the bowstring, which accordingly touches one string on the upper the other on the lower side.[91]

. . . fiddler.[92]

. . . the leader . . . plays a diminutive fiddle with one string. This string is composed of many strands of horse-hair, and over it is drawn a bow of similar material.[93]

. . . Chinese fiddle.[94]

San-hsien (most frequently referred to as a banjo[95] or guitar[96])

. . . no prettier souvenir is there of San Francisco than the Chinese banjo, a beautiful instrument of dark polished wood, with a blue snake's skin stretched over the drum.[97]

Some [guitars] have bodies of small, flat tomtoms with long neck and one to three strings, but with less frets than our guitars.[98]

On the other side of the leader are three men who "pick" diminutive banjos, and alternate this discord with performances on a species of horn.[99]

There was a grotesque guitar, something between a banjo and a Russian balalaïka . . .[100]

So-na

. . . clarionet.[101]

. . . trumpet.[102]

. . . a species of horn.[103]

In addition to these indispensable instruments one occasionally finds the use of a transverse flute. Referred to by various Western names (such as "flageolet"[104] and "fife"[105]), what is almost certainly the bamboo ti is most clearly described by Bancroft: ". . . bamboo flutes, some with lateral blow-hole, and about six finger-holes."[106] The use of the flute (and a presumptive p'i-p'a mentioned by Bancroft—see note 118) might indicate that the species of opera being performed retained vestiges of the k'un-ch'ü drama of southern China, notwithstanding the primarily Peking-opera instrumentation whose principal accompanying instrument is the hu-ch'in.

Vivid mention is made of those instruments that made the most direct and sometimes painful effect on occidental listeners—the gongs, cymbals, drums, and other percussion. Bancroft describes these in some detail:

The percussion instruments, which form the *pièces de resistance*, consist of a big tomtom standing on its end, another small and flat, like a covered tamborine, a tambour, a gong suspended by a cord, a small, sonorous mortar of wood, having the rounded upper side covered with skin, and a tiny square sounding-board, fastened to the side of a stick, all of which are beaten with drumsticks. There are also the cymbal and castanet, the latter being a heavy black piece of wood, some nine inches in length, which is held in the hand while the other piece, connected with it by a cord at the top, is made to fall against it.[107]

Thus we have the following percussion instruments still used in Peking opera: T'ang-ku ("big tomtom"), ta-lo ("gong suspended by a cord"), po ("cymbal[s]"), and pan ("castanet[s]"). The "sonorous mortar of wood" is probably a tan-p'i-ku, the "covered tamborine" a huai-ku. The "tambour" might be any of several smaller drums. It is less clear what is meant by the "tiny square sounding-board."

Extra-large cymbals were employed in certain dramas. Fitch reports that the "leader" (who he thought to be the hu-ch'in player) sometimes "seizes a pair of cymbals as big as a washtub."[108] McDowell noted that their cymbals "are much larger than ours, and beaten out artistically of brass; the dents of the hammer giving them all the effect of beaten gold."[109]

The cymbal player [in Fitch's words] is sometimes very expert, and is the only one of the orchestra who does not remain always at his post. He moves about anywhere where the inspiration of the piece may lead him, often throwing up one cymbal in the air and catching it on a flat side of the other, which he holds in his hand. As a Chinese cymbal weighs upward of ten pounds, the difficulty of this feat can well be imagined.[110]

The player of the tan-p'i-ku is correctly described by some observers as the orchestra's leader, while others guessed the player of the hu-ch'in or the gong. One writer reports that the orchestra was

conducted by a bare-legged Celestial, who sat on a stool in front of his colleagues with his coat off and his arms bared up to the shoulder, and who rapped violently all the while upon a circular piece of stone with two bits of stick.[111]

The tan-p'i-ku is otherwise described as "the ox-hide drum,"[112] the "head of polished wood" of a "small hobby-horse,"[113] an "attenuated drum with a hole in the center of the parchment,"[114] and, in Bancroft's words, "a small, sonorous mortar of wood, having the rounded upper side covered with skin."[115]

A few other percussion instruments are mentioned with less descriptive precision. Marshall makes note of an instrument that he could not see but which produced a sound "not unlike the popping of corks."[116] This may well have been the pan castanets or a mu-yü or other species of hollow woodblock. Sala reports "what seemed to be an Italian 'gauffering' iron" being struck with a pair of "tongs." He also describes one musician as sitting before "a curious metallic 'arrangement' on four legs, which bore the appearance of a miniature 'kitchener' or cooking-stove."

In the centre of the top of this weird machine there was a circular orifice with a metal cover, like a saucepan-lid, and at irregular intervals the instrumentalist lifted this saucepan-lid. . . . when he replaced [it] he brought it down with a clang, and . . . the seeming cooking-stove thereupon emitted a sepulchral and ear-piercing shriek. . . .[117]

Though the identity of the shrieking stove does not come to immediate light, one may generalize from these accounts that the typical orchestra consisted of hu-ch'in, san-hsien, so-na (or multiples of any of these), together with tan-p'i-ku and a collection of percussion instruments that always included the T'ang-ku, cymbals, and gongs. Occasional appearance of the ti and p'i-p'a[118] rounded out the ensemble. As emphasized in many of these accounts, instrumentalists were not necessarily limited to any one instrument but would double on others as the occasion demanded. The only mention of an instrument that appears truly uncharacteristic of southern Chinese opera performance (aside from the gauffering-iron and cookstove, which remain inscrutable to the present writer) is that of "two connected hautboys, like the Greek double flute," observed by Bancroft.[119]

The musicians sat on three-legged stools, barefoot and smoking at will. Marshall sums up their appearance:

Every player seemed thoroughly in earnest, and worked away at his instrument as if his very existence depended on the amount of noise he could add to the general din and confusion. But if one performer got tired, he would put down his instrument and smoke his clay pipe, and then resume his playing when he felt inclined. Not a single man among the players had a pair of shoes or stockings on.[120]

Dancing was reported to be seen only rarely on the Chinese stage. One writer went as far as to say it was nonexistent:

Do the Chinese dance? Never; neither in China nor in America, unless they have become so far denationalized as to be considered a foreign graft on the Western stalk, which occurs not once in a thousand cases. There is therefore no dance upon the Chinese stage. In all their performance, from beginning to end, there is nowhere any sort of dance. . . . The Chinese look upon such things as entirely beneath the dignity of a Chinaman, and such a performance would be received with disgust and hisses.[121]

Others, however, report the occasional appearance of dancing on stage. Lloyd states that "except for that [dancing] indulged in by the actors, it is an amusement that the race have no relish for whatever. Their strength is too valuable to be exhausted in this (to them) useless exercise."[122] Densmore concurs that actors "never do much dancing";[123] and Bancroft states that the activity "is not much in vogue, for Chinese regard it as a vulgarity and a fatiguing exercise. . . ."[124] Rare as it might have been, however, dancing of a sort did provide an occasional high point in a play's performance. McDowell describes a pageant-like "Cloud Ballet" scene in the opera entitled *Che Young Kwong Builds a Ship That Sails on Land*, but whose plot is concerned almost entirely with building a bridge. The *raison d'être* of the ballet portion, says McDowell,

is the necessity of the ocean's being calm enough to allow the building of the bridge. The King of the Eastern Ocean has been consulted, and has promised to keep the wind down. The ballet begins. Supernumeraries enter completely clothed in white, each carrying in his hands two lanterns skillfully painted in imitation of clouds. After moving gracefully about the stage for a time, meeting and retreating as if in recoil, the movement becomes definite, the clouds coming together by twos and fours, until, in the process of this movement, they spell out in five tableaux (each tableau representing a Chinese character) the glorious sentence of charity and love: "Peace on earth, good-will toward man." The allegory is complete, the clouds are resting, and the ocean is calm.[125]

If dancing was a rarity, however, tumbling and acrobatics were well-nigh ubiquitous. Hardly a description of the opera by a Western observer omits an account of such vigorous activity on stage. As we have seen, the acrobatics of the Chinese stage were the most popular of all features in the theater to occidental playgoers, from the very earliest appearance of Chinese opera in San Francisco. Such popularity had by no means declined in the later decades of the century. Acrobatics frequently coincided with battle scenes and typically were featured at a climactic point toward the end of a play.

The acrobats or tumblers make their entrance *en masse* at about eleven o'clock, and the whole stage is filled with all the members of the troupe. Their feats are wonderful. The great battle scene, an indispensable requisite in a Chinese theatre, then takes place, and a terrific display comes of banging, hammering, screaming, twanging, and tooting. . . . New armies come on as fast as the old ones are decapitated, and all the time the noise is deafening.[126]

Thomas Hinchliff, who otherwise had little good to say of Chinese opera, was highly impressed with its acrobatics:

The only redeeming feature was a group of tumblers, who, for no apparent reason, came forwards during a serious part of the performances, and did their particular work right well. They turned summersaults [sic] over the tables, alighting on the very tops of their heads, and thence taking a fresh departure with such astounding coolness that I could not help wondering at the thickness of their skulls.[127]

A more detailed description of acrobatics in a battle scene was recorded by Reinhardt:

Suddenly, in the strangest way, the fighting merges into lofty tumbling. The half-naked warriors chase each other round and round the stage, throwing double and triple somersaults high in the air, forward and backward, alighting on their feet, on their hands, and flat on their backs with

their feet stretched out straight and their arms close on their sides. Reinforcements rush out—more men, stripped to the waist, bare-armed and
barefooted, with a single, hornlike unicorn sprouting from their foreheads
and their noses painted a staring white. One huge, fat man, without a per-
ceptible bone or muscle in his body, stands on his head, walks on his hands,
or his elbows—anyway but on his feet—ties himself into horrible knots,
leaps backward over piled-up chairs and tables, throws himself into the air
rolled up like a ball, does everything but turn himself inside out, and retires, bland and expressionless, amid a storm of applause from our small
party of Caucasians, which causes all the almond-eyes to look askance at us
and a faint smile of contempt to cross a few of the placid faces.[128]

In spite of the general Chinese avoidance of stage props, special devices of various sorts were placed on the stage for acrobatic performances. The erecting of such materials would take place during
a scene previous to the entrance of the tumblers:

. . . during the singing and the capering, while the actors were engaged in
their final trial of lungs and legs [i.e., at the end of the purely dramatic part
of the program], some pigtails were busily employed in erecting poles and
horizontal bars, and in tying up ropes for performing on, so that directly
the made-up female had disappeared behind the scenes after she had made
her final bow to the audience, with scarcely a moment's pause—for everything was now ready—the stage was filled with clowns and sprites, tumblers
and turn-inside-outers, many of them bared to the waist; and I must say
that the performances they went through were executed in first-rate style. A
fearful yelling and screeching was kept up the whole time, without intermission—in short, the whole performance seemed to us nothing but a hideous
Chinese nightmare. Each tumbler had his fan, and he often managed to
tumble with it.[129]

Bancroft noted that a stranger is apt to conclude that "the strong-
est dramatic power of the Chinese actor lies in his feet" and was
much impressed by the tumblers' ability to avoid injury:

Warriors pursue warriors; high tables are cleared in a bound, and the performers land on the bare floor, falling heavily on the flat back or side with
a shock as if every bone had been broken; but ere the inexperienced visitor
has time to make an exclamation, the men are up, and pirouetting wilder
than ever; performing somersaults one over the other, spinning like tops,

wheeling on hands and feet, doing lofty tumbling, and concluding with extraordinary contortions—all in confused medley, yet in eager rivalry to surpass one another.[130]

The line between acrobatics and dancing was not always easy to draw. McDowell describes one "acrobatic ballet" in which there are forty or more tumblers, stripped to the waist, with rose-colored handkerchiefs on their heads:

Pyramids of twenty and sometimes thirty persons are formed; one little fellow carries valiantly around the stage six others larger than himself; another jumps from the apex of one of the pyramids full fifteen feet to the floor.

The acrobats amuse the audience at intervals by playing tricks on a clown, "who is as necessary an adjunct of such a performance with the Chinese, apparently, as he is in the circus with us." In the concluding event of the "ballet" two men, one atop the other, fall from a height into a "living cushion of hands" provided by two rows of acrobats.[131]

One account of theatrical acrobatics includes a man-size frog "who turned somersaults, and who was killed three or four times over, but who always came to life again in the most surprising manner."

The frog was admirably made and inflated, and exactly like the real creature, except that he had a long tail in the middle of his back. Every now and then the prince would catch hold of this in a most insulting way, and flap down on the floor with it, where he lay dead and as flat as a sheet of paper. Hardly could his enemy turn his back before he found some way to regain life and inflate his ribs, and began to frisk round, tripping up the heels of each warrior at a critical moment with the most entertaining malice, but only to be reduced to death and nothingness again on the first opportunity. Of the indescribable movement and gayety this whole scene I can give you no idea.[132]

The agility of the acrobats is helped by a particularly "springy" stage, designed with acrobatics in mind.[133]

The elaborate costuming of the players was another element that elicited admiration and awe from the audience. "The costumes are gorgeous,'' as one account has it: ''Rich gold embroidery, heavy silks and velvets, costly feathers and jewelry, form an important part of the display.''[134] Individual costumes were distinguished by complex embroidery work, sometimes representing dragons, birds, and flowers.[135] Particularly impressive was the use of gold cloth ''being picked out and heightened by innumerable silk threads of many different colors, all blending harmoniously and exquisitely.''[136] The differences between actors were marked not so much by the general cut and material of their costumes as by the head-dresses and ornamentation that they bore. Jeweled breastplates were worn by some. Pairs of peacock feathers nodded over some performers' heads and clusters of flags, flapping like wings at their shoulders, denoted high rank.[137] An emperor and his suite would wear huge hoops, which would gather in their robes just below the knee. Such actors, when sitting, would turn their shoes out well so as to display the costume to best advantage. A general's costume was perhaps most distinctive of all:

In his head-dress are four dragons rampant, and on the flap in front a lion's mouth. In time of action his sleeves are rolled up, and his loins are girded with a sash and rosette of light-blue silk. An enormous butterfly laps over and partly covers the side-pieces that protect his thighs. His boots are high-soled and add much to his stature. Two long feathers sweep from his helmet behind. As a symbol of power he wears four flags in his back, and as a token of strength a cockade of black silk on his forehead.[138]

''Beads, gilt, and spangles'' embellished the embroidery, prefiguring the almost obsessive use of sequins that would become common in twentieth-century Cantonese opera. Actors playing mandarins and governors of provinces would sometimes wear helmets, described by one observer as resembling ''the burnished copper kettles of the careful New England housewife.''[139]

Elegant as the costuming was, it was apparently not kept always in the best of shape. One critic from England was less than awed:

I had been led to expect some very magnificent costumes . . . and I was told that the entire wardrobe of the company was insured for $30,000; but in a sumptuary sense I was woefully disappointed. Some of the leading actors wore robes of brocaded damask and velvet, embroidered with gold, which had once, no doubt, been handsome, and had cost a great deal of money; but the greater number of these dresses were faded, tarnished, and disgustingly dirty. Perhaps the splendid dresses are reserved for high days and holidays.[140]

Stylized beards, then as now, were much in use: ". . . many of the performers disfigure themselves with beards and wigs of crimson, green, blue, yellow, &c., sometimes in solid colours and sometimes in bands and stripes."[141] Facial painting added to the spectacle, providing indications not only of the character's station in life but of his moral and physical ugliness; further it served to distinguish the barbarian outlanders who frequently figured in battles and other scenes.[142]

In most cases, the plots of the dramas were a total mystery to Western reporters, who could only guess at the meanings of the action on stage and contented themselves with enjoying the visual pleasures of costumery, acrobatics, and the choreography of battle scenes.[143] One misconception that one finds constantly perpetuated is that a given drama will typically run for weeks or even months before reaching its conclusion.[144] Some plays were indeed episodic, dealing in segments of a longer story, but a night's presentation was to be viewed as a complete dramatic entity in itself. The majority of plays given, at any rate, were performed in one night's staging; some, in fact, were scarcely more than curtain-raisers, as it were, taking no more than three-quarters of an hour.[145] Since there was no curtain to be raised, however, and since there was no intermission or appreciable duration of time between the performance of one play and another, some visitors were easily led to think that the story line was continuous. The conception of extremely lengthy dramatic plots may also stem from descriptions by Europeans of certain types of plays in China given by "river companies."

A band of actors, sometimes as many as a hundred, charter a flatboat and drift down one of the great Chinese rivers, playing at city after city. At each stop, they set up a tent, like the circus, and invite the whole populace to attend. Admission is free; but it costs ten cash to sit on the benches. The actors proceed with a play which lasts six days and six nights without a single intermission. The players take the part in relays—for example, one tragedian plays the hero *Jut* on the eight-to-four shift, another relieves him on the four-to-midnight shift, and another fills out the night. This is the Chinese equivalent of the circus. Doubtless, the sight of such a performance moved some early traveler to make a faulty generalization concerning the length of Chinese plays.[146]

Hazy as Western observers were about the details of plots, many of them were intrigued by reports of "indecency" on stage.[147] This little legend seems to span the whole history of Cantonese opera in the United States but is especially emphasized in the earlier decades. The story is almost always at second hand, and reporters were invariably relieved, or perhaps disappointed, to find nothing but unassailable propriety on the Chinese stage. The single incident that gave rise to the continuing "indecency" stories was the occasionally enacted birth of a baby on stage, an event whose portrayal was largely symbolic, the actual "birth" being hidden from view. A tiny doll, rather than a real baby, would be exhibited after the blessed event.[148] It is a credit to the fecundity of the Victorian imagination that such a prosaic business, as amplified through rumor, could attain the status of "indecency."

The business side of the Chinese theater lay in the hands of three men, concerned respectively with costumes, food and lodging, and finances.[149] In general, however, the affairs of the company seemed to take care of themselves without a heavy managerial hand. To McDowell it appears that: "The Chinese have little taste or talent for organization, and everything is regulated pretty much by unwritten law." The preparation and supervision of any new productions were in the hands of the author (or adapter) of the new play, generally a member of the acting company, rather than a director or stage manager.

The cast is written down in a book and hung up in a conspicuous place in the green-room. No parts are given out; the author merely tells the actor in a general way what he is to do, and that is all. The "cues," however, are written out, as well as the important sentences—*couplets de sortie.*

Once a year the company of a Chinese theater was reorganized:

The details of the reorganization are discussed at a dinner . . . at which the whole company are present. The theater is then closed for three days, at the end of which time it is opened again with great *éclat*. Very often nothing is done but to continue the arrangements of the past year; still the ceremonies of reopening are never dispensed with.

The self-management of the acting company would indicate a high degree of professionalism and skill on the part of the individual company members. The Chinese actor had to be a pretty exceptional fellow all round:

> . . . [he] must be a man of intelligence, good education, and ready wit. He must possess in addition to these qualities an accurate knowledge of the history of China, and of the etiquette and ceremonial of the the imperial court as it is popularly understood. He must be suitably dressed, and his action must conform as much as possible to the character of the personage he represents, who is often historical and well known to the audience. These requirements make acting in China no easy matter; and a really good artist is, therefore, quite properly treated with great respect by his fellows, who watch him carefully when he acts, and, in case they approve, reverently salute him with the title of "Master."

In spite of the rigid professional demands of the trade, amateur actors had at least a short-lived success on the San Francisco stage. In the early 1880s a small company of amateurs—who might be viewed as the predecessors of today's amateur opera clubs in Chinatown—gave performances on the professional stage in San Francisco. McDowell relates that:

> At first the people were delighted with them, and so great was their enthusiasm that the managers of the theater were induced to engage them in addition to the regular company. They failed utterly to realize the expectations that were formed of them, or to meet the severe exigencies of the professional stage.[150]

Then, as now, San Francisco's Chinese audiences were an exacting and highly critical community of connoisseurs. Casual as they may have seemed in their audience behavior, the regular patrons attended with keen eyes and ears, and they would accept, in the long run, nothing less than the highest quality of acting, singing, and instrumental music performance.

NOTES

1. Betty Lee Sung, *Mountain of Gold: The Story of the Chinese in America* (New York, Macmillan, 1967), p. 42.

2. London *Herald*, 17 October 1869; Julius A. Palmer, Jr., "Ah Ying and His Contemporaries," *Old and New* 2 (1870), pp. 694–95.

3. San Francisco *Post*, 9 October 1877.

4. *Alta*, 9 May 1870.

5. Richard H. Dillon, *The Hatchet Men: The Story of the Tong Wars in San Francisco's Chinatown* (New York, Coward McCann, 1962; reprinted, New York, Ballantine, 1972), pp. 85, 87. Police continue to be part of the Chinatown-theater scene to this day. The Sun Sing Theater hires off-duty policemen to collect tickets when an opera company is booked.

6. *Alta*, 25 October 1876.

7. *Alta*, 31 October 1876.

8. *Alta*, 1 November 1876.

9. *Alta*, 31 October 1876.

10. *Alta*, 1 November 1876.

11. *Chronicle*, 7 July 1877.

12. *Chronicle*, 20 September 1878.

13. *Alta*, 25 September 1878.

14. *Call*, 8 October 1878.

15. *Chronicle*, 21 October 1878.

16. *Post*, 21 October 1878.

17. *Chronicle*, 21 October 1878.

18. *Bulletin*, 10 March 1880. See also George H. Fitch, "In a Chinese Theatre," *Century Magazine* 24 (1882), p. 189.

19. *Chronicle*, 25 July 1880.

20. W.F. Rae, *Westward by Rail* (London, Longmans, Green, 1870), pp. 299–300.

21. Charles Nordoff, *California: For Health, Pleasure and Residence* (New York, Harper & Bros., 1873), pp. 86–88.

22. *Two Years in California* (Chicago, S.C. Griggs, 1876), p. 190.

23. J.W. Ames, "A Day in Chinatown," *Lippincott's Magazine* 16 (1875), p. 502.

24. *Alta*, 5 March 1875. Emphasis in original.

25. Carey McWilliams, *Factories in the Field* (Boston, Little, Brown, 1939; reprinted, Santa Barbara, Calif.: Peregrine, 1971), p. 74.

26. *Chronicle*, 29 April 1877.

27. *Chronicle*, 29 April 1879; Fitch, p. 189.

28. From clipping in San Francisco newspaper in December 1877 (newspaper unidentified, from scrapbook in Bancroft Library).

29. Map in Willard B. Farwell, *The Chinese at Home and Abroad* (San Francisco, A.L. Bancroft, 1885).

30. *Chronicle*, 25 September 1879; *Bulletin*, 24 September 1879.

31. *Figaro*, 14 November 1878.

32. *Chronicle*, 25 September 1879.

33. *Figaro*, 14 November 1878.

34. *Alta*, 8 June 1878.

35. *Chronicle*, 2 October 1879.

36. *Chronicle*, 5 March 1877.

37. *Chronicle*, 21 March 1879.

38. *Bulletin*, 10 March 1880.

39. *Chronicle*, 30 January 1881.

40. George Augustus Sala, *America Revisited* (London, Vizetelly, 1882), pp. 475–76.

41. Fitch, p. 189.

42. Sala, p. 476.

43. "Chinese Theatres in San Francisco," *Harper's* 27 (1883), p. 295.

44. Caroline H. Dall, *My First Holiday* (Boston, Roberts Bros., 1881), p. 374.

45. Henry Burden McDowell, "The Chinese Theater," *Century Magazine* 29 (1884), p. 31. Indeed, the theaters vied for the favor of the Joss:

The Joss of one of the six companies in San Francisco was asked the other day, on the occasion of his birthday, which theater he preferred to attend, the Washington or the Jackson street. The sticks were thrown up. They came down on their flat side. The Joss had pronounced for the Jackson street establishment. He accordingly was carried through the streets of San Francisco with great pomp and placed upon the receiving altar. (Ibid.)

46. Peter Chu et al., "Chinese Theatres in America" (Washington, D.C., Bureau of Research, Federal Theatre Project, Region of the West, 1936), p. 50.

47. Dall, p. 374.

48. Sala, p. 484. It was quite likely the same company that Mrs. Dall had observed. Sala notes that he did not write down the name at the time, trusting it to memory.

49. Dall, p. 378.

50. McDowell, p. 43.

51. Fitch, p. 190. Emphasis his.

52. Dall, p. 374.

53. It was probably tea. One did not drink alcoholic beverages in the theater, and Japanese sake would have been doubly out of place. "Chinese Theatres," *Harper's* 27 (1883), p. 295.

54. Dall, p. 375.

55. Ibid., p. 481.

56. Fitch, p. 190; Theodor Kirchhoff, *Californische Kulturbilder* (Cassel, Theodor Fischer, 1886), p. 102.

57. Harry T. Finck, *The Pacific Coast Scenic Tour* (New York, Scribner's, 1890), p. 119.

58. G.B. Densmore, *The Chinese in California* (San Francisco, 1880), p. 55.

59. Ibid., p. 84.

60. Edwina Booth, *Edwin Booth* (New York, Century, 1902), p. 71.

61. Ibid., pp. 483–84.

62. Kirchhoff, pp. 101–2.

63. McDowell, pp. 38, 41.

64. *Out West on the Overland Train . . . in 1877* (Palo Alto, Calif., American West, 1967), p. 184.

65. W.G. Marshall, *Through America* (London, Sampson Low, Marston, Searle & Rivington, 1882), p. 297.

66. McDowell, pp. 41, 43.

67. " 'China Town' in San Francisco," *Cornhill Magazine* 54 (1886), p. 58.

68. See above, p. 41.

69. Densmore, p. 55.

70. Ibid., p. 42.

71. Ibid., p. 192.

72. *Call*, 11 May 1882.

73. " 'China Town' in San Francisco," p. 58. Equivalence based on conversion figures in *Whitaker's Almanack* (London, 1882): one dollar equals four shillings, two pence.

74. "Chinese Theatres in San Francisco," p. 295.

75. New York *Times*, 15 March 1883.

76. " 'China Town' in San Francisco," p. 58.

77. Fitch, p. 192.

78. McDowell, p. 41.

79. I am indebted to Mabel L. Quon for having pointed out this aspect of Chinese theatrical practice.

80. *Call*, 11 May 1882. Noncapitalizations in original.

81. Benjamin E. Lloyd, *Lights and Shades in San Francisco* (San Francisco, A.L. Bancroft, 1876), p. 265.

82. Hubert Howe Bancroft, *History of California*, 7 vols. (San Francisco, History Co., 1890), 7: 372–73.

83. McDowell, pp. 42–43.

84. Bancroft, *History*, 7: 369.

85. Fitch, p. 190.

86. "A Day in Chinatown," p. 501.

87. Lloyd, p. 265.

88. Fiddles were presumably limited to the hu-ch'in. The larger spike fiddle called the erh-hu has become common in the Peking opera orchestra in the twentieth century, but it apparently was not used earlier. The instrument is said to have been adapted for Peking opera by Wan Shao-ch'ing, hu-ch'in accompanist to Mei Lan-fang. Elizabeth Halson, *Peking Opera* (Hong Kong, Oxford University Press, 1966), p. 56; Tsai-ping Liang, *Chinese Musical Instruments & Pictures* (Taipei, Chinese Classical Music Association, 1970), p. 57.

89. Marshall, p. 300.

90. "Chinese Theatres," p. 295.

91. Bancroft, *History*, 7: 370.

92. McDowell, p. 41.

93. Fitch, p. 189.

94. Lloyd, p. 265; Densmore, p. 55; Reinhardt, p. 183.

95. "Chinese Theatres," p. 295.

96. Densmore, p. 55; John S. Hittell, *A Guide Book to San Francisco* (San Francisco, Bancroft, 1883), p. 49.

97. McDowell, p. 41.

98. Bancroft, *History*, 7: 370.

99. Fitch, p. 190.

100. Sala, p. 482.

101. Densmore, p. 137.

102. Bancroft, *History*, 7: 370.

103. Fitch, p. 190.

104. "Chinese Theatres," p. 295.

105. Sala, p. 482.

106. Bancroft, *History*, 7: 370.

107. Ibid.

108. Fitch, p. 190.

109. McDowell, p. 41.

110. Fitch, p. 146.

111. Marshall, p. 147.

112. McDowell, p. 41.

113. Fitch, p. 190.

114. Sala, p. 482.

115. Bancroft, *History*, 7: 370.

116. Marshall, p. 300.

117. Sala, pp. 482–83.

118. ". . . a flat, solid, pear-shaped sounding board, with a short neck, curved at the head, and bearing four strings." Bancroft, *History*, 7: 370.

119. Ibid. The instrument in question would appear to be a shuang kuan, which would suggest the Shangtungese opera. Personal communication with Professor Chuang Pen-li, 19 May 1976.

120. Marshall, p. 301.

121. Helen F. Clark, "The Chinese of New York," *Century* 53 (1896), pp. 105–6

122. Lloyd, p. 226.

123. Densmore, p. 55.

124. Bancroft, *History*, 7: 371.

125. McDowell, pp. 38–39.

126. "Chinese Theatres," p. 295.

127. Thomas W. Hinchliff, *Over the Sea and Far Away* (London, Longmans, Green & Co., 1876), p. 212.

128. Reinhardt, p. 184.

129. Marshall, p. 301.

130. Bancroft, *History*, 7: 372.

131. McDowell, p. 28.

132. Dall, p. 377. This was apparently no everyday frog. In an article published twenty-eight years later, Will Irwin describes a similar frog and includes an illustration of it. The creature in question, "as every Chinese in the audience knows," is called "The Good Tiger," who hops on and off the stage at the bidding of the "King of the Fairies." ("The Drama in Chinatown," *Everybody's Magazine* 20 [1909], p. 866.)

133. " 'China Town'," p. 58.

134. "Chinese Theatres," p. 295.

135. Bancroft, *History*, 7: 271.

136. McDowell, p. 41.

137. Reinhardt, p. 184.

138. McDowell, p. 40.

139. Fitch, p. 191.

140. Sala, p. 486.

141. Densmore, p. 58.

142. McDowell, p. 40.

143. Attempts at plot explanation do figure in some accounts, however. The most reliable of these is McDowell, who not only relates the meaning of activities on stage, but gives a generally accurate rundown of the types of plays and the variety of roles assumed by actors. Bancroft (*History*, vol. 7) gives a lengthy explanation of a play entitled *The Return of Sit Ping Quai* (pp. 373–77). The same story is related by an anonymous reviewer for the *Bulletin*, 6 December 1856.

144. Though one is hard put to find an example of any Western observer having attended the theater more than once. Miska Hauser is an exception. See above, p. 21.

145. "What the Chinese playgoer delights in, as an evening's amusement, is a succession of plays which are more of the nature of sketches,
slight in construction and generally weak in plot, some of them based upon
striking historical episodes, and others dealing with a single humorous incident." Herbert Allen Giles, "China: Literature," *Encyclopaedia Britannica*, 11th ed., 6: 231. For a recent account of a touring Cantonese opera
troupe, see Bell Yung, "A Trip to Sok Gu Wan with a Cantonese Opera
troupe," *CHINOPERL Papers* 7 (1977), pp. 49–57.

146. Irwin, "The Drama in Chinatown," p. 869.

147. In the reports of, for example, the anonymous author of "Chinese
Theatres" (p. 295), Bancroft, *History*, vol. 7 (p. 377), Dall (p. 376), and
Henchliff (p. 212).

148. See below, p. 144. Such a scene, as observed on stage in the 1880s, is
described in Gertrude Atherton's *My San Francisco* (New York, Bobbs,
Merrill, 1946), pp. 55–56.

149. McDowell, p. 41. McDowell's observations relate from his study of
the Royal Chinese Theater. Fitch, in 1880, mentions that "the Russian who
acts as stage-manager comes on the boards and forces back the eager
crowd, in order to give the 'supers' a better opportunity to go through with
their evolutions" (p. 191). His description (relating to the Jackson Street
theater) would seem to indicate a hired keeper-of-order, not a member of
the theatrical company or an officer of the theater's management.

150. McDowell, p. 42.

3

Chinese Theater: Decline and Disaster (1890–1906)

San Francisco's Chinese drama declined inevitably in the 1890s as the decade saw the city's Chinese population cut virtually in half—reduced to about 14,000 by 1900.[1] Two theaters—one on Jackson Street, one on Washington—remained open but, by mid-decade, only on alternate nights. Performers' salaries were slashed to a half or even a third of incomes in the 1880s. Writing in 1895, one observer recalled the amounts paid to Chinese actors in the previous decade, before "the pinch of exclusion laws and hard times":

Leung Chuck . . . commanded a salary of ten thousand dollars a year, an admission fee of one dollar being charged every time he performed. . . . Pang Nga Su . . . was paid sixteen hundred dollars for a three months' engagement. . . . A celebrated tragedian nicknamed "Pock-marked Hoh" received eight thousand dollars a year . . .[2]

Formerly the theater owners would hire the players at fixed salaries, but in these lean years they took no chances. They simply rented the house, sets, and wardrobes to the touring troupes, which had to make out for themselves as regards profits and salaries. In contrast to the players' yearly incomes cited above, the top salaries now do not exceed two thousand dollars. That amount was paid to the actor Soo H. Tae, who was featured at the Jackson Street theater with a Mrs. Ah Moy, who received $1,800. The principal comedian was paid $1,500, and several other starring actors received a thousand apiece. The musicians—seven of them—got by on $500 a year each. In addition to these salaries, which were regarded as substantial in the 1890s, each member of the troupe was provided with lodging, rice at every meal, and an extra two and a half dollars given at the beginning of the month for incidental expenses.[3]

The salary cuts to one half or one third of sums received in the 1880s reflect the very difficult times for the box office. The Lung Koo Sing company paid ten dollars a night rent to the theater's manager, who engaged the company for a year. There were only thirty in the troupe, a number regarded as "much too small for the historical plays, some of which require at least double that number." All thirty had to be paid out of gate receipts of little more than $150 a night—not to speak of rent and other expenses.[4]

Accounts of the Chinese theater in the Western press during these hard times were relatively sober in tone. Several Protestant ministers applauded the theater's "morality." Frederic J. Masters, D.D.—"Twenty years a missionary to the Chinese"—compared the moral climate of the Chinese theater to that of Western drama:

The more modern dramas, notably those of the Ming dynasty, are mostly comedies, characterized by farcical dialogue, expressed in the coarse slang and colloquial of the street. Some of them abound in love intrigues, obscene jokes, and *double entendres* that justify the condemnation of stern Confucian and Buddhist moralists. Buddhist tracts, scattered broadcast, warn people against attending these plays. . . . Bad as these plays are, they are not fetid like some of our nineteenth century productions. There is nothing in the whole range of their literature that can compare with the barefaced obscenity of Wycherly, Congreve, and the comic dramatists of the Restoration, to say nothing of the Frenchy comic operas and disgusting concomitants too often seen upon the boards of American theaters. A Chinese play may be simple in plot and even silly, but it is commendably free from those nasty accompaniments of our modern stage so offensive to pure and refined taste.[5]

Furthermore, the theatrical events are advertised in a most morally approvable fashion:

A theatrical troupe starts out with a grandiloquent name and announces its *repertoire* in modest unpictured play bills. The Chinese, heathen though they are, have not become sufficiently Americanized to plaster the fences and walls with pictures of immodestly dressed actresses. The *corps de ballet* with abbreviated gauzy etherial skirts, "can-can" dancers, and other lewd spectacles form as yet no part of a Chinese theatrical entertainment.[6]

But the private life of actors is another story:

Gambling and opium smoking are the principal occupations of actors when their stage duties are done. A more dissipated, down-at-heeled class it would be hard to find . . .

Notwithstanding their "large salaries," these actors are "wretched spendthrifts" and are always in debt, having "no sympathy with the social ambitions which influence ordinary men to amass a fortune." Social ambition would be futile in any case:

They are a proscribed class and so are their children if they are so unfortunate as to have any. Wealth could not purchase the least social recognition for a Chinese actor. If his picture is bought, it is only in stage dress. His popularity is confined to the stage. He has no standing outside. Nobody ever greets him on the street. Nobody invites him to the festal board. The people that to-night laugh at his humor or weep over his pathos will to-morrow morning pass him by on the other side. He takes his pleasures sadly, keeps to his own set, and takes care not to intrude upon the other's path.[7]

As an extreme example of the lowliness of actors, an episode at a brothel is cited:

A few years ago a popular tragedian was discovered in the company of a courtesan at a notorious house on Baker Alley. The house was boycotted, nor was patronage resumed until the miserable girl had been banished from the town. The actor barely escaped the clutches of a gang of highbinders sent to avenge what was considered an outrage upon the community![8]

Another clergyman, Joseph Carey, wrote that he was pleased to find that women were traditionally barred from the stage and felt that "the Chinese are to be commended in this respect."[9]

However, visitors (including the Rev. Mr. Carey) were not barred from the stage and were often seated there, sometimes close enough to the orchestra to be quite literally shaken by the fortissimo clashings of cymbals. The children of the Chinese performers were occasional inhabitants of the stage as well, meandering about in the midst of performances. The celebrated actor Ah Chick had two little sons who were the pets of the whole company:

The stage was their playground up to 10 o'clock or so, when their mother used to enter dramatically from the wings and whisk them off to bed. They had been told not to play centre-stage; but they were regular boys, and occasionally forgot. I have seen Ah Chick, in the midst of a tragic passage, kick out surreptitiously with his foot to get one of his offspring out of the way.[10]

Musicians were visited by *their* children as well in mid-performance. One small boy bemused visitors by banging on the orchestral drums from time to time while wandering around the stage.[11]

As in earlier years, actors lived on the premises, taking their meals there as well. One observer's curiosity led him to visit first the green room, then other areas backstage and below:

Further in the rear is the kitchen, smelling of [soy sauce] and garlic, where three cooks are busy cooking the actors' meals. They all live in the theater building and board together at the manager's expense. From the green room a door opens upon a rickety narrow staircase leading into subterranean depths. The fumes of opium and tobacco mixed with an ancient and fishlike smell are, to say the least, very disagreeable. Descending the creaking stairway you creep along labyrinthian passages just wide enough to walk, with here and there a glimpse of the little boxlike apartments, not more than six feet square, where the actors are supposed to live and sleep. It is impossible to discover a single aperture for light and air or a chance of escape in case of fire.[12]

The dangers of fire were not ignored. An image of Wah Kwong, the god of fire, perched about ten feet above the stage, together with one of Tam Kung Ye, the patron god of actors in Canton.[13]

Theaters opened at five in the afternoon and closed at midnight. Admission prices continued to vary according to the clientele. The non-Chinese visitor was charged a flat fifty cents, with no return-check privileges. Chinese paid twenty-five cents if arriving during the first two hours, fifteen cents during the second two hours, and a dime for the final hour alone—all with return check included. A visiting missionary, who could read Chinese, recounted offering the price that was written in that language but was assured "with unblushing mendacity" that *everybody* had to pay fifty cents. The reverend thereupon

proceeded to read [aloud] the different Chinese inscriptions to the amazement of the door-keeper, who, convicted of extortion, gave in by saying, "Oh, he sabbe too muchee Chinee, let him in alla same Chinaman." Another time the writer was not so successful. He was recognized as a missionary and received a scorching lecture. "You Christian tellee man no go theater. Jesus man must pay welly high plice." Further protest was unavailing and the Jesus man had to pay like any other foreign devil.[14]

The biggest crowd would gather on what was called *pan hi*—benefit night. A family society or tong would hire the theater for $150 or $200, and the house was turned over to the president of the association, who would fix prices for admission and appoint doorkeepers. The image of the organization's patron god—protected from the elements by a warm fur coat—would be carried in state to the theater, amidst salvos of gongs and firecrackers. Such tradition reflected practices in Chinese towns and villages.

All their gods and goddesses are supposed to delight in theatrical entertainments and it is the commonest thing in China for a town or village to express thanksgiving to the gods for a good harvest or deliverance from pestilence, flood, or fire, by subscribing for a theatrical show to be held in their honor in a *matshed* erected in the temple yard.[15]

Even in its reduced circumstances, San Francisco's Chinese theater garnered international renown. Its actor-singers were said to have been praised by no less than Edwin Booth and Sarah Bernhardt.[16] Ignace Jan Paderewski applauded the players heartily and reported that he "had never heard any music so dramatically moving." Musical circles in San Francisco were stunned to hear Paderewski's words of praise for this alien art form. But according to Charles Caldwell Dobie: "That settled it. After that, high-brow circles affected a belief in the superiority of Chinese music.''[17] The belief was clearly short-lived.

The exodus of Chinese from San Francisco in the 1890s led to a gradual expansion of Chinatown populations in other cities, and with it the establishment of theaters. In 1900 one drama critic remarked that he had visited Chinese theaters in half a dozen American cities.[18] The theater in Portland, Oregon, had been established much earlier—1879 or 1880—and was destined to last until 1904.[19] In Boston, a Chinese theatrical troupe staged an opera in 1891, and it was well received by an audience that included Oliver Wendell Holmes and William Dean Howells. In Cuba, Havana's Chinatown was able to support the performances of a touring troupe by 1893. In the same year, Chinese opera was performed at the Columbian Exposition in Chicago.[20]

It was in New York City, however, that the Chinese theater took root most impressively. Chinese drama was by no means a new thing for New York theater-goers, as Chinese performers had come and gone ever since the initial visit of the Hong Took Tong company in 1853.[21] For most of the century, however, Chinese performers were generally presented as novelty attractions in variety shows, sandwiched between patriotic tableaux and talking-dog acts. The city would not have a Chinese population large enough to support an ongoing theater until the 1890s. Proposals and attempts to form a Chinese theater in New York date from as early as 1883, but it was not until ten years later—on 25 March 1893—that a theater would become solidly established.[22] New York's Chinese population was swelling. The official census listed a figure of 2,048 for 1890, and there was an estimated growth to over 5,000 (possibly as high as 10,000) by mid-decade.[23] The capacity-house opening of the new theater on Doyers Street in 1893 augered well for a playhouse that would see many years of successful operation.[24]

New York's blue laws were a source of irritation to the theater owners. No theatrical performances were allowed on Sunday. Despite the management's advertising of Sunday performances as ''sacred concerts,'' arrests and losses of license occurred repeatedly in the early days of the New York playhouse.[25]

In San Francisco's Chinatown, the opening years of the twentieth century saw a continued decline in both population and theater attendance. The one event that drew special attention to the theater in those years was a tong murder in the Washington Street theater in late 1903. A "hatchet man" for the Suey Dong tong stepped on the stage and, in full view of a packed house, shot down a cymbal player. Another name was added to the long list of murder victims in the Chinese theater.[26] The theater in New York became a tong battleground as well. There five men were massacred publicly during a performance on Chinese New Year's Eve in 1909.[27]

A chilling example of chicanery abetted by racism lay in the forming of a corporation in 1905 to take over the real estate of San Francisco's Chinatown—land that was estimated to be potentially worth upwards of 25 million dollars—and simply move the Chinese out en masse to a ghetto site south of the city. *World Today* reported that

The new corporation plans the acquisition of all the property in Chinatown, paying for it in preferred stock secured by bonds. Then Dupont [now Grant] street from Bush to Broadway, would be widened, giving a better outlet from the heart of the city to the northern water-front. The whole of Chinatown would be rebuilt with modern buildings and an old plague-spot—both moral and hygenic—would be wiped out of existence.[28]

Both the best and worst-laid plans were soon to be dashed, however. On the morning of 18 April 1906 the city was jolted by an earthquake whose subsequent fires wiped out much of San Francisco and completely destroyed Chinatown. Before the quake, two Chinese theaters had been in operation. The venerable Jackson Street theater was leveled, and fire destroyed the converted Bella Union on Kearney Street,

in which, in the early fifties, the elder Booth, Murdock, Jenny Lind and other famous stars appeared. A portion of this was devoted to the Chinese drama, while the remaining portion was given up to lodging purposes. This noted theater . . . went down before the withering flames, the shrieks and cries of terror of those gathered in Portsmouth Square, fifty feet away, being its only requiem.[29]

Today's San Franciscans still reckon local history in terms of "before the quake" and "after the quake," and this time division is appropriate for the history of the city's Chinese music and drama as well. After the quake, the majority of Chinatown's residents moved across the bay to Oakland and formed a ghetto settlement there. But almost miraculously San Francisco's Chinatown would be totally rebuilt on its old site within just a few years. It was clearly the end of an epoch for the area's Chinese theater in any case. Many momentous changes in Chinese life were due. The soon-to-come overthrow of Imperial China was to have a profound effect on all Chinese. And while the theater itself was to see many more years of life in San Francisco, it would soon have to face the formidable competition of motion pictures. In a few years, the first Chinese Western-style marching band would be formed in Chinatown. Its fanfares would herald changes in tastes and values among many factions of the community. Already fading were the traditions represented by the old dynastic regime and traditional Chinese music and theater. Chinatown would retain its identity as a tightly knit ethnic enclave for generations to come, but traditional Chinese music and theater would never again lead an insulated life. Since the first immigrants had arrived, the community's musical culture had remained viable but relatively static and self-contained. Its future history—like that of Chinatown in general—would be one of increasing change and adaptation to the surrounding white culture.

NOTES

1. From 25,833 to 13,984. See Richard H. Dillon, *The Hatchet Men* (New York, Coward-McCann, 1961), p. 184.

2. Frederic J. Masters, "The Chinese Drama," *Chautauquan* 21 (1895), p. 438.

3. Ibid., p. 439.

4. Ibid., p. 438. For a comparison of wages paid to actors in China (specifically Shanghai) around this time, see Frederick W. Eddy, "In the Chinese Theatres," New York *Times*, 7 April 1901, p. 16.

5. Masters, p. 435.

6. Ibid., p. 439.

7. Ibid., p. 438.

8. Ibid., p. 439.

9. Joseph Carey, *By the Golden Gate: or San Francisco, the Queen City of the Pacific Coast; with Scenes and Incidents Characteristic of Its Life* (Albany, N.Y., Diocesan Press, 1902), p. 204.

10. Will Irwin, "The Drama That Was in Chinatown," *New York Times Book Review and Magazine*, 10 April 1921, p. 3.

11. Mrs. E.M. Green, "The Chinese Theater," *Overland Monthly* 41 (1903), pp. 123–24; Helen Hunt Jackson, *Bits of Travel at Home* (Boston, Roberts Bros., 1893), p. 70.

12. Masters, pp. 437–38.

13. Ibid., p. 437, 438.

14. Ibid., 440.

15. Ibid., p. 441.

16. Will Irwin, "The Drama in Chinatown," *Everybody's Magazine* 20 (1909), p. 869; idem., "The Drama That Was in Chinatown," p. 17; Edward W. Townsend, "The Foreign Stage in New York, IV: The Chinese Theatre," *Bookman* 12 (1900), p. 42.

17. *San Francisco's Chinatown* (New York, D. Appleton-Century, 1934), p. 279.

18. Townsend, p. 39.

19. Alice Henson Ernst, *Trouping in the Oregon Country: A History of Frontier Theatre* (Portland, Oregon Historical Society, 1961), p. 98.

20. George C[linton] D[ensmore] Odell, *Annals of the New York Stage*, 15 vols. (New York, Columbia University Press, 1927–49), 15: 405, 407.

21. See above, p. 18–20.

22. The Chinese actor Loo Chin Goon tried to secure support for a company of about a dozen actors in 1883 (New York *Times*, 15 March 1883). Other abortive attempts at starting a Chinese theater in the 1880s and early 1890s are related in the New York *Times* of 10 March 1884 ("Plans of a Chinese Manager," p. 8) and in Odell, *Annals* 14: 380–81, 622; 15: 663–64.

23. Helen F. Clark, "The Chinese of New York," pp. 111–12.

24. New York *Times*, 26 March 1893.

25. See, e.g., New York *Times*, 21 January 1896 ("Five Chinese Actors Arraigned," p. 14); 21 March 1896 ("No License for Chu Fong," p. 9); 8 May 1897 ("Doyers Street Theatre," p. 2). See also Odell, *Annals* 14: 584. Accounts of New York's Chinese theater shortly after the turn of the century include Townsend, "The Foreign Stage"; Henry Tyrell, "The Theatre of New York's Chinatown," *Theatre* 3 (1903), pp. 170–72; and (retrospectively), Will Irwin, "The Drama That Was in Chinatown."

26. Dillon, p. 256.

27. C.Y. Lee, *Days of the Tong Wars* (New York, Ballantine, 1974), p. 132.

28. Francis John Dyer, "Rebuilding Chinatown," *World Today* 8 (1905), p. 554.

29. Charles E. Banks and Opie Read, *The History of the San Francisco Disaster and Mount Vesuvius Horror* (Chicago, C.E. Thomas, 1906), pp. 158–59.

4

Other Uses of Music in the Nineteenth Century

INFORMAL MUSIC MAKING

Well before the establishment of professional Chinese opera in Chinatown, music played a part in community life. Some of the newcomers had brought instruments with them, and songs and instrumental music enlivened many an hour in the immigrants' crowded quarters.[1] Amateur music making among the Chinese was, however, mentioned only in passing by observers who attempted to portray life in the Chinese community. One reporter makes note of informal playing during the Chinese New Year: "Forth from many Chinese apartments during this season, will come the sounds of their various stringed and wind instruments; and the performers seem to enjoy it, for they think it is music; there is also much of what they call singing."[2]

Another writer describes the after-hours activities in Chinatown's rooming houses:

Of an evening, the occupants of one of these small rooms gather about a common table in the centre . . . and what with smoking, gaming, and lounging on their bunks, they will pass a very pleasant hour in social enjoyments. Perchance there may be one among the number who can lightly finger the guitar, flute, or violin; if so, the harsh strains of music, that are

wafted in discordant waves on the sonorous air, together with the stifling
odors from the burning weed and drug, dispels all care from the minds of
the dreamy listeners . . . and again they roam among familiar fragrant
bowers of their native "flowery land" . . .[3]

A chronicler of New York's Chinatown in the 1890s similarly notes
that "one may enter an apartment and find two or three men smoking, and twenty or thirty who are not smoking, but are visiting,
laughing, jesting, or playing on musical instruments."[4]
   In San Francisco, the casual musicality of a Chinese businessman
was described by a visiting newspaper reporter:

. . . [The Head Manager] will even lay aside his dignity to play you a dis-
mally doleful ditty upon the Som Yen—a two stringed banjo, the small
drum of which is made of gay-colored snake skin—or upon the Good
Kim—a three stringed instrument which has a larger drum of wood. These
instruments, with several variations of them—larger or smaller—are
thrummed upon with smooth bits of bone by nearly every adult Chinese.

"Imagine," hc continues, "the head of an American trading house
of equal wealth pulling down a banjo in his back office to entertain
a stranger during business hours."[5] That instruments were played
by "nearly every adult Chinese" may be an overstatement, but the
amateur performance of music was probably much more pervasive
in the community than journalistic sources would suggest. Regularly meeting ensembles might well have been active as well as solo
performers, although musical clubs as such were not publicized until the early twentieth century.[6] Theater musicians probably performed also for funerals, banquets, and various celebrations; but it
is reasonable to expect that a body of semiprofessional players—performing from time to time when hired for specific occasions—was in existence and that such musicians might well gather
together to make music informally as well. Hints of such activity
are occasionally found in nineteenth-century sources. A *Chronicle*
account of a Chinese "conservatory of music" in Chinatown in the
1870s describes perhaps a forerunner of music clubs in today's Chinatown, since the purpose was to train musicians not only for the
Chinese opera but "to fit them as well to beguile their leisure hours
with the softening influence of music."[7]

That amateur opera groups were also in existence is suggested by the reported appearance on stage, in the early 1880s, of an amateur troupe at the Royal Chinese Theater.[8] With an attraction as popular as the professional Chinese theater in their midst, it would follow that at least a few of the thousands of faithful theater goers would be interested in making music and music-drama on their own. A Chinese "music room" on Waverly Place[9] is noted in an 1885 map of Chinatown. It may well have been a meeting place for leisure-time opera singers and other musical amateurs.

Several accounts from the turn of the century indicate that informal music making at home was a popular activity. Elmer Wok Wai recalls his father's interest in music, around 1904:

He was fond of music and in our big parlor kept many instrument: big and little violins, drums and horns. After work he would bring five or six mens up to the flat and they would raise hell with noise. And of course they would call in those no-good sing song girls. You could hear the voices, high, high, like a dog whining, clear around the corner on Dupont Street.[10]

In 1902 Joseph Carey described a "musician's shop" which he found in his wanderings around Chinatown. The "shop" consisted of a basement room about fifteen feet wide and twenty feet deep. Carey was welcomed into these quarters by a good-natured man in his fifties, who proceeded to demonstrate the yang-ch'in, the ti, the san-hsien, and the hu-ch'in. The reader is left to speculate on the purpose of the "shop." Possibly it was simply a room in a musician's home; or it could have been an instrument store for Chinese or a tourist attraction (Carey notes that he gave the musician a "suitable fee" for the entertainment). Quite likely it was a music club. The use of basement quarters (as is done by many of the music clubs today) and the presence of a number of different instruments suggest a music club with only one member present (though other members not mentioned by the writer might have been there as well). That one performer could demonstrate each of the four instruments is not in itself remarkable. In today's Chinatown a music-club member can typically play every instrument in sight, though he might do especially well on one or two.[11]

GAMBLING HOUSES

The gambling establishments, which were numerous in nineteenth-century Chinatown, offered the only source of continuous employment other than the theater for full-time musicians. Gambling halls proliferated very early in Chinatown's history.[12] Writing in 1855, Frank Soulé states that a portion of upper Sacramento Street and nearly all the east side of Dupont (now Grant) Street were occupied by Chinese gambling houses, which were crowded night and day. These halls, or "saloons," were generally small, each containing from three to half a dozen tables.

At the innermost end of some of the principal gambling places, there is an orchestra of five or six native musicians, who produce such extraordinary sounds from their curiously shaped instruments as severely torture the white man to listen to.[13]

In an accompanying line drawing, one musician is visible amidst the gambling crowd. Seated at floor level, presumably among other musicians, he is playing what appears to be a Ch'in-ch'in. The music was not purely instrumental:

Occasionally a songster adds his howl or shriek to the excruciating harmony. The wailings of a thousand lovelorn cats, the screams, gobblings, brayings, and barkings of as many peacocks, turkeys, donkeys, and dogs,—the "ear-piercing" noises of hundreds of botching cork-cutters, knife-grinders, file-makers, and the like,—would not make a more discordant and agonizing concert than these Chinese musical performers in their gambling houses.[14]

Whatever the merits of the music, it was decidedly not intended for the Caucasian ear. Non-Chinese trade was not solicited. While curious outsiders were freely admitted in the earlier days of the gambling houses, non-Chinese were excluded in the later nineteenth century as "unruly and not to be trusted."[15]

The gambling houses were illegal establishments, though their existence was common knowledge.[16]

They had little to fear . . . for the weekly fees given to the police made it to their interest to shield them, and raids were made only on delinquents for

the sake of appearance, since not Americans only, but the six companies repeatedly urged the restriction of a vice which creates so much misery, idle-
ness, and crime.[17]

Even when bona fide raids were attempted, however, police would
have great difficulty in gaining entrance and securing evidence. An
elaborate early-warning system ensured that there was little but an
empty room to confront the law when it did arrive. One particularly notorious gambling hall, located on an upper floor of the Chinese theater on Jackson Street, proved almost impenetrable to
police in the late 1860s. Time and again they had attempted without
success to raid the establishment. To gain entry was a formidable
problem in itself, and obtaining paraphernalia or catching Chinese
in the act of gambling appeared to be an impossibility. On one occasion the police succeeded only in obtaining several musical instruments that had been left behind. But this just made matters worse.
In the course of capturing the instruments, the lawmen became involved in a scuffle with the musical leader, Mr. Ah Suey, and Mr.
Suey promptly had one of their number arrested for assault and
battery. The officer had to pay a thirty-dollar fine. The notoriety of
this gambling house was caused in part by the music itself, as nearby residents complained of the "infernal din" made by the five female singer-players. (It must have been an especially puissant ensemble to be heard above the sounds of the theater below.) A successful raid was finally made on the night of 28 December 1869. A
number of individuals were taken into custody, but it was noted
that all five musical performers escaped.[18]

For female musicians and singers, the gambling houses provided
perhaps the only source of steady employment, since, with rare exceptions, the theatrical stage was not open to them. It was often assumed that female musical performers were all prostitutes. There is
no evidence to support this blanket supposition, though the name
"singsong girl" is applied loosely to all prostitutes. In any case, a
class of women-for-hire known as singsong girls figured prominently in Chinatown's nightlife, and some of their numbers were
proficient musicians and singers. Pardee Lowe has described the
behavior of singsong girls who graced the tables at an all-male banquet in the late nineteenth century:

A sense of refined gentility . . . hung over these gatherings. No word of obscenity passed the lips of these pleasure girls; they were painfully dignified and correct. . . . ungraceful gestures were conspicuously absent, and the only expressions used by the girls were those of respect. . . . Direct solicitation was never permitted at any of the banquets. These painted girls were there to entertain and to amuse. Any intimacy would depend upon arrangements made between the prospective pleasure seeker and their chaperones . . .[19]

A group of women sang and played musical instruments at the same banquet; however, these entertainers were apparently set apart from those singsong girls engaged in convivial conversation at the banquet tables.

Whether or not singsong girls functioned as prostitutes in every case, their work was inevitably associated with that area of life. With rare exceptions, unmarried women were brought to nineteenth-century Chinatown only for the purpose of prostitution, whether immediate or (in the case of female children) ultimate. Thus it may be assumed that female entertainers were either prostitutes, former prostitutes, or women who had shown musical talent at an early age (after having been brought here as potential prostitutes) and had been allowed to sing and play for a living at gambling houses and restaurants. Among Chinatown's resident women, there would appear to have been no other source of female musical entertainment than from the underworld of prostitution. Virtually the only other women living in the community were the (rare) wives and other relatives of merchants. It is unthinkable that any of these would have worked as an entertainer. An additional possibility is that some female entertainers were connected with the touring drama troupes, as family members, perhaps, of actors and supernumeraries.

Though gambling houses would continue to be found in Chinatown until recent decades, musicians of either sex were to play no role in them beyond the nineteenth century.

RESTAURANTS AND BANQUETS

An account by J.W. Ames describes an orchestra playing in a Chinatown restaurant in 1875. This again is an all-female group of singer-instrumentalists, possibly the same fleet-footed ensemble that eluded the police in the gambling-house raid mentioned above. From Ames's description, it would appear that the orchestra included drum (tan-p'i-ku), fiddle (hu-ch'in), and possibly flute (ti):

. . . near the balcony, among the jonquils, a bevy of brilliantly painted girls [were] making music. Such music! One slapped with broad pliant bamboo sticks what looked like a large polished skull, and with a force and resonance that made us jump at every blow; another sawed a one-stringed [sic] fiddle with a one-stringed bow, producing strains capable of curdling the blood of a professional saw-filer; all squalled together in voices many keys above the most ear-piercing fife. These were a few of the methods by which they wooed the dulcet Muse. Yet through it all there was a time, a swing and rhythm that suggested harmony, and made it evident that the concord of sweet sounds was the object aimed at.[20]

Gertrude Atherton recalls that entertainment was provided by a group of female singers (no instruments are mentioned) in a Chinese restaurant in the 1880s.[21] It would appear that Ames's and Atherton's experiences were unusual, however, as there is no dearth of descriptions by occidentals of eating in Chinatown restaurants in the nineteenth century; yet, no other mention is made of music during the day-to-day functioning of a restaurant (and it scarcely could have passed unnoticed).[22] H.H. Bancroft mentions "an alcove for musicians" in a Chinese restaurant. But this was "the place where the grand banquets are given," and musicians were hired presumably for special occasions only.[23] Also mentioned by Bancroft is the music issuing forth from "one of the half dozen good restaurants in the quarter." He notes that a crowd had gathered outside the establishment and that all were "entranced by the celestial strains of twanging guitars and clashing cymbals . . ." but it is not clear whether the music was for a banquet or part of the restaurant's regular fare.[24] Charles Keeler notes in 1902 that the sound of music from within a restaurant signified that a banquet was in progress. Entering, he chose a retired corner in an adjacent room, "listening the while to the high-pitched sing-song voices of the revelers, the rapping of drums, clanging of cymbals and squeaking of fiddles, and imagining myself a disciple of Confucius in the heart of the Flowery Kingdom."[25]

It is at a banquet that we find the largest Chinese orchestra reported in nineteenth-century San Francisco—forty players—for the annual banquet of the employees of a cigar-making firm on 20 February 1875. Except for the mention of cymbals, however, the instrumentation of this mammoth ensemble goes unrecorded, and the reporter's description of the music is limited to such mining-camp imagery as landslides, dynamite blasts, and planing mills.[26]

Several accounts in the 1870s mention the use of musicians and actors from the Royal Chinese Theater for entertainment at banquets.[27] In one such case the affair was held in the theater itself.[28] Bancroft in 1890 cites the use of music at an elaborate banquet held in a restaurant:

After the first course the company retires to the anteroom for half an hour to chat, smoke and gather inspiration from the cymbal clash, the twang of guitars, and the shrill strains of the singers, preparatory to another onslaught.[29]

A rare Chinese account of a banquet is given by Pardee Lowe, who recalls such an occasion in the late nineteenth century at which he first became aware as a child of the "unadorned wickedness"—in the persons of singsong girls—existing in his neighborhood.

Each of the four seasons was always formally ushered in by huge banquets given by either the district organizations, the family groups, or the fighting tongs. Such a feast was known as *Hoy Teng*, or "Opening a Reception." Father was a fixture at most of these celebrations, since he occupied the same special position in both the Masculine Concord Consolidated Districts Benevolent Association, and the Four Brothers, our clan society. He was their Secretary of Foreign Affairs.[30]

Such receptions reproduced the social atmosphere of Canton and Hong Kong while providing a setting for a variety of transactions.

Under the protective covering of good food and drink at a *Hoy Teng* gambling was permitted, assignations with daughters of joy were made, nefarious tong plots were hatched, and straightforward business deals consummated. . . . Here, lying fully exposed, were the cogs and wheels which made Chinatown's world go around.[31]

Opening a reception, Lowe found, represented "one of the wonders of pre-Revolutionary Chinatown." Always held at the largest and best-known restaurants, these affairs were the most sumptuous of all banquets and were attended by no fewer than three or four hundred guests, all of them men, who were seated at circular tables of ten. Music was featured:

A group of seven Chinese musicians, five of whom were women, sat in one corner, flanked by two luxurious bamboo couches reserved for those who were overcome by too much food or drink. These creatures were dressed in ravishing, dainty garments, the like of which I saw on no other women of the quarter. To the accompaniment of the *Law* [lo], a brass gong; the *Yuet Kum* [yüeh ch'in], the moon guitar, the Tartar fiddle [hu-ch'in]; wooden and skin drums, and clashing cymbals, they sang in shrill falsetto endless operatic ballads, mostly celebrating the past glories of the Three Kingdoms.

At least four singsong girls were seated at every table, but Lowe gives no indication that any of them sang or played an instrument.[32]

Elmer Wok Wai records his remembrance of a particular singsong girl who would sing at banquets around the turn of the century:

Beside being popular Choy Wan was a good singer and used to take me to banquets where she was hired at five dollars a song. One song would last a little over an hour. She sat with hands folded in her lap and sang through the nose a long story of love and war, sadness and joy, all mix up together. She look very serious—it would be bad manner to smile behind that face of red and white clay. Little gold bells were tied to her headdress and finger rings. On the floor beside her squatted her drummer.

According to Wai, it would cost a singsong girl "hundreds of dollars" to learn one such piece. For the instruction she would have to hire one man to beat time, another to teach the words, and still another to teach the music. It appears that such songs were in reality whole scenes from the Cantonese opera: ". . . Choy Wan would sing soprano, tenor, bass, all the parts of a song and then pick up what money the shouting banqueters threw her."[33]

A banquet of another sort—a picnic—was held by Chinese "scholars of the Mission and Sunday Schools and their friends" on 10 August 1874. Music was featured by several bands, one of them Chinese, together with singing by the Chinese, sword exercises by Chinese in costume, and—if the account is to be believed—a tumbling exhibition by "a troupe of acrobatic Bedouin Arabs."[34]

The custom of hiring musicians to play at banquets (including picnics) has continued through the present day. In the twentieth century, the practice has become to secure musicians and singers from the various music clubs in Chinatown.[35]

DANCING

As has been noted earlier, dancing was almost unknown among San Francisco's Chinese, appearing only at rare intervals even in the theater.[36] However, one account of a Chinese "dancing saloon" exists from 1854. The description is apparently of an entertainment attraction open to the public, in which sedate dancing of Chinese men and women takes place to the accompaniment of several two-string fiddles, a drum, and a gong. The account, quoted in its entirety below, is remarkable not only for its singularity with respect to dance, but because it contains perhaps the only mention in the nineteenth century of a singer using a written text (possibly with musical notation) in performance:

. . . Now let us go into the second story. Here is a long, but plain room. On the sides are coarse benches, on which are reclining a number of Chinese lasses, richly attired in silks of various colors, after the fashion of their country. Their trousers are mostly white, not very full, but heavy around the ankle, with ingenious needle-work. Their shoes are of silk, with thick, pure white soles. Their principal garment, either black, blue or green, and not made very full, extends to the knee, and is also elaborately wrought with the needle. It fits closely to the neck, and is fastened with a rich pin. This garment is not confined to the waist. Their long, glossy, black hair is combed sternly back, and bound in a knot on the crown. Each one wears a necklace, and a profusion of rings. The Chinese women are short in stature, and are by no means beautiful. At one end of the long room is a raised platform, on which are seated several musicians, each having a stringed instrument of singular construction, resembling a violin, except that the sounding-board is circular and small. It is an instrument of two strings, which cross each other below the centre. The bow-string is applied below the crossing; or it is played with the fingers like the tambourine or banjo.[37] The music made with the bow-string resembles that of the vegetable fiddle, with which lads are familiar in the gleesome days of childhood. Suspended by a cord, hangs the discordant gong. Another instrument resembles a large wooden bowl,[38] in the bottom of which is a circular opening, and over this is strained a hard, dried skin, in the form of a drum-head. It is the Chinese drum and is played with sticks, discoursing music about as inspiring as the ticking of a stout marine clock. The performers are males, neatly dressed in silks, similarly to the females, except that the trousers fit more closely to their limbs. Like all the Chinamen, their heads are shaved to the crown, and from that point, when they stand erect, their hair extends, in a long, black braid, nearly to the floor, the end of the *cue* being tastefully ornamented with ribbons. This appendage is the Chinaman's chief honor, and in defence of it he will even sacrifice his life. Another personage, habited in sky-blue silk, sits near, like a tailor on his work-table. He holds a paper, about a foot in width by four feet in length, covered with rows of Chinese characters, and folded about three inches wide, like a fan. This is a book of songs, and the person is a singer—the paper unfolding as he progresses in the performance. Now commences the dance; the young Chinamen, to the number of ten, each leads a lass upon the floor, and turns with much dignity to the tawny amateurs who are busily tuning their instruments. At this moment, another character, in green apparel, and not before observed, advances, with a very authoritative air, to a position on the right hand of the music and the figure. He looks about the room, appears to command silence, and, at the stamp of his foot, the exercises commence, with a promptness, regularity, lightness, ease, and grace, which the "outer barbarian" visitor is not prepared to witness.

It is sometimes asserted that the Chinese never dance, and probably the higher castes of the pure race do not. The amusement is by them esteemed a vulgarity. The Chinese in San Francisco are of the Tartar blood,[39] and their dances, like their games, music, and money, are unlike those of any other people; and consist, principally, in advancing and receding, changing sides, and moving down the figure, keeping constantly a kind of ambling step or motion with the feet, and bowing slightly as they pass each other. They never join hands in the dance, and appear carefully to avoid any contact. Whether this caution arises from a feeling of superiority on the part of the males, or from respect for the females, is a question for the curious. The singer makes an odd exhibition of himself, sitting, as before described, with eyes riveted to his book, which he unfolds as he proceeds—carefully refolding the extending end to render the condition of his volume convenient. His voice is like that of a squalling child, while he shakes his head, screws his face, and stretches his jaws, as if really in great distress. After passing, in the same manner, several times up and down the figure, various couples leave it and retire to an adjoining apartment, while their places are filled up by others.[40]

Later in the century, in 1870, William Frazer Rae notes the existence in Chinatown of what he terms "underground dancing saloons." These institutions are numerous, he says, "and in them are to be seen what are here significantly styled 'pretty waiter girls'." Rae gives no more description than this, but he clearly regards the "dancing saloons" in the category of vice rather than culture: "These saloons are but traps baited and set for the unwary." In this connection "there is still plenty of work for the police to perform in the interest of decency and good manners" in Chinatown.[41]

HOUSES OF PROSTITUTION

Descriptions of activities within Chinatown's brothels are almost nonexistent in the nineteenth century. Writers for Victorian readerships had to draw a line somewhere. Such observers were in agreement that the houses were evil and that there were many of them, but no details, musical or otherwise, were forthcoming. That houses in Chinatown did feature music, at least at the turn of the century, is noted in the reminiscences of the Chinese-American Elmer Wok Wai. As a six-year-old, around 1904, Wai would accompany his father on visits to brothels.

It was almost eight, evening, and streets were crowded. The Chinese theaters had been running since six o'clock but tonight we passed them up. We went on over the cobbles of Jackson Street and into "Underground Chinatown," into the Restricted District, and into Bread Alley. By that time I was skipping ahead—I knew where we were going! There was one house—dark—with iron doors where my father pulled a rope. Those heavy double door parted. We saw up a black stairway with a coal-oil lamp hanging against the wall, and mens went up and down in felt slippers without a sound. We climbed those step *and at the top was music.*[42]

Wai's father's favorite house was The Peking Boat:

The Peking Boat was big, big, with embroideries and mirrors and picture on the walls, and opium lay-outs on ebony tables. All the tea-cup, *gook jung*, had covers, very swell. There was a special room for shrine so the gods would not be shame by what they saw. Always there was much gambling and music; the mens singing for fun in the squeaky falsetto voice of womens; the womens growling in the bass voice of mens.[43]

It is entirely plausible that "Always there was much gambling and music" in Chinatown's houses of prostitution throughout the nineteenth century, but apart from Wai's account we are left generally in the dark about music as a part of brothel life. Those who frequented the houses did not write about their adventures, and those who wrote about music did not visit the houses, or at least made no mention of it. As yet, then, there is little evidence to go on. Certainly extrapolation from the present day is out of the question, as prostitution ceased to be a major industry in the area by the 1920s, and brothels as such are nonexistent in today's Chinatown.

CEREMONIAL USES

Music played an important role in such ceremonial occasions as seasonal festivals, funerals, and the dedication of new buildings in the Chinese community. Central to all such ritualistic activity were the Chinese temples, known more generally as "joss houses."[44] In San Francisco each of the Chinese Six Companies maintained a joss house within the same building as its various administrative and other offices. Sometimes the highest floor of an organization was reserved for such a sanctuary—to be as close to the gods as possible—and some associations had a specially built penthouse for this purpose. In other cases, joss houses existed as separate buildings, sometimes as mere sheds or lean-tos.[45] Within the joss house were several altars, incense burners, and representations of whichever of the Chinese gods were served by the particular joss house. The enshrined deities reflected the specific needs of the early Chinese pioneers. Particularly popular were Kuan Kuan Kung (often called the God of Literature and Valor or the God of Peace and War) and Pei Ti (God of the North). Certain gods were particular favorites of factions of the community. Hua Kuang, for instance, is the patron of actors, Hua T'u of healing practitioners. Especially popular was T'ien Hou, Queen of Heaven, who served as goddess to traveling folk in general, including sailors, actors, and prostitutes.

Often several deities were found in one temple. In addition to its own main god, a temple would honor gods of other faiths and patrons of various trades.[46]

Worship in the joss house was on an individual basis:

A petitioner entered the temple, brought incense or candles which were placed before the image of the god along with other offerings such as food, wine, or paper ''money,'' which was burned in a furnace; a kowtow was made and a prayer was murmured. Various forms of divination were available to ascertain if the petition would be successful.

A priest-custodian sold incense and candles and might provide assistance by striking a drum and gong to announce the worshiper's presence to the gods or help in divination procedures. In the day-to-day functioning of a temple, worshiping was essentially a solitary matter rather than a congregational one, although the worshiper might find himself in the midst of many others on, say, a feast day. Priests were not ordained in the Western sense, and in Chinatown a priest would purchase his joss-house position for a year at a time, sometimes at public auction.

Special services would be rendered both during festivals and on occasions when the temples were hired for the day or hour to appeal for divine aid or give thanks for favors that had been bestowed. On such occasions an orchestra would be in attendance. At certain intervals during the day, attendants would appear in robes of dark and light blue silk, marching around the images and chanting. They would then kneel before an appropriate idol, bowing a certain number of times, rise and circle around, halting before the incense table, where they would extend their arms in a ceremonial gesture. Another march around would bring them once more to the idol, to whom food would be offered. Then they would return to the incense table to consult the divining urn and a ''book of mystery,'' an activity that was alternated with several more processions, attended by chants and orchestral music. ''The music,'' in H.H. Bancroft's words, ''has in view the twofold object of rousing the drowsy god, and keeping him in good humor.''[47]

The only musical instruments normally maintained in the joss house were the gong and drum plus a mu-yü, the fish-shaped wood "temple block" that was struck for time-beating when prayers were chanted. Other instruments, such as the so-na, the hu-ch'in, the san-hsien, and various percussion instruments were used for special occasions. The opening celebration of the Ning Yeong Company's new building (including joss house) in 1864 was accompanied by "a hideous outburst of barbaric music" played on erh-hsien, san-hsien, and drums within the temple as "before the altar the heads of the companies, clad in long blue robes and black skull caps, appear daily during the festival, bowing, kissing the floor and chanting."[48] Similarly, the dedication of the Kung Chow joss house in 1879 featured the music of an ensemble made up of a hu-ch'in, several plucked string instruments, tan-p'i-ku (whose player occasionally sang also), and gong, who were seated on an elevated stage within the temple.[49] At a later stage of the festivities, a procession of priests went from shrine to shrine, forming semicircles and chanting to the accompaniment of a so-na.[50] A painting by the California artist Amédée Jullin entitled *An Interior of a Joss-House—at Prayer* shows the use of musical instruments in the 1890s. The canvas depicts a man prostrating himself before an altar-table as musicians perform on san-hsien, hu-ch'in, drum, and gong.[51]

Certain celebrations featured music and other activities outdoors, near the joss house. Such an event is described in the following, which typifies the tongue-in-cheek style affected by newspaper writers when reporting on the Chinese:

A HEATHEN JUBILEE.—The Chinese brethren instituted a pagan fete yesterday, which is to continue four days, the point of attraction being located on an alley off Sacramento street, between Dupont [Grant] and Stockton. The features of the display, and the presence of a grand orchestra, which performs continuously day and night, suggested to those uninformed in the heathen rites, who happened to pass that way, that the Chinese had opened an industrial and artistic exhibition in opposition to the Mechanic's Fair. The alley has been covered with a canopy and decorated with filagree work and paraphernalia from one of the temples. On either side are ranged groups of idols or deities, displaying a high degree of artistic skill, and, as a specimen of grotesque statuary, the exhibition is probably equal to anything that can be seen elsewhere in the city. At the end of the booth, opposite the entrance, is posted the orchestra, occupying a raised platform, who perform the sacred anthems of Pagan worship on gongs, fiddles, tom-toms, hew-gags [so-nas?], and other infernal instruments, the solo parts being given vocally with an effect that resembles the demoniacal wails of a feline conflict. On inquiry of an intelligent heathen it was ascertained that the occasion of this demonstration was the annual worship of the Yung Wo Company. Each company has four days set apart in the year for the worship of Joss, during which period their religious devotions are prosecuted with sufficient energy to satisfy the requirements of Joss for the ensuing twelve months. All the men employed by or owing allegiance to that company, if their convenience will permit, are expected to drop in at some time during the four days, offer a silent prayer and listen for a moment to the sublime music, which denotes the approving voice of the gods.[52]

Joss houses were erected in every town of significant Chinese population in California. When a joss house was dedicated in Los Angeles, in October 1878, a contingent of musicians was dispatched from San Francisco's Chinatown for the occasion.[53] Temple fairs were held during festival days in such mining towns as Marysville, Weaversville, and Oroville; and theatrical troupes would visit the various Chinese communities in the Gold Rush country and give performances.[54] Both a joss house and a theater were constructed in Oroville in the 1860s. This community had a Chinese population of ten thousand in the 1870s, second in size only to San Francisco's Chinatown.[55]

Music had a place in all the Chinese festivals, its performance ranging from the playing within the joss house for the more solemn ones to performing in the streets, sometimes on parade, for more elaborately celebrated occasions. By far the most spectacular of annual celebrations was—and continues to be—the week-long Chinese New Year, observed in February or early March, and celebrated in San Francisco since 1851.[56] Music vied with fireworks during a period in which the noise of celebration was virtually continuous.

The first morning of the year is fraught with the greatest din, but explosions are frequent all through the week, if the police permit them, and when they cease at intervals, the ear is assailed by booming drums, clashing cymbals, and squeaking fiddles, as if, as with us, enthusiasm were measured by noise, and patriotism by burned powder.[57]

Most businesses were closed for the week, and the population devoted itself to celebrating the year's most joyous occasion. Many-
colored bunting adorned windows and housetops, and Chinese lanterns of every shape and design illuminated the walks. The doors,
windows, and walls of houses were decked with placards bearing
words of wisdom and greetings. Restaurants and theaters were
gaudy with brilliant adornments, and the air was fragrant from the
courts and kitchens where banquets were being prepared.

The sidewalks, and even the middle of the streets, are thronged with
eager life. Wealthy merchants, clothed in long priestly robes of purple silk
or satin, pass to and fro, busy in conducting some particular parts of the
ceremonies of the celebration, and women and children, dressed in most
peculiar and brilliant attire, their faces painted till they look more like dolls
or toys than humans, mingle in the motley throng.[58]

Children played games and frolicked in the streets. Theaters ran
continuously night and day. Restaurants were crowded to capacity,
and the festooned gambling houses and brothels did their heaviest
business of the year—all to the accompaniment of music.

Forth from many Chinese apartments during this season, will come the
sounds of their various stringed and wind instruments; and the performers
seem to enjoy it, for they think it is music; there is also much of what they
call singing.[59]

Music and fireworks served not only to heighten the excitement and
maintain an air of gaiety but, as traditionally believed, to frighten
away all bad spirits that may have gathered about during the expir-
ing year and to ensure a fresh start without evil influences.

CEREMONIES FOR THE DEAD

Full-fledged Chinese funerals were colorful, lengthy, and expensive affairs.[60] They attracted much attention from the white press,
as the funeral was one of the most exotic-seeming of Chinese practices, and much of the funeral activity was open to public view. Actually, most Chinese were too poor to afford the sort of funerals
that received such publicity, and the deaths of children and of
women were usually attended by a minimum of ceremony and dis-

play. In the more elaborate funerals, music was performed at virtually every stage of the ceremony—first at rites over the body, then
in the funeral procession, and finally at the grave itself. (In some
cases, in which the body was to be shipped immediately back to
China, the procession and graveside ceremonies would be omitted,
as these would be eventually performed in China.[61] In other cases,
however, the complete ceremony would take place, including
graveside obsequies, after which the body would be returned to an
undertaking establishment for shipment to China.[62]) Throughout
the ceremonies, the principal musical instrument used was the
oboe-like so-na, usually played in conjunction with drums, cymbals, and gongs. In the following descriptions, quotations are used
illustratively from accounts of various funerals.

In the first part of the funeral service, music at intervals would
accompany the ritual chanting of the priest over the body. The
priest himself might mark time on percussion instruments while
chanting.

In his hands he held a small blue flag, (on which Chinese characters were
inscribed,) a pair of cymbals and a bell. Alternately accompanying himself
upon the bell and cymbals, he chanted in a crying tone of voice the good
deeds of the deceased, Wong Ah Sing, and the greatness of the Chinese
Joss, who would undoubtedly bring his assassin to justice.[63]

At this stage of the service, "Sometimes drums and gongs are
sounded, and fire-crackers exploded, to frighten off any evil spirits
that may be around."[64] A whole orchestra might also accompany
the chanting.

Four assistants . . . are ranged along the coffin. Every few minutes they
kneel to the ground, touch their forehead to the dust and give vent to their
grief in long-drawn, hideous, piercing wails, all in unison, chanting at the
same time, while half a dozen Chinamen keep time on hideous sounding instruments. When the mourners get off an unusual piercing shriek or wail,
the clarionets, gongs and one-stringed fiddles in the hands of the musicians
clang louder and more furiously than ever, and the very pavement seems to
shake beneath us.[65]

Music and priestly ceremonies might be performed not only at the
location of the body but—especially if the deceased was prosperous

and well known—at other sites in the city: "On all sides could be heard the rattle and bang of the Chinese musicians stationed in the various josshouses, where services for Tim King Yung were being held."[66] At the close of the chanting rituals, the band might play.

Finally, having finished, [the priest] gave a sign to the Chinese band, which immediately began playing what presumably was a funeral anthem, in which they were joined by the mourners, the female portion of which howled themselves almost into hysterics . . .[67]

The coffin was then placed into a hearse or wagon to be borne to the cemetery. A band of Chinese musicians marched in the procession.

[The procession] was led by a Chinese band of music consisting of five players. The chief instrument was an ear-piercing clarinet [so-na] that, as a sign of mourning for the departed, uttered wild, shrill and weird sounds, and so accompanied the mournful tom-tom and gong-gong.[68]

In the earliest decades of Chinese settlement, only Chinese musicians were used. However, from the 1870s onward, an American brass band was also hired for the procession, and it often headed the cortege, with the Chinese band immediately behind or sometimes coming at the very end of the procession.[69] The resultant clash of sounds was probably wonderful to hear.

. . . the tones of [the Chinese] instruments mingling with the notes of the brass band . . . made the funeral march played by the latter sound like the latest selection in rag time . . .[70]

Elmer Wok Wai recalls that the music at his mother's funeral in 1900 was furnished by two bands:

One was the band of my mother's Woman's Company that march in uniform; the other, the band of my father's tong, the Wah Tings. They played the famous tune: *The Di Hoy Moon*. Open the Big Gate. After the hearse walked a priest beating cymbals, a man followed him blowing a brass and bamboo horn, then came mourners, relatives and friends—and these marched two by two, the womens by themselves. One woman, with a sack over her head for manners, was Father's girl friend. There was too an open hack, holding the enlarged crayon picture of my mother, and I remember those horses got frighten at the bands.[71]

In addition to the marching musicians, one or more carriages might carry additional Chinese ensembles.

Finally, the Chinese musicians would accompany ceremonies at the grave.

It was close to 3 o'clock ere the funeral party arrived at the cemetery. There the priests held their weird service around the coffin in which lay the body. . . . Clouds of smoke from incense and punk sticks were wafted toward the sky, the feast was displayed, the Chinese musicians played their loudest and the priests chanted and intoned in a shrill tone, while the paper representing money was distributed with a liberal hand. For an hour the services continued and then the signal was given for the return to the city.[72]

INTERCULTURAL CONTACTS

The use of an American marching band for Chinese funerals provided Chinatown's residents with one of their few direct contacts with Western music. Outside of Christian missions in the community, there was little chance that such music would be heard within Chinatown's borders, and Chinese were far from welcome at those locations where Western music was to be heard—concert halls, theaters, restaurants, and gambling parlors.[73] There are some scattered instances of Chinese attending American theaters in the nineteenth century, but these were truly exceptional cases, and the events were attended with reactions of shock and indignation in the theaters and in the newspapers,[74] although Americans felt no hesitation in crossing the line in the other direction—attending the Chinese theater or, for that matter, any other attraction in the Chinese community.

In the 1850s, before anti-Chinese prejudice became virulent in San Francisco, groups of Chinese were frequently to be seen participating in parades and other events of patriotic celebration. They had made their first appearance as a semi-official contingent in August 1850.[75] Certain San Franciscans had ordered a number of pamphlets and religious tracts, printed in Chinese, from Canton for distribution to the new inhabitants of Chinatown. When the material arrived, invitations were sent out to the "China Boys," as they were called, to be present on the afternoon of 28 August at Portsmouth Square to be presented with the printed materials. The Chinese not only showed up as requested but wore their most splen-

did attire and marched to the square to receive the gifts, thereby
making a very favorable impression on the many observers who
came to watch. During this meeting the Chinese were asked by
Mayor Geary to march in a mock funeral procession the very next
day in memory of the recently deceased President Zachary Taylor.
After marching in the funeral procession, the China Boys took considerable interest in other public celebrations. With their pictur-
esque and colorful costumes, they became a popular part of many
events involving parades and festivities. They participated in the
first celebration of the admission of California into the Union, as
well as Washington's Birthday, Independence Day, and other holidays.[76] Miska Hauser described their appearance as part of a magnificent Fourth of July parade in 1853:

. . . finally the Chinese, who invariably drew the greatest attention through
the splendor and peculiarity of their part of the procession. In fact, their
appearance deserves special attention. About four hundred of them were
clothed in the finest costumes consisting of narrow pants with stocking legs
and short jackets, all done in black silk damask with embroidered flower
designs, or with wide pants and longer coats of the same material, or in
gowns reaching down to their shoes. The [colors] of these suits were predominantly light and dark blue. The headcovering, as usual, was a round
upturned hat, or small skullcap, without visor, from under which pitch
black pigtails hung down to the calves of their legs. In their hands they carried sun fans or small canes. . . . Two . . . beautiful banners carried the
inscriptions "Cheer for the Republicanism of China" and "The Chinamen
on the Fourth of July, 1853."[77]

The Chinese provided music as well as pageantry:

Between the banners of flags were . . . three carriages; in the first were
the four most important Chinamen. The second carried four musicians,
comically dressed, plus Chinese drums, cymbals, and other unfamiliar instruments. In the third carriage was a string and percussion orchestra.[78]

Earlier in the year Hauser had assembled an orchestra of Western
players from the various gambling houses and had disciplined them
to the point where they could play one of Beethoven's Leonore
Overtures. A subsequent concert

took a full four hours because I had to give in to the audience—composed of Chinese, gringoes, adventurers from every country, etc.—and play three encores to each number. When I played a composition with Chinese melodies interwoven, "Die Kinder des Himmlichen Reiches" gave way suddenly to their enthusiasm. They let out inhuman howlings and set up such a racket that I finally hid in a corner of the hall until the Chinese triumph subsided.[79]

In a story about Sunday schools for Chinese in nearby Vallejo, a reporter notes that the Chinese learn by ear "with precision after a short practice and evidently take great pleasure in exercising their musical powers."[80] It was only in church-related activities that Chinese contact with Western music was more than peripheral.[81] Here and nowhere else in the community we find Chinese singing Western songs and playing Western instruments. Newspapers typically express surprise at how well Christian hymns are rendered by Chinese singers. An account in 1878, for instance, describes the eighth anniversary celebration of the Methodist Chinese Mission School (held at the Chinese theater on Washington Street) and notes that

the performances, both in recitation and musical parts, astonished all who were present, especially those who had but little conception of the power of education, exercised upon the docile mind and voice of the Mongolian race. . . . the musical part of the programme, especially to those who were only accustomed to the nasal twangs and bagpipe notes of the ordinary Chinamen, demonstrated clearly the fact that with proper training, this race possesses voices of melody and power.

The hymns sung of the program included "Pull for the Shore," "Dark Is the Night," "The Gospel Ship," "Title Clear," "Precious Jewels," "The Bell Doth Toll," and "The Sweet By-and-By." A secular highlight was "The Whistling Farmer Boy," in which the Chinese "puckered up their lips and whistled in harmony."[82] Performing on Western instruments was more of a rarity. A Chinese pianist performed at a Sunday school picnic in 1874,[83] and in the same year a Chinese street-corner revivalist in Sacramento featured a Chinese organist and choir.[84] Composition in Western idioms was sometimes found among mission and Sunday school scholars. Thus we find "Jesus Loves Me," composed and arranged by Duck Ball, and "Shall We Meet beyond the

River?'' with music by Why Tong. An original hymn-text in English, by Hok Kan, was set by its author to a traditional Chinese melody.[85]

These are isolated examples, however, and hardly add up to any significant cross-fertilization of musical cultures. In the theater especially, the mingling of Western and Chinese traditions was almost nonexistent. The Chinese drama was as yet free of any Western tinge—though Sarah Bernhardt once gave a startling impromptu performance from the Chinese theater stage and had her good-natured Chinese audience in hysterics with her mock-Chinese singing and dancing.[86] The Chinese theater, in turn, had no influence on San Francisco's occidental playhouses, though plays and skits occasionally were based on Chinese themes, as in Bret Harte and Mark Twain's *The Heathen Chinee*. Included in a variety program at the Adelphi Theater on 13 November 1878 was a skit entitled *The Chinese Must Go*.[87] Local Chinese did have a role in lending some authenticity to a play given at the Alcazar Theater in 1897. *The First Born*, by San Francisco dramatist Francis Powers, dealt with life in San Francisco's Chinatown. Though all the Chinese roles were played by white actors, a measure of verisimilitude was given through the use of authentic costumes, provided by Chinese merchants, and an overture of actual Chinese music.[88]

The curious occidental could experience Chinese music at Chinatown's theaters and hear snatches of it from joss houses or funeral processions; more rarely, a Chinese might hear strains of Western music in church or from a white marching band; but there is no evidence that any such exposure significantly influenced either musical tradition. Except for church, in some cases, the Chinese had no use for the white man's music. And clearly the feeling was mutual, as seen in these journalistic accounts. Nonetheless, it is notable that one pro-Chinese minister, a Dr. Newman, made use of Chinese music as an addition to his lecture rebuking anti-Chinese agitators in 1879, at the height of the Exclusion movement. His lecture took place not in San Francisco—where such a call for toleration might have precipitated a riot—but in New York:

During the lecture nine Chinamen, with long queues, entered the chapel from a side room. Five of them had peculiar looking musical instruments.

After the lecture Dr. Newman introduced the Celestials, and Ye Tong, in a short address, proved himself to be quite an orator. He said he knew the instruments were peculiar, but they would make fine music. "Now give us something for the glory of God," said Ye Tong, and the company struck up a lively air, after which Eng Him played a solo on an instrument that much resembled a clarionet. This was followed by a song in his native tongue by Tom Lee, and the entertainment closed with the playing of a religious tune by Lee Quay on an instrument that resembled a cheesebox cover with four strings drawn across.[89]

The listeners' reaction is not recorded. With due credit to Dr. Newman's courage, it is doubtful whether the use of Chinese music could help elicit sympathy toward the plight of Chinese-Americans. The evidence suggests that whatever virtues the Chinese might have had, in American eyes, their music was not one of them.

NOTES

1. While the earliest well-publicized use of Chinese music was with the Hong Took Tong theatrical troupe in October 1852, the existence of Chinese instruments, as well as the performance of purely Chinese music was noted in print almost from the beginning of the immigration. G.R. Mac-Minn states that a Chinese instrumental ensemble of six players was hired in July 1851 by the management of the Athenaeum Promenade Concerts to perform "a variety of their curious national airs, in their native costume, between the parts of the concert." (*Theater of the Golden Era in California* [Caldwell, Idaho, Caxton, 1941], p. 496.) An anonymous reporter in *Blackwell's Magazine* (72 [1852]) noted that a six-piece Chinese band, seated in a wagon, performed in a parade in celebration of Washington's Birthday in 1852. ("The Celestials at Home and Abroad," p. 105.)

2. A.W. Loomis, "Holiday in the Chinese Quarter," *Overland Monthly* 2 (1869), p. 144.

3. B.E. Lloyd, *Lights and Shades in San Francisco* (San Francisco, A.L. Bancroft & Co., 1876), p. 238.

4. Helen F. Clark, "The Chinese of New York Contrasted With Their Foreign Neighbors," *Century* 53 (1896), p. 106.

5. *Alta*, 23 August 1864. The references appear to be respectively to the erh-hsien and the san-hsien. See Liang, *Chinese Musical Instruments & Pictures*, p. 73.

6. See below, Chapter 8.

7. *Chronicle*, 29 April 1877. See above, pp. 51–52.

8. See above, p. 88.

9. West side, between Washington and Clay. The map is in Willard B. Farwell's *The Chinese at Home and Abroad* (San Francisco, A.L. Bancroft, 1885).

10. Veta Griggs, *Chinaman's Chance: The Life Story of Elmer Wok Wai* (New York, Exposition, 1969), p. 26.

11. Joseph Carey, *By the Golden Gate* (Albany, N.Y., The Albany Diocesan Press, 1902), pp. 291–93.

12. Bancroft, (*Retrospections, Political and Personal*, New York, The Bancroft Co., 1912), pp. 379 ff., describes the actual gambling games. See also Stewart Culin, *The Gambling Games of the Chinese in America* (Philadelphia, University of Pennsylvania Press, 1891).

13. Frank Soulé et al., *Annals of San Francisco* (New York, D. Appleton, 1855), p. 382.

14. Ibid., pp. 382–83.

15. Bancroft, *Retrospections*, p. 378.

16. The many observers who wrote with horror of the evils of Chinese gambling rarely mention the much more numerous and flourishing gambling houses of the white population. One world traveler wrote of San Francisco's white establishments in 1853: ". . . such open and shameless enticements to evil I have never seen any where [sic] else. . . . Even the Chinese gaming-houses were more decent than the American." The writer's source of offense was the presence of women: "With respect to the furniture and decorations of these houses, it is obviously intended not only to encourage directly the passion for gaming, but also to intoxicate the senses, and entice to all kinds of sensuality. Noisy music resounds through the spacious saloons, licentiously seductive pictures hang on the walls, and beautiful girls are seated as lures here and there at the tables." (Ida Pfeiffer, *A Lady's Visit to California, 1853*, Oakland, Calif., Biobooks, 1959, pp. 15–16.) The Chinese establishments were stag affairs, furnishing only gambling and music. Chinese women were to be seen in white gambling houses, however. See Gladys Hansen, ed., *San Francisco* (New York, Hastings House, 1973), p. 126.

17. Bancroft, *Retrospections*, p. 378.

18. *Alta*, 29 December 1869.

19. Pardee Lowe, *Father and Glorious Descendant* (Boston, Little, Brown, 1943), pp. 46–47.

20. "Day in Chinatown," p. 497.

21. Gertrude Atherton, *My San Francisco* (New York, Bobbs, Merrill, 1946), pp. 53–54.

22. A correspondent for the Boston *Journal* in 1878 mentions that in a Chinese restaurant, "Amid the jargon of rude music the company, clatter-

ing like a cotton mill, sat, playing cards and dominoes." "Music" here is almost certainly a figure of speech. (From the San Francisco *Post*, 29 January 1878.)

23. Bancroft, *Retrospections*, p. 332.

24. Ibid., p. 231.

25. Charles Keeler, *San Francisco and Thereabout* (San Francisco, The California Promotion Committee, 1902), p. 62.

26. New York *Times*, 5 March 1875.

27. See above, pp. 57–59.

28. *Chronicle*, 2 October 1879.

29. Bancroft, *Retrospections*, p. 334.

30. Lowe, p. 43.

31. Ibid., p. 44.

32. Ibid., p. 45.

33. Griggs, p. 30. Wok does not mention accompaniment beyond the drummer, but it would seem unlikely that at least one melodic instrument was not present.

34. *Alta*, 11 August 1874.

35. See below, p. 199.

36. See above, pp. 81–82.

37. Here the author is mistaken. Chinese two-string fiddles are never plucked; nor are they played "like the tambourine." Perhaps a plucked-string instrument, such as the san-hsien, was also in use and the observer confused one with the other.

38. An inverted bowl: a tan-p'i-ku.

39. San Francisco's Chinese immigrants of the 1850s were of course from South China. There is no basis for Capron's description here printed. Bancroft (*Retrospections*, p. 371) also mentions dancing exhibitions by "Tartars" in the early 1850s, but his source is almost certainly the same account. There is no evidence to substantiate a "Tartar" ethnic group among San Francisco's Chinese.

40. E.S. Capron, *History of California from Its Discovery to the Present Time* (Boston, Jewitt, 1854), pp. 152–54. By some stretch of the imagination this account could be construed to be of a dance rehearsal by members of a theater company—not open to the public—into which the author happened to wander. But one would thus have to assume that the "females" were impersonators. Further, the questions arise: Why in costume? Why in a location separate from the theater? Additionally, the very concept of a rehearsal, as described, is essentially alien to traditional Chinese theatrical practice.

41. William Frazer Rae, *Westward by Rail* (London, Longmans, Green, 1870), pp. 298–99.

42. Griggs, p. 26. Emphasis added.

43. Ibid., p. 27.

44. "Joss" is a pidgin English word for any of the Chinese divinities, supposedly derived from the Portuguese "deos" or "deus," a god.

45. Thomas Chinn et al., eds., *A History of the Chinese in California* (San Francisco, Chinese Historical Society of America, 1961), p. 73.

46. C.K. Yang, *Religion in Chinese Society* (Berkeley, Calif., University of California Press, 1961), pp. 81–82.

47. Mariann Kaye Wells, "Chinese Temples in California," (M.A. thesis, University of California, Berkeley, 1962), p. 23.

48. *Alta*, 23 August 1864.

49. *Alta*, 21 December 1879.

50. *Call*, 25 December 1879.

51. Arthur I. Street, "California Artists—III," *Overland Monthly*, 2d series, 33 (1899), pp. 7–10.

52. *Bulletin*, 14 September 1874.

53. *Chronicle*, 25 October 1878.

54. Wells, p. 84.

55. Ibid., p. 82. See also Max M. Harrell, "Movements for Preservation of the Chinese Temple," *Butte County Historical Society Diggin's* 14 (1970), pp. 3–10.

56. *Alta*, 3 February 1851.

57. Bancroft, *Retrospections*, p. 302.

58. Lloyd, p. 225.

59. Loomis, "Holiday in the Chinese Quarter," p. 144.

60. Described in idem, "Chinese 'Funeral Baked Meats'," *Overland Monthly* 3 (1869), pp. 21–29.

61. See, for example, the account of funeral of Wong Ah Sing, *Bulletin*, 5 February 1880.

62. See, for example, the account of funeral of Tom King Yung, *Chronicle*, 23 September 1903.

63. *Bulletin*, 5 February 1880.

64. Lloyd, p. 228.

65. Mendocino (Calif.) *Democrat*, 14 October 1876.

66. *Chronicle*, 23 September 1903.

67. *Bulletin*, 5 February 1880.

68. I.J. Benjamin, *Three Years in America, 1859–62* (Philadelphia, Jewish Publication Society of America, 1956), p. 281.

69. Many professional brass bands were available in San Francisco, the earliest—Herr Kohler's Union Band—having been formed in 1853. Cornel Lengyel, ed., *Music of the Gold Rush Era* (New York, AMS, 1972), p. 187.

70. *Call*, 7 December 1900.

71. Griggs, p. 15.

72. *Chronicle*, 23 September 1903.

73. However, Elmer Wok Wai recalls attending vaudeville shows around the turn of the century in San Francisco with his father. He does not mention any sort of discrimination at the box office. He and his father were surprised to find that, unlike the Chinese theater, the vaudeville did not change shows every night. "We would often get stung on the same show," he recounts. On one occasion he suspected that his father had wandered into a Western opera house, as the latter's description was of total bewilderment: "It was the second inning . . . and I don't know what's the score!" Griggs, p. 31.

74. See above, pp. 38–39.

75. Soulé et al., p. 288.

76. Dobie, *San Francisco's Chinatown* (New York, Appleton-Century, 1936), pp. 37–38. Their first use of music in a parade appears to have been in the Washington's Birthday celebration of 1852. An observer noted: "Seated in an express waggon were six musicians, playing tunes which to them seemed most soul-stirring, although to us most heart-rending." ("The Celestials at Home and Abroad" [*Blackwell's Magazine* 72 (1852)], p. 105.)

77. Miska Hauser, *Letters of Miska Hauser, 1853* (New York, AMS, 1972), pp. 63–64.

78. Ibid., pp. 64– 65.

79. Ibid., p. 30.

80. *Alta*, 2 November 1875.

81. Christian missionary work in Chinatown dates almost from the earliest arrival of the Chinese in San Francisco. See, e.g., Albert Williams, *A Pioneer Pastorate* (San Francisco, Wallace & Hassett, 1879). Among the earliest churches established in Chinatown were those of the Catholic and Presbyterian faiths, both in 1854. A Young Men's Christian Association center was established in Chinatown in 1870. Clifford Drury, *San Francisco YMCA: 100 Years by the Golden Gate* (Glendale, Calif., Arthur H. Clark Co., 1963).

82. *Alta*, 8 June 1878.

83. *Alta*, 11 August 1874.

84. *Alta*, 1 March 1874.

85. *Alta*, 5 March 1875.

86. San Francisco *Examiner*, 26 April 1891.

87. Peter Chu et al., *Chinese Theatres in America* (Washington, D.C., Bureau of Research, Federal Theatre Project, Region of the West, 1936), p. 40. Comic roles for stage-Chinese are found in plays produced in San Francisco throughout the second half of the nineteenth century, beginning

with Alonzo Delano's *A Live Woman in the Mines; or, Pike County Ahead*, produced in 1857 and including in its dramatis personae a character simply labeled "Chinaman," who exclaims at one point: "Chinaman no fight; Chinaman skin good skin; keep him so. Mellican man big devil—no hurty bullet him." Stuart W. Hyde, "The Chinese Stereotype in American Melodrama," *California Historical Quarterly* 5 (1955), pp. 357– 67.

88. Edward M. Gagey, *The San Francisco Stage* (New York, Columbia University Press, 1950), p. 175.

89. *Call*, 6 May 1879.

Part II

THE TWENTIETH CENTURY

5

Chinese Theater: Regrowth and Survival (1907– 1945)

Although San Francisco's Chinatown was devastated by the earthquake and fire of 1906, the Chinese community was not long without a business and residential neighborhood. Thousands of Chinese rendered homeless by the catastrophe fled to Oakland, across the bay. Within a few weeks a new Chinatown began to grow in this East Bay city while San Francisco's Chinese neighborhood was being rebuilt. Four months after the earthquake a New York *Times* reporter wrote with astonishment of the size and sudden rise of Oakland's Chinatown:

It begins on the water front, and for many blocks it extends quite into the heart of the town, only one block from Broadway, the main avenue of the city. It was all done so quietly that Oakland sits up in amazement, and with a gasp of astonishment realizes that for good or evil . . . Chinatown is here to stay.[1]

Oakland's Chinatown occupied a larger territory than the old San Francisco neighborhood. Residential houses were quickly transformed. Extra stories were added, and shops appeared on ground floors, surrounded with alleys and fronted with wide awnings. Club houses, restaurants—with music—, tong headquarters, gambling dens, opium dens, and brothels were said to re-create the atmosphere that had prevailed in San Francisco. The area did not lack for theatrical entertainment, as a theater was soon established in the top floor of a three-story building that contained over six hundred rooms and featured shops on its ground floor.[2] While some Chinese were to settle permanently in Oakland, the majority of the newcomers came there simply to bide their time until a new Chinatown could be established in San Francisco.

Scarcely had the dust settled in San Francisco when plans were at work to rebuild the Chinese quarter. A syndicate of Hong Kong merchants was reportedly prepared to purchase a new site for the neighborhood. Mayor Schmitz was in favor of a plan to relocate the Chinese on the coast away from San Francisco. A considerable residue of Exclusionist sentiment still festered among many San Franciscans who favored ridding the state of the Chinese completely.[3]

In the end, however, San Francisco's Chinatown arose on the same site that it had occupied for half a century. Gradually the emigrants to Oakland and other communities found their way back to San Francisco, and the new Chinatown flourished again as both a business and a residential enclave and as the city's most colorful tourist attraction. Indeed, it was a far more "Chinese"-looking neighborhood than was its earlier version. The new buildings were modern; but balconies, balustrades, and pagoda-like roofs incorporated Chinese architectural and decorative features.

The old Chinatown of gambling halls and opium dens was now history. Illegal operations would continue to some degree in the new Chinatown, but the Chinese made decided efforts to create an image of reform and rectitude in the rebuilt neighborhood. A tourist's pamphlet of 1909 urged visitors not to search for the sordid:

A suggestion:—Bad sights can doubtless be found in any part of town—in San Francisco or anywhere else. There are plenty of interesting sights in Chinatown, as you will see from the list we have herein. If, however, you MUST see bad sights, well—no doubt it is possible to find them; but the respectable Chinese of San Francisco beg to suggest that these sights be left for exploration by those to whom decency and right-living do not appeal. In others words: Do not leave your morals at home when you visit Chinatown.

Safety for travelers was assured: "Visitors in Chinatown need fear no harm from members of the Chinese race. As to members of other races who often haunt Chinatown's streets, the visitor must use ordinary prudence." Visitors were urged to see (and get a whiff of) Fish Alley, off Washington Street, just below Grant, but were warned: "Visit this part only in the daytime, as white 'sporting women' live on this street in considerable numbers." The editors boasted of Chinatown's new cleanliness:

San Francisco's *reconstructed* Chinatown is composed of modern sanitary and attractive buildings. A Chinese lodging house recently constructed by Chinese owners on Clay Street has bathtubs on each floor—something novel in Chinatown.

The editors added: "There are no underground opium dens in Chinatown—haven't been any since the fire."[4] Indeed, vice was in for hard times. By the time of the Opium Act of 1923, the drug had been priced and taxed virtually out of existence. Brothels were dealt a death blow by the state legislature's Red Light Abatement Act of 1914, though occasional raids on houses of "slave girls" continued to be made until 1925.[5]

That Chinese drama was still produced in Chinatown is indicated in various sources, but there is no evidence that the theater enjoyed the continuity and steady patronage that had characterized the attraction even during the declining years of the nineteenth century. There appears to have been no permanent base for theatrical performances during the first two decades of the twentieth century. There were high hopes for building a new theater during these years, but these were not fulfilled. In April 1907—one year after the fire—plans were being made to erect a new theater on the old site on Washington Street, and other theaters were being envisaged as well;[6] but matters did not get beyond the planning stage. Two years later it was reported that "among the buildings recently completed is the theater of Chinatown, being constructed at a cost of $50,000 at Clay and Stockton Streets."[7] But no subsequent word appears about the project. Like previous such structures, it is likely that the building was converted to other uses. San Francisco's City Directory mentions one theater in 1912 (at 813 Kearny Street), and does not again mention a Chinese theater until 1930. Tourist guides, which had previously given much attention to Chinese drama, notably omit mention of the theater during these years. *The San Francisco Standard Guide* of 1913, for instance, dwells at length on the attractions of Chinatown but does not mention Chinese theater.[8] Ruth Kedzie Wood, in *The Tourist's California* of 1914, wrote that the theater, like the "precarious balconies" of old Chinatown, was only a memory.[9]

Though a permanent base for the opera is missing during these years, however, there are occasional reports of Chinese theatrical performances. An advertisement in a 1909 Chinatown pamphlet for visitors publicizes the show at the Oriental Theater (at 1035–1037 Grant Avenue): "Chinese Vaudeville performance from 1 p.m. to 11 p.m. Don't fail to see our troupe of Chinese Actors, including our famous Chinese lady, MAR YIT OR."[10] In 1910 a group of Chinese actors performed at the Palace Hotel for a convention of the Hotel Men's Mutual Benefit Association. The occasion featured a miniature theater complete with Chinese orchestra.[11] In February 1913 a Chinese theatrical troupe performed in a huge tent erected at the corner of Grant and Jackson.[12] Five years later, a tent on Grant Avenue served similarly as a Chinese theater.[13] (Both of these tent performances occurred around the time of the Chinese New Year, always a prosperous period for the Chinese opera.) From desultory mentions in various sources—and from the memories of elderly Chinese in today's Chinatown who recall that the theater was indeed alive during these years—we can infer that the drama was a sort of floating phenomenon in Chinatown—a month here, a one-night stand there, in Western theaters, in tents, and in other temporary locations.

Clearly the times were not economically propitious for ongoing Chinese theater. The population of Chinatown was at low ebb—around eight thousand in 1913,[14] compared with the boom days of the nineteenth century when there were sometimes over thirty thousand potential patrons for the theater.

Another factor that undoubtedly hindered the establishment of a full-time theater was the rapidly growing competition of motion pictures. Even before the fire, movie performances had attracted attention and patronage in Chinatown. In a nostalgic piece on the Chinese theater *prior* to the earthquake, Will Irwin stated flatly that "The Chinese theater in America is forever gone, and the cinema did the business." He recalled his first notice of a movie theater in Chinatown:

One night, walking home from a performance at the Jackson Street Chinese Theater . . . I noticed that what had been but last week a Chinese grocery store was curiously transformed. It was painted with great, gaudy posters; it blazed with electric lights illuminating the legend "Moving Pictures." I paused to admire and to smile, for the commercial movie was then a novelty.[15]

A Chinese writer remembers attending movies in 1908 in Chinatown: "In those early days the motion picture company would hire an empty store in Chinatown and run a few reels of film. There were no seats. Peoples stood on boxes." Neither movie houses nor theaters had reserved seats: "If you wanted to save a bench before someone else grabbed it, you spread a baby's diaper over it."[16] By 1909 a "five-cent theatorium" was established in the neighboring Barbary Coast district, and the reign of the motion picture was well under way as a powerful competitor of the live theater.[17]

In 1916 a building at the corner of Washington and Kearny streets served as a setting for Chinese theater. It was here on the night of 6 March that the sanguinary reputation of the Chinese theater as the scene for tong violence was brought up to date. One death and four injuries by bullet wounds occurred during "The Tragedy of the Seven Emperors," as reported by the *Examiner*:

It was just after the evening meal and the smoky little theatre just across the street from the Hall of Justice was crowded with more than 500 Chinese—men, women and children. The tom-toms and the cymbals were pounding and sqeaking [sic], and the tragedy of the third emperor had reached its thrilling climax when the disturbance came.

Fong Wing, a gun man of the Suey On tong, had been insulted.

Some one had taken his seat, he declared. He ordered five Hop Sing men sitting in a row to make way for him. They gazed stolidly at the story-teller on the stage and ignored him.

Fong Wing whipped his "gatling gun" from his voluminous clothes and fired five shots. Every shot took effect. Five Chinese fell off their seats and lay groaning on the floor. Fong Wing looked around to see if anyone dared to follow him and walked out of the theater.

The play never stopped. No one paid any attention to the five Chinese on the floor. A woman with two babies in her lap who was sitting just across the aisle never left her seat, never screamed or did anything that might be expected. She just sat there and looked at the stage.[18]

Although tong murders would continue to capture headlines in San Francisco newspapers until the last one in 1922, the theater had seen its last real-life killing.

The 1920s were to see a renaissance of sorts in the Chinese theater of San Francisco. The early years of the decade saw much box-office success in the performances of Chinese troupes at such theaters as the Crescent, the Liberty, and the Orpheum. Chinatown, slowly growing in population, began to look as if it could once again support full-time drama. Spurred by such optimism, local promoters built two Chinese-opera theaters in the mid-1920s. The reawakening of interest in Chinese theater also led in 1925 to the founding of what would become Chinatown's largest amateur music club, the Nam Chung Musical Society, in which Cantonese opera would continue to be performed and promoted to the present day.

Perhaps no feature of the Chinese theater of the 1920s represented a more profound break with the past than the emergence of the female actor as a dominant figure on the Chinese stage. As we have seen, women had appeared in Chinatown theaters since the late nineteenth century, but only as novelty attractions. Until the 1920s the Chinese stage was still primarily a man's world, with female parts played by specially trained male actors. After the Chinese Revolution in 1911, however, women became increasingly accepted on the Chinese stage, to the degree that female actors were becoming leading box-office attractions, both in San Francisco and China, and were commanding salaries that were often higher than those of any male actors in the troupe. In fact, the resurgence of interest in the Chinese theaters of the 1920s has been attributed directly to the flowering of authentic womanhood on the Chinese stage. The new attitude toward women was further reflected in the fact that audiences were no longer segregated by sex, and—not long after the earthquake and fire—women were even hired as usherettes.[19]

The featuring of women on the stage quickly caught the attention of the daily press. The *Chronicle* in April 1922 announced that "China Now Has Stage Door Johnnies" and quoted Je Quon Tai, new prima donna of the Orpheum Theater:

"Up to about eight years ago there were no stage-door 'Johns' in China, because all of the female parts in Chinese plays were taken by men, female impersonators. Since that time the Chinese theaters using women in their productions have their 'Johns' just as the American theaters."

The speaker was Princess Je Quon Tai, the Orpheum prima donna, who, in discussing the differences between American and Chinese theaters, finds the John an interesting difference.

"In China no man would ever think of approaching a stage door with flowers meeting a woman for the first time in that manner. The Chinese custom of the male who would woo the actress is to send costly gifts daily for weeks, none of which bear the name of the giver. Then, suddenly, the generous soul would appear at the stage door and say:

" 'Here I am, the man who was sent the beauteous gifts.' " . . .

Miss Tai says that there are noticeably few "Johns" in San Francisco, and also emphatically states that no one here has showered her with gifts at the Orpheum. Possibly conditions are better for the Johns in this country, but the Chinese actress has an advantage and custom makes being a Chinese John something of a burden.[20]

In the same year, the *Chronicle* also did a lengthy illustrated feature on Tam Wai Jon, "the new leading lady of the Chinese dramatic company playing at the old Crescent Theater, where she charms the theatergoers of Chinatown." The story reveals that Chinatown's actors are no longer quartered in the theaters themselves. In various nineteenth-century accounts of Chinatown's theaters, reporters had been appalled at the tiny and crowded living quarters allotted in the theater buildings to even the most highly paid actors. Actors now stayed at a boarding house on Pacific Street:

The actors' boarding house is palatial compared with the average Chinese lodging quarters. The halls are wide and light and clean—the hall floor looked as if it had been scrubbed within the hour—and the players have their own rooms, comfortable little cubby holes, decorated with pictures and souvenirs.

As in earlier days, actors brought their families with them on tour. The *Chronicle* reporter noted that "the friendly company of players wandered back and forth into each other's rooms and two pigtailed little girls shepherded a perfectly spherical baby up and down the hall"—these being part of one actor's family of seven.[21]

Even as interest mounted in full-time Chinese theater, however, attendance was by no means guaranteed, and hard times were often in evidence. In 1923 the company at the Crescent Theater was described as "penniless," owing to the near-empty houses to which they had been playing. When a sympathetic "angel" extended help, however, the actors flew the coop:

It appears that Chung Yick, feeling sorry for . . . [the] penniless members of the "Juck Wah Ning" company . . . dug down yesterday morning and came up with $2,600. The money was to be used to keep the company together for another week. When Yick produced the cash Chu Fun, leading man, wept with joy. . . .

At 3:01 . . . Yick . . . learned that Chu Fun and eight other artists . . . had packed their scenery and trunks and were on their way to Portland. . . . When the Shasta Limited steamed into Port Costa, the fearless Constable boarded it and debarked with Chu Fun, eight other Chinese actors, including two dainty feminine stars, the Misses Lee Wai and Wong Gow.[22]

However, the Crescent Theater was to have better success in the same year with the Lee Sut Moey company, named after the sixteen-year-old female star of the troupe. Reporter Idwal Jones described an evening at the Crescent in which he was seated on stage, just as visitors frequently were in the nineteenth century. He described the teenage star as "made up like a marionette." Miss Lee, he said,

piped away in a shrill voice . . . achieving, for some obscure reason, a tremendous success. She was the daughter of the wicked tax collector in the play, "Disaster Springs From Evil Wrought," and the Nemesis, a huge paper dragon, was dragged on the stage by the property man, and at the dramatic moment it opened its mouth and figuratively bit off her head.

The orchestra accompanying Miss Lee was an unusually large one for the Chinese theater:

Fifteen impassive youths in college-cut suits, tight and pichback, rent the atmosphere with discordant drums, saw-fiddles and brass gongs. Considering that the star was paid $500 a month for the excellence of her speaking voice, that seemed a pity.

The principal "angel" for the Lee Sut Moey company was Tai Kee, who put up the $30,000 bond to admit the troupe into America. Tai, who had been a butcher in a Chinatown fish market prior to his theatrical successes, was also one of a group of Chinatown businessmen who raised a quarter of a million dollars in 1923 to build the Mandarin Theater, the first theater to be built specifically for Chinese drama since the 1870s.[23] The new house, at 1201 Grant Avenue, opened in June 1924. In the same year still another new Chinese theater—the Great Star—was erected on Jackson Street. Thus Chinatown once again had a substantial base for the production of Chinese drama, and the two theaters would remain active for decades to come.[24]

The opening of the Mandarin Theater ushered in a whole new concept of Chinese drama. "For instance," wrote Franklin S. Clark in 1925,

the Chinese theater now uses scenery that is identical with that used in our own modern drama—drops and sets portraying interiors and landscapes. It is, however, combined with the imaginative scenery of the ancient Chinese drama. The venerable Chinese property man is still in evidence. He comes out now and again to put a label on a bench or chair, transforming it from what it appears to be into a bridge, a boat or a pagoda. And the actors may prance about on purely imaginary steeds. But the modern scenery of the west is used too. In the "Broken-Hearted Mother," a play recently produced at the Mandarin theater, no less than four complete changes of scenery were made behind drawn curtains by regulation scene shifters.[25]

Usherettes escorted customers to their seats and also dispensed popcorn, ice cream, and lemonade. With an eye to meeting the competition of movie houses and variety theaters, the managers set aside part of the week for lighter fare, which would appeal to a wider range of clientele:

Vaudeville of a sort, or rather, humorous tabloid drama, enlivens the patrons three evenings a week. The twenty tragedians in the company, who wear, not toppers and furs, but brown shirts, caps and frayed overcoats and are indistinguishable from boss crab fishermen, pitch in and make the best of this concession to vulgar popular taste.[26]

The actress Cheung Sook Kun was the first star of the Mandarin Theater. An exceptionally versatile performer, Miss Cheung epitomized the new importance of women in the Chinese theater. She was billed as "The Mary Pickford of southern China" and paid $17,000 a year,[27] reportedly the highest salary paid to any Chinese actor in the world, with the exception of Mei Lan-fang of the Peking opera. In addition to having remarkably expressive hands and an unusually wide vocal range (enabling her to sing in a "male falsetto" voice and take men's parts) Miss Cheung exemplified both the skilled improvisatrice, in the classical tradition of Chinese acting, and the actor-playwright. Though performing traditional plots, Miss Cheung would write out the parts for the other players, who would learn them as if in a Western play. "At the Mandarin," noted Franklin Clark,

Cheung Sook Kun dominates the rest of the cast. She is virtually the author of the plays in which she stars. And because the others cooperate with her and speak the lines in the play as she has written them rather than following the ancient and honorable custom of interpolating and improvising as the spirit moves them, the plays to be seen here have genuine plot.

As in the nineteenth century, American playgoers were astonished to see childbirth enacted on the stage.

In westernizing her plays Cheung Sook Kun hasn't by any means done away with the symbolical, suggestive acting of the Chinese drama. Only in the most starkly realistic of our drama, with our realistic acting, could the heroine portray the travail of giving birth to a child. Yet Cheung Sook Kun goes through this ordeal in the "Broken-Hearted Mother," in the end actually producing an infant, a large doll. And the audience doesn't seem shocked at all, or to consider the pantomime obscene—or, on the other hand, to find anything to titter about or snicker at even though every small detail is portrayed and ten or fifteen minutes are taken up by this scene.[28]

The price of admission, as in previous years, was reduced as the evening progressed. Performances began at six-thirty and continued until midnight, but most of the audience would arrive around nine o'clock, and many would leave before the play's ending. An outline of the play for the next evening would be distributed at each performance, a gesture that was undoubtedly useful for the next evening's latecomers or early-leavers.[29]

The success of the Mandarin Theater was an impetus for further theater building in 1924. A group of Chinatown businessmen erected the rival Great China Theater at 630 Jackson Street to house the Yen Shiu Nin company, for whose production rights the financing group had paid ten thousand dollars. Throughout the rest of the 1920s the rivalry between the two theaters was intense. Stars were paid ten to fifteen thousand dollars a year, and sometimes double the latter amount. Both sent road companies to Los Angeles and elsewhere. Each featured vaudeville acts to alternate with the Chinese drama. The two theaters were even reportedly political rivals, the Mandarin retaining imperialistic sympathies while the Great China was thoroughly Republican in sentiment.[30]

An important event in Chinatown's musical history was the founding, on the Fourth of July in 1925, of the Nam Chung Musical Society, a group that has long been the largest and most active of Chinatown's music clubs. Nam Chung's founders were a group of Cantonese-opera devotees who sought to raise the level of musicianship among the community's amateur players and singers. In time, the club was to win the praise of highly critical professionals and to stage productions on its own. (See Chapter 8.) Its inception was another indication of the renewal of enthusiasm for Cantonese opera in the Chinese community.

The upsurge in theatrical activity in the 1920s had a special impact on the social life of Chinatown. It is reported that the younger women of the community made the opera an occasion for the display of their latest gowns and accessories in the Western mode. "Soon all were busy 'keeping up with the Joneses'. The opera soon changed the evening life of Chinatown."

"Before the opera came the Chinese people stayed home in the evening and social intercourse was within the family," a Chinese friend explained recently. "After the opera came the young people began giving supper parties and inviting friends to each other's houses.

"That made them want finer homes, so they could entertain, and pretty soon Chinatown had several class A apartment houses with elevators and high rents. Next they wanted country homes and now many Chinese families have homes across the Bay or down the Peninsula."[31]

Despite the westernization of playhouse and stage, audiences remained thoroughly Chinese in their undemonstrative mien and their habits of talking during performances, reading newspapers, and snacking on various edibles that were hawked by peddlers in the aisles.[32] The commercial rivalry of the motion picture continued to make inroads on the attention of Chinatown's theatergoers:

. . . down the block the whirring motion picture projector is more agreeable to the ears of Young China. Jung Shook may shrill never so loud and Ong On roar his fiercest, but Bill Hart and his pony have the edge. The Chinese theater will flourish nevertheless, for there are the oldsters . . . and always the tourist.[33]

Remarkably, the 1930s—the Great Depression notwithstanding—did not see the close of the Chinese theater in San Francisco. Throughout the decade, both the Mandarin and Great China theaters continued to import troupes from China, thus maintaining continuity for both the growing population of Chinatown itself and for the continuing parade of tourists that still nourished San Francisco's economy in spite of the nation's financial woes. Both theaters would have their ups and downs during the decade. The Great Star in particular would have such problems that it would switch for long periods to an exclusively movie format. But the Chinese theater would continue, its presentation becoming increasingly westernized: Elaborate and often incongruously Western stage sets would become standard, and the orchestras of the period would adopt the Western violin as a permanent fixture for Cantonese opera and would also make use of the saxophone, clarinet, and other Western instruments. Musical life in general actually experienced something of an upsurge in the 1930s, although much of the increased activity was partly or entirely Western—as in marching ensembles, night clubs catering to the occidental trade, and swing-era dance bands made up entirely of Chinese youths.

The year 1930 saw the most widely heralded event in the history of Chinese theater on this continent: the American tour of Mei Lan-fang, China's greatest living theatrical performer. With appearances first in New York, then Chicago, San Francisco, Los Angeles, and Honolulu, Mei won critical plaudits everywhere that he appeared; and the performer was the object of much curiosity and interest among Western theatergoers who otherwise had no use for the Chinese drama. An array of dignitaries and celebrities were among his sponsors. In New York, Mei was welcomed by the likes of John Dewey and Mrs. Woodrow Wilson; in Los Angeles, by Douglas Fairbanks, Jr., Mary Pickford, and Charlie Chaplin.[34]

Mei's arrival in San Francisco on 20 April was a spectacular event. Among the notables gathered at the Ferry Building to greet him were the mayor, the chief of police, several city supervisors, and the president of the Chinese Chamber of Commerce. From the Ferry Building to the Great China Theater Mei was escorted by a parade which featured bands from the Six Companies, the Chinese Boy and Girl Scouts, and the Chung Mei School. Chinatown was draped with flags and bunting, and the ceremonies at the Great China included the mayor's presentation to Mei of the key to the city.[35] During his three weeks in San Francisco, Mei played to enthusiastic crowds at occidental theaters (Tivoli, Liberty, Capitol) and the Great China Theater in Chinatown—his only appearance at a Chinese theater in the United States.

Mei's opening night at the Tivoli was a gala social event. A *Chronicle* society reporter devoted the bulk of her column next morning to describing the gowns of the women attending the concert, noting that "The exquisite gowns and thrill of expectancy in the audience were reminiscent of an opera season's first night."[36] Reviewers were enraptured. George G. Warren commented in the *Chronicle*:

The gorgeous costumes and settings introduced by Mei Lan-fang and his company, and the strident, fluttering off-stage orchestration, give these plays an exotic quality. They should be seen by anyone who loves the theater, not, however, because of their novelty. Mei's acting is a revelation in style and a source of definable pleasure to the spectator, even to the benighted Westerner.[37]

Mei's weeks in San Francisco were busy ones, with the famed performer being honored at numerous luncheon and dinner affairs and making appearances at civic organizations in various parts of the city.[38]

As in New York and Chicago, Mei's performances served to acquaint a wide segment of the theatergoing public with Chinese dramatic traditions. However, this introduction to Chinese theater was tailored somewhat to the Western audience. Sketches or one-act plays were presented to showcase Mei's talents. The orchestra was hidden in the wings at stage right rather than performing visibly on stage, and cymbals and other percussion instruments were considerably underplayed, in consideration of the occidental ear.[39] The use of the property man was unobtrusive, and such symbolic stage properties as a curtain representing a wall were not in evidence. If the tradition was thus somewhat diluted, the performance was nonetheless not without integrity and considerable artistic merit, as noted by Chicago columnist Chester Rowell, who had observed Mei's work in China as well as during the American tour:

. . . the essentials remain, presented by the most perfect actor in China. There will not be one thing in it, not even the human voice or face, like anything you ever saw before. If you think being different means being bad, the Chinese play is not for you. Thronging audiences of the most cultivated people in New York and Chicago thought it was for them, and were delighted with the experience.[40]

When Mei left for Los Angeles in mid-May, he had concluded a notably successful run in San Francisco and had promoted good feeling in general for China and its cultural traditions.[41] Though largely oriented to Western playgoers, however, his performances—entirely in the Peking-opera tradition and in the Mandarin dialect—did not leave an appreciable impact on the playgoing habits of San Francisco audiences. There was no observable carryover from the enthusiasm for Mei to Chinatown's theaters, which had presented Chinese drama to the public for nearly eighty years. To most non-Chinese, the drama in Chinatown continued to be merely a loud and colorful novelty attraction, in spite of the praise and artistic hullabaloo that had accompanied Mei's sojourn in America.

While the visit of Mei Lan-fang was a celebrated event in Chinatown, the arrival the following year of the great *Cantonese* actor-manager Ma See Don (Ma Shi Tsiang, in Mandarin) was of much more importance to America's predominantly South-Chinese population. Ma's name reportedly meant as much in Southern Chinese theatrical tradition as did Mei Lan-fang's in the North; and Ma had broken all gate-receipt records and become "the most popular and highest paid matinee idol of all South China."[42] Ma brought his own troupe with him and held forth for eighteen months at the Mandarin—greatly eclipsing the triumph of the Great China in presenting Mei Lan-fang. Ma is generally credited with (or blamed for) some of the more Western features that have become entrenched in Cantonese-opera tradition, such as the use of the violin and other Western instruments in the orchestra. A flamboyant personality himself, Ma would sometimes perform in modern Western garb, amidst his traditionally dressed supporting players, adding further anachronism to a stage already graced with Western backdrops featuring skyscrapers and trolley cars. It is interesting to note that Ma See Don's arrival and performances went unheralded in the non-Chinese press, in ironic contrast to the publicity that was given Mei Lan-fang, although Ma's cultural traditions were precisely those of America's own Chinese, while Mei's style and dialect were of North China—scarcely more familiar to America's Chinese than to the largely occidental audiences for whom he performed.

The rivalry between the Mandarin and the Great China theaters continued through the early 1930s, until 1934, when the Great China reportedly "gave up the ghost entirely," although the theater continued to show motion pictures and present sporadic offerings of Chinese drama.[43] It would reappear in the late 1930s again as a full-time Cantonese-opera theater.

Many interesting notes on performances at the Mandarin were recorded in 1934 by Katherine Hill in the *Chronicle*. The troupe then in residence numbered twenty-two actors, seven of them women. An unusual recourse, not previously reported in Chinese drama, was the occasional hiring of a Caucasian actor. This intrusion went unnoticed by audiences, however, as the temporary thespian would be heavily made up and in Chinese costume—and he would speak no lines.

At the time, the Mandarin had one visiting star from Peking: Owyong Kim; all the rest of the actors were from Canton. The reporter noted that the highest paid actor in the Mandarin's history received thirty thousand dollars a year, but "They lost money on him." (The actor is not named but quite likely was Ma See Don in 1931–1932.) The present star with the highest income was a young actress who received sixteen thousand. "Attendance is good at the Mandarin," the reporter adds, "and such salaries seem warranted by results."

Actors were brought from China under an arrangement with the United States government by which the theater would post bond for each artist brought in. Under this bond an actor could remain as long as three years in America, but three to six months was the usual time that the Mandarin needed them. The longest staying performer at that writing was a young woman whose engagement had already run eighteen months.

The policy continued of lowering admission prices as the evening wore on. From seven until around eight-thirty, choice seats went for $1.50 and $1.25. From that time on, rates declined sharply, and by nine the best seats could be had for fifty cents or a quarter. "By 9 o'clock the lobby is usually packed with Chinese families, waiting for admission."[44]

Later in 1934 the Mandarin was embroiled in a dispute with a group of its actors who claimed to the State Labor Commission that the theater had reneged on its guarantee of a year's employment and return passage to China. The troupe of twenty-two—apparently the same as described by Katherine Hill in the above paragraphs—claimed back wages totaling $19,511.93.[45]

Around this time, one book on San Francisco states, "There are two Chinese theaters, one of which features chiefly stock played by local actors, and the other more elaborate productions played by the great stars of China."[46] The latter theater is clearly the Mandarin; the other the Great China, which—far from having "given up the ghost"—continued to make a go of it throughout the 1930s, whether through films, imported drama, or (if this account is accurate) the experiment of using local talent on the Chinese stage. However, it appears that in the mid-1930s only the Mandarin was a full-time theater for Chinese drama. In 1935 it advertised itself as "The Only Chinese Opera in America."[47]

The westernization of Chinese actors took some steps forward in 1935 when some members of the Mandarin's troupe began to study American ballroom dancing with an instructor in Chinatown. The community's English-language *Chinese Digest* commented:

To these enthusiastic tyros of western dance it must afford a great deal of fun, and not a little relief, also, to be able to use their feet in a natural, graceful manner instead of the studied, robot movements of our ancient dances which Chinese actors and actresses have practiced for many centuries.

The new fancy for American dancing may not infuse new life into the slowly ebbing popularity of Chinese opera, but at least these performers of the Chinese stage are keeping in step with the times.[48]

By 1936 Chinatown's one remaining full-time theater, the Mandarin, was feeling the financial pinch of the depression. The theater was forced to dismiss its expensive troupe and negotiate for players on a new percentage basis. In spite of hard times, however, a future was still seen for Chinatown's drama. In Peter Chu's words:

The incomes of the present Mandarin actors [in 1936] may not be as princely as formerly but the houses are fair, the troupers young and enthusiastic, and the country fresh and new to them. The theatre troupe is constantly augmented by new stars to offset possible boredom of an elusive but generally loyal public.[49]

The growing competition of motion pictures continued to plague live theater in general and to draw younger Chinese away from the Cantonese opera. In addition to the standard Hollywood product and imported films from China, Chinese movies made in the United States began to make their appearance. One such film, shown during an off-night at the Mandarin, was advertised as follows:

Watch for
HEARTACHES

A Soul-Stirring Epic of the Chinese Wars
'First Chinese Singing-Talking Picture in Technicolor'
Starring
WEI   KIM   FONG
Formerly of the Mandarin Theatre

Produced by
QUON   YUM   LIM

Released by
Cathay Pictures, Ltd.
Hollywood, California[50]

In July 1936 the fate of the Great China seemed to be sealed. The *Chinese Digest* reported:

It was announced two days ago that the Chinese-American United Theatrical and Film Corporation, Ltd. of San Francisco will very shortly open its theater at 360 Jackson Street, formerly the Great China Theater, showing motion pictures produced in China. It was also learned that films made by this company in the United States will be sent to China for showings.[51]

The remaining theater, the Mandarin, would continue to produce live drama throughout the 1930s. In August 1936 the immediate future of the theater was threatened when immigration authorities showed reluctance to renew the permit of a Chinese theatrical troupe. The issue was short-lived, however. Chinatown theatergoers were gratified not only by the subsequent decision to renew the permit but by the large measure of public support that the issue had aroused. The San Francisco Chamber of Commerce rallied to the theater's defense. In a letter to the commissioner of immigration, the chamber's executive vice-president stressed the importance of the Chinese theater to San Francisco as a whole, pointing out that occidentals as well as Chinese attended the theater and that it "has long been a featured attraction in the local life."[52] Strong emphasis was given to the theater's attraction as a tourist landmark. The *Chinese Digest* further pointed out that the Mandarin was "the only place outside of the Orient where such entertainment is offered" and that "it is the ONLY form of entertainment that breaks the monotony of everyday life for the older Chinese."[53] Editorials in the occidental press as well showed widespread support in the community for the theater's continuance.[54]

At the Mandarin, plays were presented every night of the week. A complete calendar of productions for January through April 1936 indicates a different play every night, with additional matinee productions during the Chinese New Year. Once or twice a month, a night was left free for a movie. The rarity of cinema performances suggests that the purpose was simply to provide a night off for the acting company rather than yielding to a public demand for movies.[55]

The performances at the Mandarin balanced traditional Chinese practices with twentieth-century technology and westernized stage innovations. The Mandarin was equipped with a "picture-frame" stage with proscenium arches designed by an American-born Chinese in collaboration with a non-Chinese American architect. Its Western-style appearance was modified with a relief design of gilt and lacquer-red dragons. A departure from traditional theater was the front curtain, "a gorgeous blue satin or sateen affair with yellow, red and fringed bands horizontally at bottom." The stage was donated to the theater by a firm in Canton, and viewers were reminded of its source with both a conspicuous advertisement in Chinese and the following legend in English:

Heart Brand Skin Disease Solution
Dependable for Curing All Kinds of Skin Disease
The Wai Shang Yuk Ching Tonic Juice
Safe and Highly Recommendable for Nourishing the
Blood and Brain

Aukah Chuen   Canton, China[56]

The curtain was equipped with American rigging and was drawn from stage left at the play's opening and to allow for changes of scene.

Painted backdrops appeared incongruous to many. They are described in one source as "naively realistic" and "painted after the fashion of the murals sometimes met with in small Italian restaurants, utterly Occidental and utterly out of keeping with what one imagined a Chinese theater to be."[57] Just inside the proscenium arch was a "grand Valence," and beyond that another, cut from canvas and painted in imitation of draped and pleated red cloth. Upstage at each side was a canvas wing drop containing a doorway, with the top of each drop painted to suggest more red draperies looped back.[58]

Beyond these entrance and exit drops, which formed a more or less permanent setting, was a whole collection of painted backdrops, featuring scenes with no reference whatever to traditional Chinese life—false perspective, retreating vistas of rooms, chandeliers and electric wall-fixtures, conglomerates of American-style furniture, and various landscapes and seashore scenes.[59] A Chinese observer at the time describes the theatrical effect of such a mixed bag:

An example of the unfortunate possibilities of this type of staging may be cited from a recent play [in 1936]. An official of the imperial court, in a particularly gorgeous and striking costume and a long beard, appeared on the stage with that beautiful stylistic "manner" of Chinese actors, carrying in his hand the much-tasselled wand which indicates that he is riding on horse-back. The scenario evidently called for a street scene. Hence the back drop was a painted representation of a modern city with boulevard lamps and contemporary vehicles in the street. One American spectator remarked, as a comment was made on the significance of the "whip,"—"Why does he ride a horse when he could take the bus?"[60]

Some of these all-purpose backdrops continue in use even today in the same theater, though the trend has been toward more neutral outdoor settings in place of the detailed city and interior scenes.

The Mandarin in the 1930s was equipped with regular theater seats with backs—no longer the benches of earlier Chinatown theaters. The theater was unheated, a condition that doubtless caused occasional discomfort but was not a major problem in San Francisco's Mediterranean climate.[61] Shows commenced at 7 P.M. Prices of tickets ranged downward from one dollar for a box seat to twenty-five cents in the second gallery. A reduction of price occurred at eight-thirty, and at nine-thirty all seats were available for a quarter.

A "New Year's Greetings" sheet issued by the Mandarin Theater in 1936 lists the complete cast and company of the Great Stars Company, then in residence. Twenty-five actors and seven musicians are listed, plus the director and four assistant directors, making a grand total of thirty-seven.[62]

A representative theater program of 4 March 1936 gives a rounded picture of the entertainment to be presented. The fare for the night was "A Good Wife is Hard to Find," which the program describes as a "Newly revised melodrama—the best play ever presented." The program contains a lengthy synopsis of the play, preceded by the following words, which stress the morality and high tone of the production:

Dramas and other plays exist for the purpose of offering a mental repast; they are also invaluable for the training of the family and cultural background of society. This cultural background is reflected in the performances upon the stage. This show does not present anything that is detrimental to public morals. The troupe sacrificed everything that is not of benefit to the public, to show the public what is right and what is wrong. Plays that are detrimental to the morals of the public are cast aside by the troupe. But if a play is excellent and of benefit to the public, it must be presented and played in the best and most enjoyable manner. . . . Is it not fortunate that there is nothing in this play that will cause any shame? Ladies and gentlemen of the critical theater audience, kindly come early and enjoy yourselves.

The program is adorned with photographs of the leading man and leading lady. A dramatis personae of twenty players is listed, followed by a schedule of prices for various kinds of seats at different times of the night, together with announcements of forthcoming plays. The printed program ends with a restaurant advertisement and an announcement of some furniture for sale.[63]

Such illustrated programs, combined with commercial advertisements, were printed for each night's performance. An official photographer for the troupe took pictures for display outside the theater as well as for the programs. The actors themselves were given the lion's share of publicity. One advertisement for the Mandarin Theater is completely taken up with the announcement of a new "well-known comedian"—Fung Yue Lung—soon to arrive. After a lengthy and rhapsodic section of praise for the actor's talents and fame, a bit of biography is added:

. . . Born at Hawk Sun district, Canton, China. While a youth, he was very intelligent in his studies, and unlike many youths he liked to study. He graduated from the Nom High School at Canton City, Canton, China. He realized that the Chinese public as a whole needs moral teaching, so he took it upon himself to do his part to help his people. He, although of southern birth, has acquired the northern art of self-defense. His fame for good acting spreads like fire and is well received by the general public. His songs are educational and of proved far-reaching effect. . . . Previous to his coming to this theater, he was touring Siam and its neighboring countries. Fung Yue Lung is here to fulfill his agreement with this theater and The Great Stars Company. Don't miss him at the Mandarin Theater.[64]

The late 1930s were a relatively uneventful time for the Chinese theater in San Francisco. The period saw the emergence of several music clubs in Chinatown, whose inception was much influenced by the traveling troupes of actors that performed professionally.[65] The actors and musicians of the theaters were among the thousands of Chinatown residents who participated in the "Rice-Bowl" festival of 1938, an elaborate fund-raising drive to benefit war-ravaged civilians in the home country.[66] The Rice-Bowl party was an all-night affair, attended by some 200,000 San Franciscans, featuring a multitude of attractions by some ninety-two organizations in Chinatown on 17 June. Motor traffic was blockaded, the streets renamed for the occasion, and the whole area—and its residents—were decked out in traditional Chinese decoration and raiment. Together with restaurants, teahouses, temples, and various family and district associations, both the Mandarin and Great China theaters stayed open all night. The Mandarin featured continuous Chinese opera with its resident company, and the Great China presented an American-flavor show with performers from San Francisco's nightclubs.[67]

By 1938 the Great China Theater once again attempted a policy of Chinese opera full time, and operated thus in competition with the Mandarin. The reborn competitor was able to make a go of it for about a year before lapsing once more into a movie theater with only occasional visits from opera troupes.[68] Both theaters were usually crowded, and visitors were shown not only the classic plays but an occasional modern stage creation as well.

During the years of World War II, the character of San Francisco's Chinatown was enlivened by a wave of prosperity, which stemmed from the new availability of jobs at shipyards and other war-related industries. The boom in employment was reflected in the profitable nightclub business that Chinatown enjoyed[69] and in the proliferation and increased activities of the community's music clubs.[70] War-bond drives and other patriotic activities served as a uniting factor to many factions in the community, as the Chinese backed the American war effort—which included many young men from Chinatown who had enlisted or been drafted into the armed services.

Chinese opera continued throughout the war years at the Mandarin, with occasional performances at the Great China as well, though the latter featured movies for the most part. The opera rarely attracted large crowds to either theater, however, except for Friday nights ("Actors' Night") at the Mandarin, when special attractions were offered.

The movies and other entertainment attractions vied for attention as never before, and the Chinese theaters counted largely on a faithful middle-aged clientele from the community as well as a sprinkling of tourists to provide an audience. The personnel of the theatrical troupes were effectively stranded here throughout the war: Players who had arrived here prior to the hostilities were constrained to stay in the United States for the duration, creating in effect a captive dramatic community.[71] Some of these players found more lucrative work in American war industries; others became American citizens; but a large number simply bided their time until they could return to China to resume their careers there.

Throughout the war, Chinese drama was made available live to Bay Area listeners through the Golden Star radio station in Chinatown, which had established a direct line to the Mandarin Theater shortly after the station's founding in 1939. Such broadcasts continued until the radio station's demise in 1979 as theatrical troupes visited the theater (later renamed the Sun Sing Theater) though the usual fare from the radio station consisted of the Chinese movies being shown at the theater—a somewhat frustrating circumstance for the community's listeners, as most of the movies made use of the Mandarin dialect (with subtitles—for the paying customers—in both Chinese and English), which can be understood only intermittently, if at all, by most of Chinatown's Cantonese-speaking residents.

The theatrical companies' stranded stars served in some cases as advisers and members of Chinatown's growing music clubs. This infusion of professionalism in the amateur clubs was reciprocated somewhat by the occasional work by the clubs' singers and musicians in the professional theater. Alfred Frankenstein noted such informal sitting-in in 1943:

I was amazed . . . to discover that the yee-wu [erh-hu] player in the orchestra was the very same James Fong who had been playing the oboe [so-na] at the Flying Dragon Club just five minutes before. I asked him if he was engaged there, but he said no; he had just dropped in for a while. One of the actors from the stage had also dropped into the orchestra to play the drums for a while, to the great delight of the regular drummer, who was lying on a table and reading a newspaper, and to the distaste of the stage manager, who showed up in the middle of the performance and protested against such goings on.[72]

A notable portrayal of Chinatown's theater during this same year appears in Jade Snow Wong's autobiography, *Fifth Chinese Daughter*. In her description, printed below in its entirety, she talks not only of the stage practice in general but of the audience and, finally, of the significance of the play's denouement and message with respect to traditional Chinese values. (Jade Snow Wong always refers to herself in the third person; "Jade Harp" is the name that she has given to a Caucasian friend whom she has met during her first year out of college.)

The Chinese opera was one of the experiences Jade Harp shared with Jade Snow. As a child, Jade Snow had been to the theater once or twice, but she didn't have any real understanding of the opera and the language of the stage was not their daily Cantonese. However, she delighted in the brilliant costumes, the bizarre make-up, snow-white or jet-black artificial hair and beards, and jeweled headdresses.

Now, returning as an adult, she was able to pick out the plot and to see the audience as well as the performance with new eyes.

The girls arrived one evening a few minutes after the opera had begun, but they alone were the audience. The players were singing solos, without apparent effort or thought. They stared curiously at the two girls, until Jade Snow felt that they instead of the play were under observation. The property man wandered around on the stage unconcernedly, straightened a pillow or a chair here and there, and joined the actors in staring at the punctual members of their audience. One of several standard sets of painted scenery formed the stage background. Now it was the interior of a home. To the left, a five-piece orchestra played on the stage; one of the traditional string instruments had been replaced by a violin, which echoed the others in Chinese harmony. Brass cymbals broke into loud clanging whenever a character was about to enter the scene.

About half an hour after the performance had begun, a few old Chinese women drifted in to join the girls and the ushers. Some of these older inhabitants of Chinatown came regularly every night, for the opera was the center of their social life. For another hour, more people drifted in and sat anywhere they wished in the almost-empty theater. Those who recognized friends went over to chat with them. Children who didn't have tickets gathered together, first in the boxes. Then, as ticket holders of those seats came, they ran to front seats on the main floor, and later as these seats were claimed, they went to the balcony. Sometimes, they chased the cats which wandered about in leisurely fashion. People freely left their seats to purchase peanuts, soda pop, or candy. The cracking of melon seeds was a distinctive minor note. Mothers nursed babies with bottles and fathers read Chinese newspapers. A few young girls, whispered about as flirts, paraded up and down the aisles in new form-fitting silk Chinese dresses, which covered them completely except where the high side slits revealed shapely limbs as they walked. The older men gave them appreciative glances. It was a relaxed gathering, with everyone in high spirits. The seats were only half filled an hour and a half after the performance had begun, and the actors and actresses were still playing their roles with half a heart. Small wonder, for no one could tell that the audience was paying any attention.

Then it was nine-thirty, and a horde of people swarmed in suddenly to fill all the unused seats, which went for reduced prices at this hour. Some came because of the lower prices, others to see the better acting. For now both performers and audience settled down to the business of the evening. The actors gave a quick résumé of what had happened, and then worked toward the climax. Whenever a scene of importance was beginning, the cymbals obligingly announced it with a great flourish. The men quickly folded their papers and the women turned from their babies and visiting to pay undivided attention. Like the Chinese novel, the opera, which was based on great Chinese legends, offered many side excursions and indulged in subplots which it never intended to finish. As a matter of fact, the last hour was really the best and most exciting.

Jade Snow interpreted to Jade Harp and explained the profuse use of symbolism: the little wand with varicolored tassels which indicated a horse, the pacing back and forth on the front part of the stage which indicated a journey, the women who were acting as men, the men who were acting as women, and the costumes which were the key to the positions of the actors—a nobleman, a warrior, a scholar, a princess, a servant girl, a messenger.

The play was a bedroom farce, wherein a beautiful young wife, rebelling against her "blind" marriage to an old wealthy landowner, surreptitiously carried on an affair with a handsome young scholar whom she met at the garden wall. Rightfully, she was trapped in her unfaithfulness by her husband. The climax was reached when the downcast sinner was chastised in the privacy of their bedroom by her wrathful spouse. He strode up and down indignantly, hurling scornful denunciations, with his hands tucked importantly in his elaborate belt. The audience now paid undivided attention.

Then a most terrible fate was announced by the husband: "You deserve the action I am going to take—I shall report this to your honorable father!"

So the curtain dropped on the triumphant husband and the pleading, weeping wife, who could not have heard a more severe and disgraceful sentence. The audience nodded in approval. Then, at a quarter to one in the morning, the crowd prepared to leave for a midnight snack or to return home.[73]

NOTES

1. M.E.C., "The New Chinatown of the Pacific," New York *Times*, 16 September 1906.

2. Elinor H. Stoy, "Chinatown and the Curse that Makes It a Plaguespot in the Nation," *Arena* 38 (1907), pp. 361, 364.

3. New York *Times*, 21 April 1906.

4. *San Francisco's Chinatown: An Aid to Tourists and Others in Visiting China Town* (San Francisco, Portola Editions, 1909), p. 1.

5. Richard H. Dillon, *The Hatchet Men: The Story of the Tong Wars in San Francisco* (New York, Coward-McCann, 1961), p. 266.

6. *Chronicle*, 14 April 1907.

7. *Chronicle*, 3 October 1907.

8. *San Francisco Standard Guide* (San Francisco, North American Press Association, 1913).

9. Ruth Kedzie Wood, *The Tourist's California* (New York, Dodd, Mead & Company, 1914), p. 47.

10. *San Francisco's Chinatown*, p. 1.

11. Peter Chu et al., *Chinese Theatres in America* (Washington, D.C., Bureau of Research, Federal Theatre Project, Region of the West, 1936), p. 71.

12. *Examiner*, 12 February 1913.

13. *Examiner*, 5 February 1918.

14. *San Francisco Standard Guide*.

15. Will Irwin, "The Drama that Was in Chinatown," *New York Times Book Review and Magazine*, 10 April 1921, p. 3.

16. Veta Griggs, *Chinaman's Chance* (New York, Exposition Press, 1969), pp. 49, 50.

17. Rufus Steel, "The City That Is," *Sunset* 22 (1909), p. 14.

18. *Examiner*, 7 March 1916.

19. Griggs, p. 50. The emergence of the Chinese actress is viewed in historical perspective in George Kin Leung, "The Chinese Actress: Social and

Dramatic Factors in Her Slow Rise to Fame," *Pacific Affairs* 4 (1931), pp. 394–407. The "liberating" effect of the 1906 earthquake on Çhinatown's women is noted in M.E.C., "The New Chinatown of the Pacific," New York *Times*, 16 September 1906. See also "Flappers of Chinatown," *New York Times Magazine*, 27 May 1923; "Chinese Women's New Freedom Leads Them into Male Roles," New York *Times*, 15 May 1927; Frank J. Taylor, "San Francisco's New Chinese City," *Travel* 52 (1929), pp. 18–21, 54.

20. *Chronicle*, 9 April 1922.

21. *Chronicle*, 15 December 1922.

22. *Chronicle*, 6 April 1923.

23. Idwal Jones, "The Chinese Theater Advancing," *Chronicle*, 25 December 1924, p. 20.

24. Both are in operation today. The Mandarin has been renamed the Sun Sing Theater and operates mainly as a movie house, though it retains the layout and equipment for live drama and abandons the movie format several times a year for highly publicized performances of touring groups from Hong Kong, which will play for ten days or two weeks. The Great Star Theater on Jackson Street was bought by the Shaw Brothers interests of Hong Kong and modernized. Now it shows movies only, as the remodeling has removed all possibility of stage performance.

25. Franklin S. Clark, " 'Seats Down Front!'," *Sunset* 54 (1925), p. 33.

26. Jones, "The Chinese Theater Advancing," p. 20.

27. According to Franklin Clark (" 'Seats Down Front!' "). Idwal Jones gives the figure of $20,000 ("The Chinese Theater Advancing").

28. Franklin S. Clark, p. 33. See also above, p. 87.

29. Ibid.

30. Chu et al., p. 77.

31. Taylor, p. 21.

32. Idwal Jones, "Cathay on the Coast," *American Mercury* 8 (1926), p. 460.

33. Jones, "Chinese Theater Advancing," p. 20.

34. The success of Mei's tour is recounted in A.C. Scott, *Mei Lan-fang* (Hong Kong, Hong Kong University Press, 1959), pp. 105–13; Barbara E. Scott, "We Bow to Mei Lan-fang," *North American Review* 229 (1930), pp. 572–75. See also Ernest K. Moy, ed., *The Pacific Coast Tour of Mei Lan-fang* (San Francisco, The Chinese Dramatic Club, 1930).

35. *Chronicle*, 20, 21 April 1930.

36. Lady Teazle, "Fashionable Throng Greets China's Distinguished Actor," *Chronicle*, 24 April 1930.

37. "Mei Lan-fang Charms in Capitol Bill," *Chronicle*, 6 May 1930.

38. See, e.g., "Famous Actor Will Be Guest of S.F. Center," *Chronicle*,

20 April 1930; "China Actor Stresses Art as Best Aid to Understanding World Affairs," *Chronicle*, 2 May 1930; "Mei Lan-fang Host to S.F. Sponsors," *Chronicle*, 10 May 1930.

39. Mei's practice of concealing the orchestra is said to have left a permanent mark on Chinese dramatic practice in the twentieth century, as, for instance, in today's Chinese-opera performances in San Francisco's Chinatown, in which the orchestra is concealed or partly concealed in the wings at stage right. Mei is also said to be the main influence in introducing the now-pervasive use of the mellow erh-hu in addition to the hu-ch'in in the performance of Peking opera. See above, p. 92 note 88.

40. Quoted in *Chronicle*, 30 April 1930.

41. Though a critical success, Mei's American tour was a financial loss for his backers. See "This Is Scarcely in Best Hollywood Mode" (editorial), *Chronicle*, 5 March 1931.

42. A detailed biography and publicity note in English on Ma, published by the Mandarin Theater, is included in Chu et al., pp. 80–81. See also Alfred Frankenstein, "Flying Dragons and Sounds of Silver and Fine Wood," *This World* (*Chronicle* magazine), 7 March 1943, p. 30.

43. Chu et al., p. 83.

44. Katherine Hill, "Putting on Chinese Play at Mandarin," *Chronicle*, 24 February 1924.

45. *Chronicle*, 2 January 1934.

46. Basil Woon, *San Francisco and the Golden Empire* (New York, Harrison Smith and Robert Haas, 1935), p. 47.

47. *Chinese Digest*, 15 November 1935, p. 12.

48. *Chinese Digest*, 6 December 1935, p. 10.

49. Chu et al., p. 83.

50. Ibid., p. 85.

51. *Chinese Digest*, 31 July 1936, p. 7.

52. *Chronicle*, 22 August 1936.

53. "Preserve the Chinese Theater!" (editorial), 23 August 1936, p. 8.

54. E.g., "Let the Play Go On," *Chronicle*, 22 August 1936.

55. Chu et al., pp. xxii–xxiv.

56. Ibid., p. 88.

57. Alfred Frankenstein, "An Operatic Cycle of Cathay by Benefit of Symbols and Cymbals," *Chronicle*, 19 January 1936.

58. Chu et al., p. 86.

59. Alfred Frankenstein ("An Operatic Cycle") noted: "According to the backdrop, the furnishings in the palaces of ancient Chinese emperors were made in Grand Rapids in 1904."

60. Chu et al., pp. 87–88. See also Charles Caldwell Dobie, *San Francisco's Chinatown* (New York, Appleton-Century, 1936), p. 277.

61. Dobie, p. 282.

62. Chu et al., p. i—appendix.

63. The complete program is included verbatim in English translation in Chu et al., pp. xii–xvii.

64. Ibid., pp. ii–iii.

65. See below, Chapter 8.

66. The Rice-Bowl parties were a nationwide affair, held in some seven hundred localities in the United States between 17 and 30 June 1938. See "S.F. Chinatown's 'Bowl of Rice' Pageant," *Chinese Digest*, July 1938, pp. 12, 19. San Francisco's Rice-Bowl benefit was the most successful, raising $50,000.

67. *Chronicle*, 14, 17 June 1938. A second Rice-Bowl benefit was held in 1940 to coincide with the Chinese New Year celebrations, from 2 through 11 February.

68. Alan Tory, "A Visit behind Scenes at the China Theater," *This World* (*Chronicle* magazine), 20 July 1952, p. 12; Alexander Gross, ed., *Famous Guide to San Francisco and the World's Fair* (New York, Geographia Map Co., 1939), p. 86.

69. See below, Chapter 7.

70. See below, Chapter 8.

71. Some had been stranded here as early as 1937, unable to return because of the Chinese-Japanese War in China.

72. Frankenstein, "Flying Dragons," p. 30.

73. Jade Snow Wong, *Fifth Chinese Daughter* (New York, Harper & Bros., 1945), pp. 214–16.

6

Chinese Theater: The Postwar Years

The end of World War II saw an exodus of San Francisco's professional Cantonese-opera performers back to China. This move coincided with new social changes in the Chinese community to signal the end of the already declining full-time theater. Not all performers returned to China, however. Some settled down as partners in restaurants and other enterprises. For some of the female performers, marriage and home life necessitated professional retirement. In many cases, the formerly full-time actors and musicians continued to make occasional appearances in professional opera performances—temporarily augmenting the personnel of touring companies, and their membership in the community's music clubs gave a welcome infusion of experience and expertise.

Already beleaguered by the continuing competition of motion pictures and the attraction of home entertainment media, the theater of the late 1940s fell prey also to demographic shifts and new living patterns, which would diminish in number the once-captive ghetto audience. No longer was the population virtually all male. Increasingly, the growth of family life among San Francisco's Chinese served to deplete the theater's clientele. The evening life of individuals was more and more spent at home with the family, rather than at the theater. Although the population continued to be balanced heavily in favor of men (who still outnumbered women by nearly two to one by 1950),[1] an easing of immigration restrictions in the 1940s finally allowed for the arrival of women in significant numbers. In 1943 the Exclusion Law that had been in effect since 1882 was repealed, and a federally enacted War Brides Act further swelled the immigration rolls and helped change the character of America's traditionally bachelor-dominated Chinese communities.

Another factor that served to draw Chinese away from the theater was a burgeoning movement of middle-class Chinese to homes in neighborhoods some distance from Chinatown. In San Francisco, a restrictive covenant that had prevented Chinese from buying homes outside Chinatown was lifted in 1947. Individuals with the means began moving to the quieter and more expensive residential neighborhoods of the city. Especially favored by the Chinese have been the Richmond and Sunset districts of the city, suburb-like areas of private homes and relative tranquillity. Others moved even farther away to communities in the East Bay, the Peninsula to the south, and Marin County to the north.[2]

With the return of opera performers to China and the gradual shift toward domestic living patterns for San Francisco's Chinese, both theaters in Chinatown were forced to adopt a policy of showing movies most of the time. This prime entertainment fare was set aside only during the occasional visits from opera companies from Southern China. (Some of these companies emanated from Canton itself prior to the 1949 Revolution. Since that time most visiting companies have been from Hong Kong. In the 1980s, Cantonese opera from the Mainland has begun to reappear.)

As if to take up the slack, Chinatown's opera clubs proliferated and swelled in membership, now admitting women—usually from families of already enrolled members—and becoming a setting for family life rather than a substitute for it. Meetings and musical get-togethers now rang with the shouts of children at play as well as the sounds of Cantonese opera and conviviality.[3] The continuing popularity of Chinese theater—despite its disappearance as a full-time attraction—was reflected in the vigorous growth of the clubs and by the substantial attention to Cantonese opera on radio and on commercial recordings.

In the theaters themselves, the postwar years have seen an adoption of a new modus operandi. Visiting opera troupes are booked for only a week or ten days. San Francisco is typically only one stop on a tour that will include Vancouver (British Columbia), Chicago, New York, and Boston; on occasion, such other cities as Seattle, Portland (Oregon), and Houston might also be included. (Before 1956, Havana was often on the itinerary as well.) That full-time Cantonese opera in San Francisco is no longer commercially feasible has generally been a foregone conclusion. Nevertheless, as late as 1952 there continued to be hope in some quarters that the continuous theater of old would come back to life. In July 1952, for instance, the local theatrical impresario Lok Yip opened the Great China to Cantonese opera again, using an array of stars from Hong Kong and expressing the hope that operatic offerings would command enough patronage to justify a year-round season.[4] His hopes were in vain. The professional opera would continue in San Francisco, but only sporadically.

The settlement of professional actors and musicians in the San Francisco Bay Area from the late 1930s through the war provided the oppportunity for a new pattern of performances. In many cases, only a few well-known actors would arrive from abroad for a run of performances, and local émigrés were used to flesh out the rest of the cast and to provide instrumental music. This practice has clear advantages in cost and logistical simplicity, but it has been an unpopular one with the opera clientele—some of whom feel cheated—and is practiced less in recent years than during the 1950s. One Chinatown columnist has noted: "Chinatown has been bamboozled many times by opera stars who come alone to set up shop with local pick-ups. The problem is that the locals, long retired and out of practice, are out of gas before the night is over."[5]

Until recent years, both the old Mandarin (now the Sun Sing) and the Great China theaters continued as settings for the occasional visits of opera troupes. However in the late 1960s, the Great China was extensively remodeled and geared totally to movie showings; the present set-up will not allow for any kind of stage presentation. The Sun Sing Theater, however, remains little changed since the 1920s. Many of its props and backdrops are survivors of the full-time era of opera. The Palace Theater on Powell Street has also served as a location for professional Cantonese opera, as have the Victory Hall on Stockton Street and the city's Masonic Auditorium.

As in earlier days, it is the individual opera stars that are the prime attractions. Today's Cantonese-opera actors rarely confine their work to opera alone. Many of them are recording artists in Hong Kong—as the vocal quality required in Cantonese opera does not differ significantly from that used in westernized popular music in Hong Kong and other Cantonese settlements. Acting in motion pictures is also a part of the lives of many Cantonese-opera stars.

The better-known actors are greeted with some ceremony in the Chinese community, although their arrival goes unheralded outside Chinatown. They are taken as guests to various associations and are greeted with special welcome at opera clubs, where they will perform as featured guests with the club's ensemble. An opera star is also feted at the family association of his or her surname. Typically, the actor or actress will disperse complimentary tickets at the associations visited, and in turn the various associations will make up elaborate decorative "floral" pieces of dollar bills which the performer will wear during the opera performance. These creations appear in various fanciful designs (such as hearts or fans) and may contain as much as a thousand dollars in bills of various denominations. They are worn for a few minutes when an actor makes his or her initial appearance, then inconspicuously set aside during a moment when attention has shifted elsewhere. Each of these stylized garlands is tagged with the name of the donor organization, which is written in large characters on a red tassel. The practice of presenting these creations dates from the 1950s, when members of a local opera club decided to fabricate such tributes as a highly practical supplement to the elaborate displays of real flowers that have traditionally been presented to the performing artists and which continue to be placed outside the theater and in the lobby.[6] Presentting gifts of paper greenery as well is said to have begun in Honolulu, where an opera club came up with the idea of presenting leis made of dollar bills instead of flowers.

A principal difference in the performing abilities of today's actors and actresses lies in the dynamic-range potential of their voices. Before electronic amplification became a standard feature of Cantonese-opera theaters, singers had to possess especially powerful voices, capable not only of being heard at a distance but of rising above the very audible instrumental accompaniment and the rarely quiet audience. Before amplification, according to one Cantonese-opera aficionada,[7] one of the prime criteria of greatness was the carrying power of the voice. After that came appearance and acting ability. Nowadays, of course, audibility is no problem, even for the most subdued of voices; and sheer lung power is no longer rated high on the list of necessary attributes.

Another difference in today's Cantonese-opera performances is a lesser degree of the use of the Mandarin dialect, formerly found quite often in the midst of the Cantonese dialogue. (One amateur singer who has a modest command of Mandarin relates that she learned the dialect almost entirely from hearing it used within the Cantonese opera.) Mandarin continues to see some use, but it appears relatively rarely, usually in situations of great pomp and ceremony.

No longer is the orchestra placed squarely in the middle of the stage, as was the case in earlier years. Since the 1920s the orchestra has occupied the wings at stage right, in full view of the actors but out of sight to most of the audience. Today's orchestra typically numbers between six and nine players and travels as part of the dramatic troupe. The eight-piece ensemble that accompanied a recent visiting troupe may be said to typify the makeup of the modern Cantonese-opera orchestra. Two of the instruments were Western—violin and tenor saxophone. Other melodic instruments were the Ch'in-ch'in, the cello-like chung-hu, and the double-reed kuan. Both the saxophone and kuan players doubled on so-na, which was used during military scenes and for brief, curtain-raising pieces. It may be noted that the general tessitura of the melodic instruments is that of alto and tenor—a consistent sort of mellowness that blends well with the relatively low ranges of voice that are used. The ''leader'' of the orchestra, as in the past, is the tan-p'i-ku player, who is flanked by two other percussionists who handle the gongs and cymbals and also double on other instruments such as the ta-ku and the hsing. The tan-p'i-ku player himself commands a battery of percussion instruments which are grouped conveniently around him as with the traps of a jazz drummer: three wood blocks of different tones, two mü-yu (''temple blocks''), a tomtom, and a single, small cymbal, which rests on an upright rod (as a cymbal is typically supported in a trap-drum set) and is struck from time to time with one of the sticks that are used on the tan-p'i-ku.

The overall sound of this orchestra is in interesting contrast to that of the Peking-opera orchestra. In the latter, the tessitura is high—the shrill hu-ch'in and high-range vocalization predominating. The sound of the Cantonese-opera orchestra, by contrast, is relatively bottom-heavy. The sonority is remarkably homogeneous as well, with a blend of instruments of similar range and tone color. (The use of the so-na is counter to this homogeneous sound, but it occurs relatively infrequently.)

Also in significant contrast is the variety of functions served by the respective types of orchestra. A person accustomed to the Peking-opera type of ensemble might be surprised to see the use of music stands by the Cantonese. Sheet music is indeed used from time to time, but not for the bulk of the musical fare, which is based on melodic formulas which are thoroughly familiar to all the performers.[8] The notation occasionally referred to by the musicians is for interpolated songs that have been composed especially for the opera or which have been borrowed from current South Chinese popular music or even Western music.

The functions of the Cantonese orchestra are a bit more varied than those of its Peking counterpart. As with the Peking-opera orchestra, the melodic instruments accompany the vocal line at the unison or octave and provide melodic interludes of varying length. However, this function is only one of several in the Cantonese opera. Much of the singing in modern productions is of an antiphonal nature, with the singer trading phrases with the orchestra, sometimes overlapping at the beginnings and endings of phrases. (The singer is thus singing a cappella for brief periods. Additionally, a song may be sung without accompaniment throughout, with no answering phrases from the orchestra, but this practice is less frequent.) Still another function of the orchestra would appear to result from the influence of motion pictures (and perhaps radio and television drama): "background" music to spoken narration, in which, after an aria, the musicians softly continue the melody of the song, while players talk in normal conversational tones. The effect is remarkably similar to that of a movie soundtrack and is often found in scenes of romantic love. Finally, the orchestra provides appropriate music for battle scenes and for episodes of dancing and stylized pageantry. (Dancing occurs rarely and is neither elaborate nor lively. The small size of certain stages—as with that of the Sung Sing Theater—would inhibit the use of dance, in any case, for more than incidental adornment to the drama.)

The use of electronic amplification has been mentioned with reference to its part in changing the decibel-power requirements for singers. One may conjecture another effect that is less obvious: It may be noted that singers seldom wander far from the microphones, which are set up at the front of the stage. Since present-day voices are developed in relation to microphone-availability, it would appear that the singer is constrained to stay within a few feet of a standing microphone whenever singing. The resultant effect may well cause a generally more static stage situation than might be the case if no microphones were being used.[9]

Stage practices in modern Cantonese opera often parallel Western techniques. There remains a primary reliance on symbolism and pantomime instead of stage properties; but Western-style backdrops are used, and the rise and fall of the front-curtain signals a drama's beginning and end. Another curtain is sometimes used in the midst of a play to allow for scene-changing. An intermission of ten to twenty minutes is made at least once in the course of an evening's entertainment. During this break, the patrons will stroll to the lobby, where various items of food and drink are available. During an intermission, some patrons choose to stay in their seats to view the presentation of money bouquets to various of the performers and to hear brief eulogies from representatives of Chinatown associations, extolling the virtues of the dramatic company's players and management.

As in the past, costuming is elaborate. An extensive use of sequins (a Cantonese costuming practice that stems from the 1930s) presents a glittering spectacle under the theatrical lights. The embroidered silks and satins of old are still very much in evidence, but nylon has become preferred for much of modern costuming and headgear.

There is little apparent change in the behavior of audiences since the accounts of Western observers in the nineteenth century. A constant hum of conversation is heard throughout the evening. The audience very rarely applauds, but there are occasional spontaneous ovations after a particularly affecting aria or impressive bit of stage gymnastics. There is no longer a price reduction for late arrivals—and Cantonese opera does not come cheap. Though a balcony seat may be had for $5.00, ground-floor seats are at least in the twelve- to fifteen-dollar range.

Many of the customers are elderly. Chinatown columnist Manchester Fu noted in connection with one visiting opera troupe: "We know of four little old grannies, living on pensions, breaking their piggy banks to take in the shows three nights in a row. Nothing like instant nostalgia."[10] All age groups are represented in the audience, however, and the opera does continue to attract a sprinkling of Caucasians. The presence of a number of children in the audience is explained in part by the general propensity of Chinese parents to take children along on such occasions. But the children are not mere indifferent observers. Allowed to congregate in small groups of their own in the balcony, they often sit transfixed in fascination by the action on stage, especially during battle scenes and acrobatics. Although the Cantonese opera is frequented most by the older age groups in Chinatown, it is unlikely that any Chinese growing up in the community will not have some direct exposure to it.

In recent years, companies of *Peking* opera have played to good audiences in the Bay Area as troupes have made tours from Taiwan, Hong Kong, and most recently the People's Republic. Public performances by Peking-opera amateurs are also given, notably at colleges and universities in the Bay Area and on noncommercial television by the various Peking-opera clubs that have been formed locally since the 1960s. The vigorous activity and interest in this operatic form results directly from an influx of Mandarin-speaking Chinese from North China and Taiwan since the 1960s, as the result of liberalized immigration laws.[11] Another dramatic form, the "liberation operas" of the People's Republic, aroused interest among Chinatown's youth in the 1970s, and musical, dramatic, and dance excerpts of such works were given amateur performances locally.[12]

Cantonese opera, however, remains the primary dramatic form that engages the interest of San Francisco's Chinese community. One is accustomed to hear of Cantonese opera as being a "dying art," and indeed its present-day status may seem relatively insignificant in comparison with its former years of glory and prosperity. Yet the tenacity of the tradition is remarkable. Though the traditional form was largely suppressed in the People's Republic in the 1960s and 1970s and elbowed aside by the movies and other forms of entertainment in Hong Kong and overseas settlements, the form not only survives but continues to recruit young actors and musicians who must undergo many years of training.[13] In recent decades the opera clubs of Chinatown have had a principal role in keeping Cantonese-opera traditions alive. Efforts in several other quarters, however, have been made to promote the form to a wider audience. The Chinese Cultural Foundation has sponsored Cantonese-opera performances at its auditorium in San Francisco's Chinatown and has offered instruction in dramatic and musical techniques associated with the form. The production of full-length Cantonese operas has been successfully effected by Richard Yee, a professor of philosophy at Oakland's College of Holy Names. Using the services of professional Cantonese-opera performers who have settled in the Bay Area, Yee has mounted productions at his college for a predominantly non-Chinese audience.[14]

Clearly, the demise of Cantonese opera in San Francisco is not yet in sight, although its activities in recent years represent a descending curve of interest in the form when viewed in the context of the century and a quarter in which the Chinese theater has existed in the United States. Though young Chinese are not strongly attracted to the form and it is generally unknown outside the Chinese community, it continues to provide cultural identity and memories to older Chinese as professional troupes make their sporadic appearances and several of the opera clubs of Chinatown continue to give the form a flourishing, though unpublicized, existence. In the early 1980s, San Francisco has hosted for the first time professional Cantonese opera from the People's Republic of China, in which the traditional form has been allowed to make a gradual comeback since the death of Mao Tse-tung in 1976. Subsequent policy changes on the Mainland have made it possible for various regional-opera genres, such as the Cantonese, to be performed again in their traditional styles.

NOTES

1. Seventy-seven-thousand-and-eight men, 40,621 women in the United States as a whole. Figures from Betty Lee Sung, *Mountain of Gold* (New York, Macmillan, 1967), p. 320.

2. See e.g., Victor G. Nee and Brett de Bary Nee, *Long Time Californ'* (New York, Pantheon, 1972), pp. xxiii, 155; Richard Springer, "The Migration to the Other Chinatown," *East-West*, 27 March 1974, 10 April 1974.

3. See below, Chapter 8.

4. Alan Tory, " A Visit Behind Scenes at the Chinese Theater," *This World* (*Chronicle* magazine), 20 July 1952, p. 12.

5. Ken Wong, "The Orient Express," *East-West*, 9 August 1972, p. 3.

6. See below, p. 200.

7. Mrs. Mabel Quon, interview, 22 August 1975.

8. See Lim Chew-pah, "The Main Singing Styles in Cantonese Opera," M.A. thesis, University of Washington, 1973; Bell Yung, "The Music of Cantonese Opera," Ph.D. dissertation, Harvard University, 1976.

9. At the Sun Sing Theater in the summer of 1975, three standing microphones were used, spaced equidistantly at the front of the stage. An additional standing microphone was positioned at the edge of the stage-left wings, and three hanging microphones were in use as well. Two loudspeakers were used, placed high up on the walls on either side of the stage. That modern performers are extraordinarily dependent on amplification can be noted in Richard Yee, "Staging a Chinese Opera," *California Living* (*Chronicle* magazine), 24 February 1974, p. 14.

10. Manchester Fu, "Manny, Celestial," *East-West*, 12 August 1970, p. 7.

11. See below, pp. 200-201.

12. See below, pp. 217-18.

13. For notes on the declining popularity of Cantonese opera in Hong Kong, see Fu, p. 7; Wong, p. 3.

14. Yee, pp. 12-15; Frederic A. Moritz, "Chinese Opera for Americans," *Christian Science Monitor*, 21 March 1975.

7

Other Uses of Music in the Twentieth Century

In the new, post-earthquake Chinatown, many of the settings in which music once played a vital part have either passed out of the picture entirely or have ceased to be associated with music.

The rebuilt community presented a considerably less sordid face to the outside world than that of the old Chinatown of gambling halls, opium dens, and open prostitution—exaggerated as those aspects may have been in the accounts of nineteenth-century observers. Music was still to be found occasionally in restaurants, especially for banquets, but much less so than in the earlier decades. Westernized nightclubs did become part of the scene in the 1930s and 1940s. These offered music with superficial oriental touches but drew their repertoire primarily from Tin Pan Alley. The decline of music used in ceremonial settings has been almost total. Music disappeared from joss-house activities except for the minimal role of gong, drum, and wood-block to summon spirits and accompany chanting. Though the more elaborate funeral processions would feature marching bands, even to the present day, Chinese orchestras were to become less and less a part of these ceremonies as the century progressed, and in the present, the music for funerals is entirely in the province of occidental musicians performing a strictly Western repertoire.

Gambling-house activities became increasingly covert after the turn of the century, and music was no longer offered for the customers. The association of music with gambling continues in a mild fashion in some of the community's private music societies, in which the clacking of mahjong tiles can sometimes be heard from an adjoining room as other members absorb themselves in the performance of Cantonese-opera songs and interludes.

Institutionalized prostitution has long ceased to exist in Chinatown, and with it the singsong girls who added music to the other attractions of the nineteenth-century brothels. The virtual death knell to organized prostitution in Chinatown was given by the passage of the state legislature's Red Light Abatement Act of 1914, although the final raid on a house of prostitution in Chinatown would not be made until 1925.[1] In any case, there is no evidence to suggest any association of prostitution with music making in the twentieth century.

Live music has appeared in Chinatown's restaurants from time to time since the earthquake, but most of the community's eating houses in the twentieth century have settled for recorded music if they furnish music at all.[2] Ensembles have continued to be hired for special occasions, however, to add to the festive nature of banquets for which a restaurant or section thereof is reserved, as in Jade Snow Wong's notes on a banquet around 1940:

The wedding banquet was held on the top floor of Chinatown's oldest restaurant. . . . Here on this evening a Chinese orchestra was seated comfortably. Every time a guest arrived, the music was punctuated by huge brass cymbals which clanged to announce him.[3]

In the present day, ensembles from Chinatown's music clubs are hired to entertain at banquets—especially around the time of the Chinese New Year—held in restaurants, in the headquarters of various associations, and at picnics.

NIGHTCLUBS

While live music has not been a regular feature of Chinese restaurants, a related enterprise—the nightclub—did prosper with music of a sort for several decades in Chinatown. About a dozen Chinese nightclubs catering largely to a Western trade featured music and floor shows during the 1930s and 1940s. The most prominent were the Sky Room, Forbidden City, Kubla Khan, Club Shanghai, Club Mandalay, and the Lion's Den.[4] With Chinese owners often serving as masters of ceremonies, the clubs would feature a show starring a male or female singer and an acrobatic or magician act. Often a chorus line featured young women who were Chinese, part Chinese, or at least bearing temporary Chinese names. Orchestras were invariably all-white and featured current American pop tunes, although occasional hints of the orient were heard through heavily Westernized Chinese popular songs.

Chinatown's nightclub era began in 1936 when Charlie Low opened a cocktail bar on Grant Avenue. Having secured much success with tourists, Low opened his Forbidden City nightclub two years later. According to writer Jim Marshall:

At first, only tourists patronized Chinese night clubs, expecting to whiff opium smoke and maybe see a hatchet or two flying. All they saw was Miss Joy Ching (Home Economics, University of Chicago) doing a strip tease as The Girl in the Gilded Cage; and Miss Mary "Butch" Ong dancing along with the Misses Ruby Chew, Rose Chan, Ruth Lee, Minnie Yuke, Eleanor Wong and Faye Ying, who were being the Chinese Floradora Sextet at the moment.

After a while, "the San Franciscans themselves began dropping around to Chinese night spots, and finally the older Chinese themselves peeked in to see what was going on and became regulars." By 1942, Marshall observed, half the patronage was Chinese in some clubs. The principal entertainers in the shows generally imitated American celebrities, and the club floors were crowded with "Chinese Bing Crosbys, Chinese Sally Rands, Chinese Maxine Sullivans and Chinese Fred Astaires."[5]

After the war years the clubs went out of business one by one, and Chinatown's nightclub industry was dead by the 1950s. San Francisco's other large-scale nightclubs—such as the Mocambo, Bimbo's 365, and the Latin Quarter—similarly ceased to be paying operations. and the old-time cabarets have been replaced in general (in the words of Manchester Fu) "by the topless, bottomless and the tasteless."[6] Chinatown continues to have cocktail bars and small clubs, some of which will occasionally feature a live singer with a small combo. These are often Chinese, Japanese, or Korean entertainers. What little Chinese music is heard in such bars and clubs is modern Westernized popular music from Hong Kong and Taiwan. One interesting exception in the early 1970s was the occasional appearance of members of the local Chinese Classical Music Club at the Seven Divinities, a theater-restaurant in the North Beach area, adjacent to Chinatown, which featured various kinds of music from the Far East.[7]

DANCING

Dancing as an entertainment attraction was a rare part of the Chinatown scene in the nineteenth century,[8] and social dancing among the Chinese was unheard of. In the twentieth century, however, dance performances have been featured in several contexts, notably in the Westernized nightclub acts of the 1930s and 1940s and in several folk-dance clubs that have been popular among young people since the late 1950s. Starting in the 1920s, social dancing has gained popularity among the younger Chinese and may be viewed as a significant measure of acceptance of Western customs among the community's youth.

Dance has continued to be seen as an incidental part of Cantonese operas, but, as in the previous century, it plays a relatively small part in the productions, ranking in importance far behind acrobatics and elaborately stylized stage battles.

A vestige of the occasionally mentioned public-dance activities of the late nineteenth century may be seen in the mention by Elmer Wok Wai of Chinese children, in embroidered costumes, dancing in Chinatown around 1908:

In our block was a cellar joint where a company of thin little boys and girls sang and danced for pay. Guides use to bring strings of tourist down there at night. Those tourist thought they were nice childrens, Ah Wa, Ah Mee, Ah Bick, growing up there in the dark like mushroom. I can hear their weak voices now, in the song to the Sacred Lily:

> "*Suey-sin-fa-a-a-a-a*
> *How ye ga, suey-sin-fa.*"[9]

During the ten years or so after 1938 that large nightclubs operated in Chinatown Chinese and other Asian women comprised chorus lines and also danced solo numbers, including stripteases, in
imitation of prevailing styles in conventional nightclubs. This innovation in Chinatown apparently caused difficulties in the beginning
with respect to learning the standard routines. Jim Marshall writes
in 1942:

It was tough going, because the ban against Chinese girls in such barba-
rous places still held. . . . When Charley [Low] did succeed in getting a
dozen girls as dancers and singers, it still was hard to teach them American
dance steps—although they were all American-born and educated. A Chi-
nese-girl dance line still is far behind the Rockettes, but . . . nobody minds
much.

During the war years, around one hundred Chinese young women
worked in these establishments. They were described as being different in attitude from their counterparts in the more standard
nightclubs:

. . . the night-club idea still is so new that there is, among the girls, none of
the hard-boiled sophistication that is the trademark of their white sisters in
Eastern American cities. They're more like a bunch of college kids having a
good time—and in fact, more than two thirds of them are graduates of
Western universities.[10]

Fan dancers and strippers garnered the most publicity in these
clubs. Most celebrated of all was Joy Ching and her striptease routine, "The Girl in the Gilded Cage," which was given national attention in *Newsweek*.[11] Whether all the girls were really Chinese is
much disputed. Manchester Fu cites names such as Kay Origami,
Juanita Gomez, Soon Kim Chee, and May Monahan. They weren't
real orientals, he says, "but they wore so much makeup and the
lights were so dim you really couldn't tell."[12]

Social dancing among young people, a practice alien to traditional social patterns, began to take hold among Chinatown's native-
born in the 1920s as local Chinese youth thus followed national
trends. One reporter wrote in 1929:

Not long ago the windows of Chinese shops bore huge posters showing a young Chinese girl, flapper type, dancing with a Chinese young man in formal clothes. The headline ran:

"Chinese Collegiate Shuffle!"

What would old John Chinaman think, could he see one of these lively dancing parties of the Chinese students of the San Francisco district, jazz music, bright costumes, beautiful young women, gaiety on every hand. "Everything but hip flasks," someone said of the dance.[13]

In general, the penchant for ballroom dancing among Chinatown's youth was not notably different in character from the practices of young people throughout America. Dancing, to American popular music and jazz, was a prime organized social activity of Chinatown's American-born youth. Dancing lessons were offered in the community, and swing-era bands were organized among young Chinese to meet the demand for dance music.[14] The most popular of the local bands were the Cathayans and the Chinatown Knights—both offsprings of the Cathay Club.[15] These groups performed widely in San Francisco's Chinatown and in other Chinese communities in Northern California. The popularity of social dancing in the 1930s is reflected in the social columns of the *Chinese Digest*, the English-language newspaper of Chinatown published from 1935 through 1940.

Ballroom dancing has long ceased to be a novelty in the Chinese community, and social-dance activities have become a normal part of school and club functions. The usual musical fare at such dances—from the 1920s through the present—has been indistinguishable from that of dances outside Chinatown. In the 1970s, however, the Westernized popular music of Hong Kong and Taiwan was featured by one youthful ensemble in Chinatown: the Chung Sai band, which included yang-ch'in, erh-hu, and ti as well as such Western instruments as the saxophone, amplified guitar, and trap drums.

An interest in Chinese folk dancing has made itself felt over the past several decades with the formation of the Chinese Folk Dance Association and the Chung Ngai group, both of which give frequent concerts both in Chinatown and elsewhere in the Bay Area. The Chinese Folk Dance Association, which dates from 1959, is of special musical interest, as it includes within its activities a large and active orchestra, entirely of Chinese instrumentation, which rehearses regularly and accompanies the dancers in public performances. The popularity of both dance groups in recent years is one of the many indications of the burgeoning interest in cultivating and affirming Chinese identity among Chinatown's young people.

CEREMONIAL USES

Music associated with Chinese temples has become virtually nonexistent in twentieth-century Chinatown, except for the occasional use of gong, drum, and wood-block during certain services. The few traditional temples, or joss houses, remaining in Chinatown serve the needs primarily of older Chinese and also function as tourist attractions. They are no longer a locus for ceremonial music as was the case in the nineteenth century. About the only occasion of even peripheral musical importance in Chinatown's year now is the celebration of the Chinese New Year, which involves a parade that features various marching bands and drum-and-bugle corps from the Chinese community, together with a Miss Chinatown pageant and contest, whose concluding ceremonies invariably include the services of a non-Chinese dance orchestra.

Only the funeral, of various Chinese ceremonies, retains music as an integral element. As always, however, only the funerals of the fairly well-to-do and prominent will feature a procession complete with music. For a while in the twentieth century, a Chinese orchestra and a Western marching band were typically both used in a large-scale funeral. However, since about 1940, a Western band alone accompanies the funeral cortege. The Chinese boys' band of the Cathay Club furnished Western-style funeral marches from the founding of the group, in 1911, until the early 1960s, when the club became musically inactive. Today's funeral music is typically furnished by a small marching band (eight to twelve pieces) hired directly from the Musicians' Union by the funeral home in charge. The repertoire of the band for such occasions is of standard Western hymns and dirges, such as "Nearer My God, to Thee," "Flee as a Bird," "Departed Comrade," and "Rock Hill."[16] Although Chinese music and instruments have been visibly missing from Chinese funerals here for some forty years, a survival of past practices occasionally is found in which a so-na player performs in one of the closed cars of the funeral procession. The practice is in consideration of the wishes of the deceased, in cases where a strong adherence to old Chinese customs has been pervasive in the person's life. This rare practice will probably not be seen many more times, however, as there are very few so-na players in the Chinese community, and the instrument sees little use locally these days, ritual or otherwise.

INFORMAL MUSIC MAKING

In the twentieth century, music played by amateurs for their own pleasure is concentrated in large measure in music clubs, in which performers can enjoy socializing along with music making and can sing and play to their hearts' content away from the crowded living quarters of Chinatown. (The subject of organized amateur ensembles is treated in some detail in the next chapter.) In some cases, performers—especially beginning players—have congregated very informally in the evenings in such locations as the Chinese Library of America or the Chinese Progressive Association. While Western music-making at home is not a Chinese family tradition, those Chinese with the means and the space will sometimes buy a piano and arrange for lessons for their children. Many Chinese children now study the violin and other Western orchestral instruments as well. In general, patterns of informal Western music making have become, especially among the suburban middle-class Chinese, Americanized and unexceptional.

CONTACTS WITH OCCIDENTAL MUSIC

The effects of westernization, especially among American-born Chinese, are seen increasingly after the turn of the century, as Chinese become less confined to the ghetto and as the movies, radio, and finally television have brought Western music into the community. Chinese ensembles for the performance of Western music find much popularity among the younger Chinese even early in the century. We find, for instance, the formation of the Cathay Club band in 1911 and a chamber orchestra at the Chinese YMCA by 1916. In

1909 "Chinese vaudeville performance" is advertised by the Oriental Theater on Grant Avenue.[17] In 1915 Chinese and Westerners alike applauded the appearance at the Orpheum Theater of the Chinese girl Chee Toy who performed in conjunction with her magician father and sang "It's a Long Way to Tipperary."[18] A "Chinese Jazz Band" from Chinatown was featured in theatrical performance in 1919.[19] By the 1920s, Western music was no novelty to the Chinese community, as American tunes were brought by radio, hymns were sung in the churches, band music was provided by the Chinese themselves in parades and concerts, and jazz was heard in Chinese restaurants.[20] An amateur performance of Cantonese opera was accorded Western treatment in November 1927, as fifty performers of the Chinese Presbyterian Church presented *Little Almond Eyes* completely in English, after three months of rehearsal.[21] Even a blackface minstrel show was not beyond the ken of the Chinese. In what the *Chronicle* heralded as probably "the first attempt of Orientals in blackface," Chinese boys from the Chung Mei Home in Berkeley presented in 1928 a complete minstrel show in San Francisco and East Bay cities.[22] The all-Chinese swing bands and the Western-style nightclubs of the 1930s completed the invasion of Western music in the community, and Chinatown has long since ceased to be a musical ghetto. Since the 1950s, the Chinatown Optimist Club has put on annual productions of Broadway musicals with all-Chinese casts.[23] Over the past decade, symphonic ensembles of Chinatown musicians have rehearsed regularly and given frequent public performances.[24]

For the visitor to today's Chinatown, the most pervasive Western musical influence is heard in the performance of street musicians—itinerant individuals and groups who appear during all seasons on Grant Avenue and offer classical chamber music, jazz, rock, country music, and combinations thereof to the sidewalk passersby. Street musicians entertain throughout San Francisco, especially where tourists are likely to be found, and have become as typical of the San Francisco scene as cable cars and al fresco flower stalls. In Chinatown the musicians station themselves at various spots along the sidewalk and offer entertainment day and night. There is no active solicitation of money, but an open instrument-case or other receptacle is conveniently in sight for contributions. An *East-West* reporter has written of their reception in Chinatown:

The invasion of the "street musician" in Chinatown is not as welcomed by some residents as it is in other parts of San Francisco.

Shopkeepers declined to say how they feel about the musicians playing in front of their stores. Many of the youth, however, felt strongly against them. One young Chinese girl said they were "ripping off from the Chinese."

She admitted that they do attract tourists, but they also take the money the tourists would otherwise spend on the Chinese goods sold in the stores the musicians play in front of.

"They not only obstruct traffic, they degrade from the cultural atmosphere of Chinatown," she said, wishing to remain unidentified.

One other girl pointed out that it was unfair because city cops would "kick out the young Chinese kids who hang around the streets but let the beggars stay."

"Besides," she continued, "they play lousy music."

Of course there are varying opinions among the youth. One 19-year-old resident said he felt the street musicians added to the "quaintness" of Chinatown. He said he really had no opinion on how they played, but he doesn't object to them playing in Chinatown.

"Just because they are white doesn't mean they arc no good. They don't bother me. It's better than outright begging for money," he said.[25]

Now an established part of the Chinatown ambience, the street musicians, with rare exceptions,[26] are non-Chinese, and their music is strictly of Western and Afro-American traditions.

From time to time, one hears recorded Chinese music issuing from a loudspeaker on a balcony or rooftop on Grant Avenue or Waverly Place, but such musical background generally heralds a special occasion, such as an association's anniversary or a Chinese holiday. No one has followed up on a suggestion made to the San Francisco Chinese Community Citizens' Survey and Fact Finding Committee in 1969 that "the playgrounds and even the streets be wired for playing of Chinese music in a low key."[27]

RADIO AND RECORDINGS

While radio has had a substantial role in bringing Western music to the attention of many Chinese, it has also functioned to some extent as a medium for Chinese music itself. Until very recently, there was no full-time radio station in Chinatown. But for forty years the Cantonese-speaking community was entertained and informed by a regularly scheduled program called "The Chinese Hour," which emanated from the Golden Star radio studio on Clay Street and was supported through commercials for business firms in Chinatown.[28] The studio was founded by Mr. and Mrs. Thomas Tong, and Mrs. (May) Tong served as the program's announcer from the beginning until the studio's operations were closed in 1979. During this span of years, the program provided the only important radio contact with the world for much of Chinatown's population, and many individuals in today's Chinese community speak with nostalgia of "growing up to the sound of May Tong's voice."

"The Chinese Hour" was actually a two-hour program, broadcast every weeknight and on Saturday afternoons. Mrs. Tong featured recordings of Cantonese opera and Chinese popular music, together with her regular coverage in Cantonese of world and community news. Various community-service programs were offered, and remote broadcasts were made from the Mandarin (later the Sun Sing) Theater. In the earlier years of the program, Chinatown still supported full-time live Cantonese opera at the Mandarin, and the Tongs' studio made frequent broadcasts of the medium. In the postwar years, when the theater changed its fare to Chinese movies, alternated only occasionally with live opera, the studio retained its direct line to the theater, broadcasting the movie soundtracks as well as the infrequent live performances of Cantonese opera. Also heard live in the early years of the program was music performed by several of Chinatown's amateur music clubs.

Today's radio-listener in Chinatown is offered daily programming in Cantonese from 9 A.M. to midnight every day of the week through a listener-subscription service called SINOCAST, which was introduced to Chinatown in 1977. The SINOCAST subscriber pays a monthly fee for the use of a special FM set which can receive no other station. (The station's signal can be picked up only on these special radios.)

Chinatown's SINOCAST studio is part of a network of stations which has developed since 1976, when the Sino Communications Group was organized in New York City to establish listener-supported radio for urban areas with large Chinese populations. Four SINOCAST stations have been founded so far: in New York, Boston, San Francisco, and Toronto; and the corporation's plans include extending the service to such other cities as Chicago, Los Angeles, Seattle, and Vancouver, British Columbia. Each SINO-CAST station has a listening radius of some fifty-five miles, extending well into suburbs as well as the city.

With the exception of occasional newscasts and public-service programs, which are broadcast live from the local station, SINO-CAST's material is all of Hong Kong import. Taped programs are flown from that city directly to the New York headquarters and then distributed to the member stations, whose program schedule is uniform throughout the network. The subscriber is, for all intents and purposes, listening to a Hong Kong station once removed. The majority of the programming is devoted to Hong Kong popular music, though about two hours a day (spread over several time segments) are devoted to Cantonese opera. Additionally, radio drama—Chinese soap opera—is included in each day's programming, as is some material for children, the latter consisting mostly of storytelling with music.

The forty-year reign of "The Chinese Hour" and the current SINOCAST service represent the most significant use of radio as a medium for music for the Cantonese-speaking majority of San Francisco's Chinese. Chinese music may also be heard from time to time on the Bay Area's noncommercial FM stations, which will sometimes feature music from Cantonese and other Chinese traditions and offer explanations and commentary on the music in English.[29] Radio in the lives of most of San Francisco's Chinese, however, has simply reflected what is current in Hong Kong. With rare exceptions, it has not been a vehicle for the expression of a specifically Chinese-American musical culture.

For some years, the Golden Star company, which broadcast "The Chinese Hour," also made and marketed recordings of Cantonese opera. It appears to have been the only Chinese recording company in North America.[30] The record-making operation began in 1949 with 78-RPM recordings of visiting artists at the Mandarin Theater and also performances by the Flying Dragon Music Club of Chinatown. Later, the firm issued a number of LP albums and continued in the recording business until 1961. Some of the Golden Star's albums can still be found on sale in Chinatown stores. The firm also maintained a background-music service for a few years in the 1950s. Music taped by a sister studio in Hong Kong was relayed by telephone line to various locations in Chinatown, including the many small garment factories, which are a principal source of employment for Chinatown's women of all ages.

NOTES

1. Richard H. Dillon, *The Hatchet Men* (New York, Coward-McCann, 1961), p. 266.

2. The use of a Chinese orchestra in a restaurant in Oakland's post-earthquake Chinatown was noted by Elinor H. Stoy in "Chinatown and the Curse that Makes It a Plague-spot in the Nation," *Arena* 38 (1907), p. 361. Charles Caldwell Dobie complains of "jazz orchestras" in Chinese restaurants of the 1930s. *San Francisco: A Pageant* (New York, D. Appleton-Century, 1934), p. 292.

3. *Fifth Chinese Daughter* (New York, Harper & Bros., 1945), p. 142. Wedding-banquet music also figures in C.Y. Lee's novel, *Flower-Drum Song*, set in the Chinatown of the mid-1950s. (New York, Farrar, Straus and Cudahy, 1957, p. 292.)

4. Manchester Fu, "Manny, Celestial," *East-West*, 30 September 1970, p. 3.

5. Jim Marshall, "Cathay Hey-Hey," *Colliers* 109 (28 February 1942), pp. 13, 53.

6. Fu, "Manny, Celestial," p. 3.

7. "Multi-purpose Theatre-restaurant Debuts," *East-West*, 12 June 1973, p. 5.

8. See above, pp. 113–15.

9. Veta Griggs, *Chinatown's Chance* (New York, Exposition Press, 1969), p. 47.

10. Marshall, p. 53. Chinese women who were recent college graduates in the war years ran into much difficulty finding jobs above the menial level, owing to racial prejudice. See Wong, *Fifth Chinese Daughter*, pp. 188–89.

11. 24 November 1947, *Newsweek*, p. 24.

12. Fu, "Manny, Celestial," p. 3.

13. Frank J. Taylor, "San Francisco's New Chinese City," *Travel* 52 (1929), pp. 18–21, 54.

14. "Young China Dances Now," *Chinese Digest*, 6 December 1935, p. 4.

15. See Chapter 8, below, regarding the Cathay Club and other music clubs in Chinatown.

16. As heard by the present writer in a funeral in Chinatown in the summer of 1974.

17. *San Francisco's Chinatown.*

18. *Examiner*, 26 January 1915.

19. See below, p. 207.

20. Dobie, *San Francisco: A Pageant*, p. 292.

21. *Chronicle*, 29 November 1927.

22. *Chronicle*, 27 February 1928.

23. See, e.g., " 'Boyfriend' Premieres at Bimbo's," *East-West*, 6 June 1973; "Optimists Doing 'Call Me Madam' This Year," *East-West*, 29 May 1974.

24. See below, pp. 204–5.

25. *East-West*, 6 September 1972, p. 1.

26. As with a Chinese folk singer noted in June 1974. *East-West*, 19 June 1974, p. 6.

27. Lim P. Lee et al., *Report of the San Francisco Chinese Community Citizens' Survey and Fact Finding Committee* (abridged ed., San Francisco, H.J. Carle, 1969), p. 195.

28. The actual broadcasting was through the facilities of local full-time stations. In its final decade, the program was broadcast over KBRG-FM, having previously been heard on KSAN (from 1939 to 1960) and KLOK. "The Chinese Hour" is described in Terence O'Flaherty, "The Golden Voice of Chinatown," *This World* (*Chronicle* magazine), 11 March 1951, p. 31.

29. Notable in this regard have been KALW-FM, KPFA-FM, and KQED-FM. Chinese-opera films and other Chinese-music programs can be seen occasionally on the educational television station KQED. Television has not yet played more than an incidental role in disseminating Chinese music, however. The SINOCAST network hopes eventually to include television stations in its North American network. The corporation's programming would presumably reflect current Hong Kong tastes, through videotapes flown from that city.

30. Supplementing the large import trade of Chinese records from China and Hong Kong. Regarding imported records, see Lim Lai, "The Talking Machine Goes East," *East-West*, 8 January 1969, p. 7; "Nee, Nee, Nee," *New Yorker* 28 (1952), pp. 29–30.

8

Music Clubs and Performing Ensembles[1]

The most outstanding feature in the musical culture of San Francisco's Chinese community in the twentieth century has been the growth of amateur music clubs and ensembles. These comprise the principal focus of musical life in today's community. Especially since the 1940s, when public performances of professional Cantonese opera ceased to be offered full time. Chinatown has turned inward for its sources of musical creativity and entertainment. Because of the vigorous activities of musical societies in the community, it is likely that today's Chinatown eclipses in musical life that of any urban neighborhood in North America for the sheer quantity of music sung in non-Western tongues and played on non-Western instruments. Yet this lively musical milieu is largely hidden from the eyes and ears of outsiders. The community's musical activities are rarely glimpsed by the daily torrent of tourists who invade the neighborhood, and the doings of music clubs and organized ensembles have gone unchronicled in both the musicological literature and the popular press.

The information in the present study has been gained primarily through firsthand accounts and from direct observation. It would be useful to supplement and compare these findings with other studies and observations, but such sources are virtually nonexistent at the present writing.[2] It is known that Chinese music societies function in a similarly active and unpublicized fashion in other North American cities (such as New York, Honolulu, Los Angeles, and Vancouver, British Columbia), but as yet there is little in print that would permit comparisons with them. It is hoped that the growing interest in the music of urban ethnic minorities might eventually result in material that could shed light on the musical culture of overseas Chinese communities in general. The present exploratory study could then take its place as raw material in a more comprehensive investigation of the musical life of the overseas Chinese.

TODAY'S COMMUNITY

Census reports in the 1970s recorded a total of 58,696 Chinese living in San Francisco. A true figure, however, would probably be closer to 70,000 or even 80,000, owing to the reluctance on the part of many Chinese to give census information and also allowing for population growth in subsequent years. In any case, the Chinese make up at least 8 and probably from 10 to 15 percent of San Francisco's population, one of the largest such percentages in any city outside of Asia.[3]

A little over half of San Francisco's Chinese were born abroad (in Chinatown itself, a large majority are foreign-born), and a continuing influx of immigrants serves to provide direct contact with Chinese cultural patterns. This continuing immigration also perpetuates the need for such a protective environment as Chinatown, in which it is possible to conduct most of one's affairs in the Cantonese tongue and to minimize contacts with non-Chinese.

As a family prospers, however, it rarely elects to remain permanently in Chinatown. Eventually, when finances permit, the family will settle in a quieter part of the city or elsewhere in the Bay Area.[4] Ties to Chinatown are retained, however, as former residents visit and shop there. Many also maintain their connections with the multitude of Chinese clubs and organizations based in Chinatown. More than an ethnic neighborhood, Chinatown is the headquarters for virtually every Chinese association—family (clan), political, commercial, social, and cultural. The area's complicated infrastructure of such organizations is to some degree a vestige of earlier years when Chinatown existed as a virtually self-contained principality, governing itself in many respects and remaining effectively sealed off from the larger community by barriers of language and custom, as well as by discriminatory laws, which discouraged any attempt of Chinese to move from the protective ghetto.[5]

While legal restrictions have been removed and many Chinese no longer reside in Chinatown, the elaborate network of social and quasi-governmental organizations remains, though many of its institutions have diminished in their usefulness as Chinese have learned to relate directly and effectively to the larger society. Among the associations headquartered in Chinatown that do continue to serve much-needed functions for their members are the community's numerous music clubs, whose private activities provide a lively world of socializing and amateur music making.

MUSIC IN THE COMMUNITY

The professional Cantonese opera was the conspicuous center of musical activity in Chinatown's earlier years. Although opera companies now visit San Francisco only a few times a year, the legacy of the earlier reign of the Chinese theater is strongly felt in Chinatown's musical life. Professional opera performances, though infrequent, are well attended; and interest in the genre is further reflected in the sale of phonograph records of Cantonese opera, the popularity of radio broadcasts of opera, and the appearance of an occasional opera film at one of the community's movie theaters. The opera becomes an even more direct element of many individuals' lives through their participation in music clubs whose main fare is Cantonese opera.

Most of Chinatown's music clubs are formally organized but informally conducted. The formalities include a charter, bylaws, an elected slate of officers, dues and initiation fees, and a specified procedure by which new members may be admitted. Such clubs commonly maintain a rented headquarters, which serves for general social get-togethers as well as music making. Foreign-born Chinese form a large majority in almost all of the music clubs. At present, there are about fifteen music clubs in more or less active existence. The clubs are of three general types, as will be discussed below: Cantonese opera, Peking opera, and instrumental music.

Less distinctively Chinese but not to be overlooked in any study of Chinatown's musical mannerisms and tastes are those organizations that are cast in a Western mold and which exist as part of larger institutional programs: for instance, the choirs of Chinatown's eight Christian churches; the drum-and-bugle corps which are sponsored by Chinese-language schools and civic groups; and the marching bands and other musical organizations of the local public schools.

COMMUNITY ORGANIZATION IN TODAY'S CHINATOWN

In order to understand the functions of music clubs in Chinatown society, it is useful to distinguish such groups in general from other types of associations and to view them in an overall social perspective. In some cases, the functions of clubs organized ostensibly for musical purposes will be seen to overlap with those of other types of clubs. In other cases, one may note definite interaction between music clubs and other types of organizations.

The most all-encompassing and powerful of Chinatown's associations is the Chinese Consolidated Benevolent Association, usually referred to as the Six Companies. The Six Companies was formally organized in 1882 as an amalgam of district associations (or hui-kuan) representing the principal areas of Kwangtung province that are the ancestral homelands for Chinatown's residents. In earlier years the Six Companies had an all-important administrative and adjudicating role in the Chinese community, serving as advocate and go-between with the larger community. However, its power and importance have receded in the years since World War II, as Chinatown has become less socially insular and families have moved elsewhere. The district-association constituents of the Six Companies are in turn made up of groups whose membership is based on a common surname (thus "family association," whether or not actual kinship) or common origin from within a given area of the district in question. By virtue of surname and region of ancestral origin, every Chinese is thus an ipso facto member of several organizations. In practice, many Chinese, especially the American-born, do not choose to participate actively in these homeland-oriented groups. Some ignore them completely; others pay only nominal acknowledgment (as with attending only the annual banquet of the family association).

Separate from regional and surname considerations are the fraternal societies known as tongs. These groups, descendants of Chinese secret societies, emphasize ceremonial and social functions. They were once a powerful force in Chinatown life, largely through control of gambling, prostitution, and other illegal activities that flourished in the community's earlier years. Like the Six Companies, the tongs have seen a decline of power and purpose over the past decades (the last of the notorious West Coast "tong wars" ended in the 1920s) and now consist mainly of middle-aged and elderly members. The tongs own a great deal of Chinatown's property, as do the family associations, and continue to exert a degree of influence through such ownership.[6]

Among other organizations are political associations, religious groups, merchant associations (such as the Chinese Chamber of Commerce), and a wide variety of clubs organized for social services, hobbies, athletics, and other common interests. It is in this category of social or "voluntary" organizations that we find music clubs.

It is typical of members of music clubs to emphasize the autonomy of their groups. Heavily stressed is independence of political ties and general avoidance of political issues. The validity of the claims notwithstanding, there are many interactions and interconnections between music clubs and other organized groups in the Chinese community. For instance, one orchestral group is given rent-free rehearsal space by a family association. Another ensemble is provided quarters by the local Salvation Army; still another meets in the headquarters of a political party (though the group itself has no official ties to the party). Music-club groups are hired by the Chinese Chamber of Commerce for functions involving parades or ceremonial events. A family-association banquet will sometimes feature a hired performance by music-club members. Athletic activities provide a notable overlap of functions between music clubs and other groups. Some music clubs put much emphasis on interclub sports (volleyball and bowling are favorites) and hold competitions with other clubs, some of them musical, some not.

A music-club member not uncommonly belongs to at least one other voluntary organization in the Chinese community. However, (with rare exceptions) no one is formally a member of more than one music club at a given time. Observed by custom in any case, this exclusivity is written into the bylaws of at least one of the music clubs (Nam Chung). However, such restriction does not apply to the participation of members in other clubs as guests. The practice of sitting in as a musician with another club is quite common.

Music clubs do not, as a rule, unite for common purposes. There are exceptions, however: During World War II, clubs worked together during war-bond drives and other patriotic functions, and in more recent years Peking-opera clubs have often shared resources in order to stage a production.

TYPES OF MUSIC CLUBS

Chinatown's music clubs do not always fall conveniently into categories, as the types mentioned are not necessarily mutually exclusive. Instrumental solos and ensemble pieces are sometimes played at Cantonese-opera clubs, for instance; and instrumental-music associations will typically feature a vocal selection or two—sometimes from Cantonese opera—on a program. Further, one could make a case for lumping Cantonese and Peking opera clubs into one general "music-drama" classification; yet, the differences extend well beyond musical styles, as will be discussed.

CANTONESE-OPERA CLUBS

The Cantonese-opera clubs are the oldest and most populous of the clubs whose music is strictly Chinese. Their music reflects the South Chinese origins of most of San Francisco's Chinese. For immigrant members, who make up the majority of the Cantonese clubs, the clubs are often a direct carry-over of village traditions. Many of the Chinatown members first sang and played Cantonese-opera music in village clubs in Kwangtung.[7]

These groups are the most culturally insular of Chinatown's music societies. The spoken language is Cantonese. The music is generally for the membership only. Privacy is valued and publicity shunned. While a club's policy is ostensibly to promote the appreciation and performance of Cantonese opera, in practice the association typically serves a more heavily social function. Each of these groups has a rented headquarters to which every member has a key, and the club rooms see much use as informal havens for relaxation and conversation, with or without music. Although members may bring family and guests at will, the clubs are not otherwise accessible to nonmembers.

There are presently six Cantonese-opera clubs in San Francisco's Chinatown.[8] Membership figures, as given by members of the respective clubs, vary from ten to slightly over two hundred, but such figures are necessarily approximate, as "membership" may be held by individuals seldom or never seen: Such a member will always pay dues initially but become inactive eventually, with respect to both finances and participation. In some cases, members have moved to distant states or to other countries, yet are not dropped from the membership rolls. In practical terms, no more than twenty or thirty active members of the clubs could function comfortably in the rather uniformly small quarters: typically one general-activities room (with couches, chairs, and a small stage for singers and musicians) and one or two other smaller rooms in which mahjong and general socializing can go on. Kitchen facilities are ubiquitous. Hot coffee and tea are always available, and various snacks are sometimes prepared in the kitchen. The largest club, Nam Chung, serves a full meal, buffet-style, to its members at midnight on Saturday nights.

Actual performing ability in Cantonese opera is never a requirement for membership, and many members are devotees only, with no special training in music or acting. The experience of those who do perform is often limited to amateur participation in the club itself. Every club takes pride in having at least one member who has a professional background in the field, however, and some have a number of such members. The former professionals serve as a guiding force musically and provide instruction and coaching to other members on an informal level. They are sometimes among the elected officers of these clubs.

One group, the Flying Dragon Club, which was founded in 1942, achieved a measure of local renown for its professional activities during the war years, when it was coached by members of opera troupes from Canton and Hong Kong who had been stranded in the United States during the war. The ability of some of the Flying Dragon members was advanced to the point that the club is remembered by some as being a sort of informal booking agency for the professional theater, as its musicians and singers were prepared to fill in for full-time professionals. So well regarded was the Flying Dragon that it became the only Chinatown music club to be substantially publicized in the English-language press. Its credits include a spread in *Life* magazine and a long, detailed, and favorable article by the *Chronicle*'s principal music critic, Alfred Frankenstein.[9]

The Flying Dragons performed on the local Golden Star radio station and even made some professional recordings with the record company associated with that station.[10] With the virtual disappearance of the live Cantonese theater from the San Francisco scene, however, the Flying Dragon Club became less active musically and admitted many nonperforming members. In recent years it has existed in a sort of semi-retirement, and the character of this once lively organization is not markedly different from that of other Cantonese-opera clubs, as the group has become largely devoted to social activities.

During the earlier days when professional opera was flourishing in Chinatown, there was initially little direct interaction between the professionals and the local amateurs. It was in the nature of the professional performers to associate only with their own colleagues and to guard jealously the various secrets of their trade. In time, however, a degree of association did develop between amateurs and professionals. When the Nam Chung Club was first formed, in 1925, its members would attend the Chinese theater nightly in hopes of learning techniques by watching and listening. Members would secure seats as close as possible to the performers. Particularly important to the aspiring amateurs was learning the actions of the orchestra's percussionist, whose role is central and directive to the other performers, as in other Chinese-opera traditions.

Such learning by observation was the only recourse for the early Nam Chung members, as the aloof professionals refused to give direct instruction in their esoteric and oral-tradition art. After a night of intense observation, the Nam Chung members would return immediately to their club and spend hours in imitation of the techniques they had been observing. Alternately, members would listen to recordings of Cantonese opera and perform along with them. They were otherwise limited to the rudimentary techniques

that some of the members had learned in their Kwangtung villages
and in Canton.

After some months of this imitative self-teaching, the Nam
Chung neophytes were able to persuade members of an opera company to come to the club headquarters to hear the amateurs perform. The professionals were surprised to find at least occasional
competence among the fledgling players. This initial encounter led
to friendly relations between professional performers and Nam
Chung members. In time, it was not uncommon for theater musicians and singers to visit Nam Chung in off-hours and join in with
the amateurs.[11] Such a relationship continues to this day, as members of the —now infrequent—visiting troupes are guests at the
club, which has acquired an international reputation among Cantonese performers and in time has welcomed a number of professionals and former professionals to actual membership in the club.
This association has been of considerable benefit to the competence
of Nam Chung performers, who eventually developed the ability
and confidence to stage occasional full-scale opera productions,
renting a local theater for the night of the performance.

The musical activities of the Cantonese clubs center on re-creat-
ing scenes from operas through singing songs with orchestral accompaniment. They do not extend, in recent years, to costuming
and staging. During informal sessions, on weekend nights, the accompanying orchestra will consist of simply anyone who shows up.
(In Nam Chung, the largest club, the orchestra rarely numbers less
than seven and sometimes includes as many as fifteen musicians.)
The Cantonese tradition does not have stringent specifications for
melodic instruments, and the typically versatile players will sometimes switch from instrument to instrument, even as singing is in
progress. The favored instruments are the Chinese spike fiddles of
various sizes (especially the erh-hu), the yang-ch'in dulcimer, and
the banjo-like san-hsien. Notated music is rarely in evidence, but
singers will often read texts from a sheet or keep one handy for reference. Singers always use a microphone, and each club has an amplification system. It is characteristic of the Cantonese clubs to
have a stock of musical instruments for performers to play, though
musicians may occasionally bring their own.

Non-Chinese instruments are rarely heard in such clubs. This situation is in interesting contrast to an earlier period, which reached
a peak in the 1940s, when Western instruments were a vogue in

Cantonese opera. In Nam Chung, which has used the same quarters almost since its founding in 1925, there is a decorative, glass-fronted display case for instruments, which is prominently placed near the stage. This case has been there for nearly the whole history of the club. In a commemorative volume published by Nam Chung for its members in 1945,[12] a photograph shows the display case to contain, in addition to Chinese instruments, a tenor saxophone, a trumpet, and a clarinet. (For a while during this period a xylophone was also put to use by the club, and Nam Chung even possessed a grand piano for a number of years.) Today, only the clarinet remains, and it has seen no use for many years.

In spite of the continuing use of Western instruments in some Hong Kong operatic troupes, San Francisco clubs gradually have abandoned the use of such instruments. "We learned from the Communists," states one opera-club member. It seems that much of the Cantonese-opera music from Mainland China (prior to the Cultural Revolution of the mid-1960s) was esteemed by San Francisco opera fanciers, whose interest transcended political considerations. Recordings from the Mainland featured only Chinese instruments, and the local clubs followed suit in gradually abandoning the westernization of their orchestras. An exception is the Western violin, which has found a more or less permanent place amidst the Chinese instruments in present-day accompanying groups. More exceptional, but sometimes found, is the use of the saxophone and the Western four-string banjo.

Instruction in Cantonese-opera techniques is given both formally and informally in the opera clubs. The apprenticeship system, which still holds sway in professional Cantonese opera, is obviously impossible for part-time enthusiasts. Each of the Cantonese clubs has at least one person who will teach on a fairly regular basis. One of the smaller clubs (Hoy Fung), which has had the financial problems and dwindling membership common to these groups, now remains in existence in large part to provide a place for the club's president to teach. Another club (Chung Sing) has formed in recent years as, in effect, an alumni club of students who studied with the teacher, Wun Gee-chung, who taught in San Francisco in the late 1960s.

Though each club has its own special features, one can generalize a Saturday-night get-together that would not be unlikely at any of the more active clubs. A number of activities will be in progress at once. While a group of musicians accompanies a singer, children will be playing games and running to and fro. In the midst of this—in the main room—several members may read newspapers or magazines, others will chat, a few will sit (perhaps with eyes closed) and listen to the music. In an adjoining room, the punctuating click of mahjong tiles will be heard. In the kitchen, other members may be putting together a snack or late supper. Coffee and tea are being consumed in large quantities. The mélange of children's cries, mahjong, and kitchen activities is of no apparent consequence to musicians and singers as they proceed uninterruptedly through twenty- or thirty-minute musical sections of a Cantonese-opera scene. As members tend to bring their whole families to such meetings, there is a mixture of sexes and generations. Singers and musicians are, however, unlikely to be under forty.

Such a picture is in striking contrast to what meetings must have been like in the earlier days of Cantonese-opera clubs. The most noticeable difference is the presence of women and children. The Cantonese clubs of earlier decades were founded in a predominantly male society, before the repeal of immigration laws that excluded women. (It is only since the early 1940s that women have become part of the clubs' memberships.) The clubs served as centers for social and recreational activities for their men without families. During the war years, some of the clubs were active around the clock, as jobs were plentiful in Bay Area defense industries, and many workers were employed in shifts that necessitated seeking recreation at varying times of the day and night.[13] Today's club members remember the early 1940s as a sort of golden age of opera-club activities, with music going on every night of the week, in contrast to today's entertainment only on weekend nights.

The gradual decline of activities in the Cantonese-opera clubs following the war years may be attributed in part to the relaxation of immigration laws in 1945 and 1946, one result of which was to admit thousands of Chinese women as war brides.[14] As members of the opera clubs married and became increasingly involved in family life, the need for such gathering places diminished; and the presence of wives and children gave a changed character to those clubs whose members did continue to attend.

Music making per se is not always the predominant concern of some of the present-day associations. General socializing and mahjong occupy the time of many of the members. For those who no longer live in Chinatown, the club is useful as a stopping-off place, before or after shopping or appointments, and as a generally convenient place to relax with friends. In several of the clubs, athletic pursuits are emphasized. Trophy cases, celebrating triumphs in bowling or volleyball, are conspicuously displayed in such clubs. Picnics and excursions also occupy members' time. Thus music as a specific activity varies in importance from club to club. In all cases, however, a stage, instruments, and sound-amplifying equipment are available for whoever wishes to perform, and there is a core of the membership that continues to perpetuate the musical traditions within the club.

What singing and playing does go on is rarely heard outside the circle of club members. Their performances, in some cases, might quite literally be termed "underground music," as clubs tend to be located in inexpensive basement quarters. Even the most reclusive of clubs, however, will generally surface around the time of the Chinese New Year. During this period the family associations of Chinatown give their spring banquets, and it is traditional for a Cantonese-opera club to provide performers for these affairs. The family association in turn makes a donation to the club's coffers. The income that a group derives from such a performance is an important part of the club's annual budget, usefully supplementing the dues and donations that pay the rent and other expenses.

It is thus as the Chinese New Year approaches that many get-togethers may assume the character of rehearsals. Otherwise, musical activity, when it exists, is purely recreational and is decidedly private. Notwithstanding the emphasis on privacy, many club members are welcomed as performers in other clubs. At the Saturday-night meetings of the well-attended Nam Chung club, the opera orchestra is often made up in large part of guests from other clubs. In some cases, members of the smaller groups use their own club rooms for socializing but go to Nam Chung to make music.

In general, the membership of San Francisco Cantonese-opera clubs is middle-aged or older. Although children and other younger relatives are often brought to club functions, interest in Cantonese opera among younger people is in rare evidence.

Most of the clubs require regular, standardized dues of their members. Annual dues typically range between ten and twenty-five dollars, but additional donations are sometimes solicited. One club has no set requirements for dues but expects each of its members to make a pledge twice a year, when the contributions range from five to five hundred dollars. Money problems have always plagued the opera clubs. Over the years, a number of clubs have quietly expired, having been crushed between rising expenses and dwindling income from members who have lost interest in the club's activities.

A prospective member of a Cantonese-opera club must first be recommended by at least one present member of the club. His or her application is then voted upon by the club at large. Typically, such votes must be unanimous. In mentioning desirable qualities for new members, present members put high priority on good character and the ability to get along with others. Also stressed is the apolitical nature of the club (at least one association forbids membership to any member of a tong or purely political group). While "love of music" is mentioned as desirable in a new member, no other musical criteria apply.

The Cantonese-opera clubs are of course prime sources for audiences when an opera troupe visits San Francisco from Hong Kong. The act of distributing tickets has evolved into a sort of ritual in San Francisco. While tickets are available to the general public at the theater box office, opera-club members will often receive them directly from the opera performers themselves—ostensibly as a gift—the tickets having previously been purchased from the opera company by the performer. Well in advance of opening night, individual singer-actors from the company will appear as guests at opera clubs and other associations in Chinatown. During such a visit to an opera club, the performer will sometimes sing with the group's orchestra and will distribute tickets as gifts. In turn, the club members respond with corsages and wreaths, adding to these (since the 1950s) "floral" and other creations made from dollar bills.[15]

PEKING-OPERA CLUBS

Chinese of North China origin, whose dialect is Mandarin, have never formed a sizable part of the Chinese population of the San Francisco Bay Area. Those who now reside locally have for the most part immigrated after 1950, having been admitted as parolees who had previously immigrated to Hong Kong from the Mainland. These newer immigrants, typically middle-class merchants and professionals, have generally settled not in Chinatown but in other neighborhoods of the city and surrounding areas. That such individuals have been relatively rare in this area is reflected in the fact that no locally organized performance of Peking opera had been held until the 1960s.

Late in 1960, a lecture-demonstration of Peking-opera techniques was given in Berkeley by Dr. David Huang, a Berkeley radiologist who had immigrated to the United States two years previously. The interest aroused by Dr. Huang's demonstration led to the formation of the Chinese Center Opera Group in the same year. The group held monthly meetings at the Berkeley Chinese Center, an organization founded in 1959 as a volunteer-staffed agency for assistance to newly arrived Chinese immigrants. The Opera Group's meetings were informal, as participants simply met to make music together rather than rehearse for public performance.

In 1963, coinciding with a Peking-opera performance in Berkeley by the Fu Hsing Opera Company of Taiwan, a group of the Center Opera Group members decided to form an independent club which would devote itself to perfecting Peking-opera techniques and to rehearsing for eventual public performances in the Bay Area. The new group found quarters in San Francisco's Chinatown and began holding frequent training sessions and rehearsals. Members pooled their resources to buy costumes and instruments necessary for the mounting of full-scale productions. In 1967 the San Francisco group was incorporated and registered with the State of California as the San Francisco Chinese Opera Association.

In the same year, one faction of the new association resigned to form a separate group, giving itself the name of the Mandarin Opera Society of San Francisco. Other groups have subsequently come into being, as factions have split off from the earlier organizations, so that five distinct Peking-opera clubs were in existence in the Bay Area by the late 1970s. There is frequent interaction among these five and also with the relatively young Peking-opera clubs in Los Angeles, Seattle, and other West Coast cities, and the various associations have given many full-scale opera presentations, together with less formal demonstrations of Peking-opera techniques for civic organizations and educational institutions in the Bay Area.

Markedly different in attitude and approach from the Cantonese societies is the Peking-opera groups' penchant for public performance and goal-directed training and rehearsing (for which, unlike the Cantonese clubs, they collectively own their own theatrical costumes). The Peking-opera clubs are anxious to bring this aspect of Chinese cultural tradition to the attention of non-Chinese as well as to Chinese in the Bay Area.

The meetings of the local Peking-opera clubs are more likely to be intensively musical affairs, less purely social than those of the Cantonese societies. Such contrasts do not extend to the age groups of memberships, however. Like the Cantonese clubs, the Peking-opera groups comprise mostly middle-aged or older individuals. They have not significantly elicited the interest of younger-generation Chinese in carrying on the traditions of Peking opera.

In general, the sociological aspects that characterize members of Peking-opera clubs are those of the Mandarin-speaking community as a whole: largely first-generation, middle-class, often college-educated, and living in outlying residential areas of San Francisco or in suburban communities—rarely in Chinatown itself. Contact between the two types of opera club is almost negligible. There have been a few instances of Cantonese-speaking Chinese who have attended meetings of Peking-opera groups out of curiosity and a desire to extend their understanding of different aspects of Chinese culture. There is no evidence that members of Peking-opera clubs have shown similar interest in the Cantonese opera. In short, there is no significant mixing of the two operatic traditions, just as there is little social interaction of any sort between local Chinese of Northern and Southern backgrounds.

INSTRUMENTAL MUSIC CLUBS

Cantonese orchestral music in the twentieth century appears to be a fairly recent tradition. The Chinese instrumental music clubs that have shown remarkable growth and popularity since the early 1960s stem ultimately from the Cantonese opera, as it appears that Cantonese orchestral music as an independent form developed after the 1911 Revolution, having arisen from the need to provide instrumental interludes between acts of the Cantonese opera and to furnish accompaniment for dancing, battle scenes, and other stage activities.[16] The appearance and growth of instrumental groups outside the opera context since the 1920s in China might well be seen as deriving from Western influence, as Western orchestras and chamber-music groups were encountered in China's larger cities.[17]

In San Francisco, Chinese instrumental music groups were heard as early as 1851 (when an ensemble of six players was hired by the management of the Atheneum Promenade Concerts to perform "a variety of their curious national airs, in their native costume, between the parts of the concert.")[18] Chinese bands have played in parades since the early 1850s.[19] An ensemble rehearsing in a "Chinese Conservatory of Music" was noted by a *Chronicle* reporter in 1877.[20] However, instrumental-group playing in the nineteenth century was overshadowed by the dominant musical life of the Cantonese theater and appears to have played a minor part in the community's musical culture.

The founding of ensembles to play strictly Western music during the second decade of the twentieth century reflects both the general Chinese tendency toward westernization after the 1911 Revolution and the emergence of a small group of American-born Chinese. The pioneer Western-music group was the Cathay Club, which formed its first band in 1911.[21] Shortly thereafter, the Chinatown branch of the Young Men's Christian Association established an orchestra which by 1916 comprised twenty members, including a twelve-piece string section.[22] It was in the 1930s that the greatest proliferation of Western-style groups in Chinatown took place. While music for entertainment and parades was provided by the Cathay Club and other bands in the community (such as those of the Boy Scouts, the Girl Scouts, and the Chung Mei School), the increasingly westernized social life of the community's youth was being accompanied by swing-era dance bands of young Chinese. Parties and amateur shows were enlivened by harmonica bands, including one that was sponsored by the YMCA.[23]

Receiving the most attention and the greatest participation, however, were the numerous drum-and-bugle corps which sprouted up among various organizations, such as the Chinese language schools (whose combined corps numbered 120 in 1938), the YMCA, and

the Chung Mei School.[24] The most attention-getting of the corps
has been the Chinese Girls' Drum Corps, organized in 1940 by the
Paulist Fathers of Old St. Mary's Church. The group, composed of
some fifty girls from ages four to twenty-one, parades in gleaming
red and gold satin costumes, elaborately embroidered with peacocks and flowers, the costumes having been patterned after the
uniforms of the Palace Guard of China's last empress, the dowager
Tsu Hsi of the Ch'ing dynasty.[25]

The drum-and-bugle corps, which continue to flourish in the
present day, have had enormous appeal for Chinatown's young
people. Such ensembles—whose melodic instruments consist of
only bugles and glockenspiels—are within virtually every young
person's reach with respect to musicianship. They owe much of
their attraction to the eye appeal of precision marching and costumes that are similar to the more colorful creations worn by Cantonese-opera stars. The hundreds of youths who participate in these
groups exemplify the love for parades that has been exhibited by
the Chinese community since its very beginning in San Francisco[26]
and continues in the extensive Chinese participation in every civic
parade during the year and makes its most spectacular appearance
in the annual parade in conjunction with the Chinese New Year.

Membership in a drum-and-bugle corps is an important facet of
young Chinatown's social life. (Sometimes it has appeared as a
glamorous alternative to more prosaic activities. For instance, students at the Hip Wo Chinese School in the 1940s who did not participate in parades had to do calligraphy lessons.)[27] The musical
repertoire of the drum-and-bugle corps consists mostly of well-
known popular tunes. Favorites include "When Irish Eyes Are
Smiling," "Chinatown, My Chinatown," and—in recent
years—"I Left My Heart in San Francisco."

In the 1970s several Western-style chamber orchestras were
formed in Chinatown and enjoyed a good measure of popularity
and community support. The Chinese Community Chamber Orchestra was founded in 1973 by conductor and cellist Sidney Wong
and was active for several years. The group of about twenty musicians held weekly rehearsals and gave a number of concerts which
were well attended by the Chinese community. Primarily Chinese in
membership (though strictly Western in instrumentation), the
group included several Caucasians and several Japanese.[28] In con-

cert, the orchestra sometimes joined forces with the Dragon Singers, a Chinese chorus of some forty members, also founded in 1973 and directed by Ting Fai Lam, who had previously taught music in Taiwan and Hong Kong.[29]

In the late 1970s both Western classical music and arrangements of Chinese melodies were rehearsed and performed by the Chinese American Youth Orchestra, conducted by Timothy Chan and sponsored by the Chinese Cultural Foundation. The orchestra was comprised of some twenty-five young Chinese, aged ten to seventeen. From 1974 to 1979, the orchestra gave four or five concerts a year, before having to suspend operations because of funding difficulties. The existence of both the Community and Youth orchestras in the 1970s demonstrated a growing interest by the community in performing Western art music and also reflected a high, often professional-level degree of musicianship among Chinese American conductors and instrumentalists.

Ensembles formed for the purpose of playing *Chinese* music outside the opera setting were, by contrast to the Western-music groups, relatively rare until the 1960s. On two occasions—in 1919 and 1922—the Cathay Club organized ensembles of Chinese instruments, but these were short-lived efforts for specific occasions.[30] The first purely instrumental ensemble of consequence was a Chinese music class established by Old St. Mary's Church in 1934 consisting entirely of girls. This group of eight, half of whom played the yang-ch'in, soon acquired a measure of local fame, in and out of the Chinese community, performing on radio shows and before various civic and fraternal organizations. The players, all in their teens, were featured in the 1936 motion picture, *Grand View of San Francisco*, produced by a group of Chinatown merchants for the upcoming International Exposition in 1939. International publicity was to follow a year later, in 1937, when the St. Mary's class was featured in the Hollywood production, *Stowaway*, starring Shirley Temple.[31]

The Cathay Club. Now existing in semi-retirement is the Cathay Club, the oldest music club in Chinatown. The group was formed in 1911 by teenagers as a marching band with a totally Western repertoire. From its beginnings until 1963, when it ceased its band activities, the club provided music for virtually every major holiday and festive occasion observed in Chinatown. Additionally, it was much in demand for the elaborate funeral processions that have been a part of the Chinatown scene. Its performing members were of high school age for the most part and almost all of American birth. After their years of playing with the band, members would typically maintain their ties with the club. Even today, two decades since the club has existed as a band, the organization has about a hundred "alumni" members who hold meetings from time to time, participate in the club's golf and bowling teams, sponsor social events, and maintain the club's meeting hall. The Cathay Club's headquarters is the largest among Chinatown's music clubs, the only one to have two floors. In the downstairs rehearsal room—now a vacant, cavernous hall empty of chairs or instruments—is the band's library of sheet music, now archived in a large, standing cabinet. Another cabinet holds behind its glass doors an array of trophies from band-competition and athletic events. The walls are lined with photographs of the band performing over the years and of such club events as dances, parties, and anniversary banquets.

In its half-century as a performing organization, the club was locally renowned for the splendor and color that its band added to parades and celebrations. With its active music-making days over, the club now functions socially in a manner not unlike that of the other older clubs in Chinatown. Members have keys to the spacious quarters and drop in whenever it suits them. The large living room on the ground floor, adjoined by a well-equipped kitchen, contains comfortable chairs and couches, a television set, and plentiful reading material.

The Cathay Club's repertoire was always geared to band music by Western composers, with marches, overtures, and concert waltzes providing the bulk of its fare. The band made a notable exception to this approach in 1919, when members of the club decided to form a Chinese-instrument ensemble as a novelty attraction. The club bought two yüeh-ch'ins ("moon guitars"), several bamboo transverse flutes, spike fiddles in two sizes (a hu-ch'in and an erh-hu), a san-hsien (three-stringed "Chinese banjo"), and a set of Chinese percussion instruments. The players were taught the use of the instruments by a local merchant who performed Chinese music as a hobby. A handful of Chinese pieces were learned by the boys, for whom one of the club members made transcriptions from

Chinese number notation into conventional Western staves and symbols.

No direct desires for resuscitating Chinese culture motivated these activities. Rather, this band-within-a-band was formed as a novelty group in preparation for a four-month national tour of vaudeville houses on the Orpheum Circuit. The Chinese-instrument group was typically to provide only one or two numbers within a program of the band's more conventional offerings. Twenty of the Cathay youths participated in this tour, which was widely advertised and successful throughout many cities of the Midwest and South. Directed by a U.S. Navy bandmaster, the group was variously billed as "A Chinese Band," "The Chinese Military Band," and "The Chinese Jazz Band." The last-named title was hardly in keeping with the band's foursquare fare of overtures and marches, interspersed with a Chinese bagatelle, but the youngsters would strive to justify their modish title with an energetic finale of *Trombonium* or another syncopated novelty of the day.

The vaudeville-house tour brought a degree of national fame to the Cathay Club and added considerably to the club's treasury. Only on one occasion, however, did the club venture again into show business. In 1922 the band—now gorgeously arrayed in silk Chinese costumes—played a two-week engagement at San Francisco's Golden Gate Theater. Once again, the ensemble of Chinese instruments added flavor to the program. Chinese music and musical instruments were scarcely less exotic to these American-born bandsmen than to their vaudeville-house audiences, however, and the celestial ensemble—abortive precursor of today's instrumental music clubs—did not survive its brief career as a vaudeville novelty.

For much of its existence, the Cathay Club sponsored a senior band, a junior band, a glee club, and two dance bands (the Cathayans and the Chinatown Knights). The last-named groups were full swing-era dance bands which led a busy professional life during the 1930s and early 1940s. Bowing to coeducational trends, the club also sponsored a girls' auxiliary band, which began in 1939 with twenty-one members. The girls' unit proved enormously popular in subsequent years, trebling its membership by 1942.

The club was nourished in its beginning years by the Six Companies, which had been content previously in sponsoring a conventional drum corps for parades. The Six Companies supplied the band with its first instruments and provided rehearsal space in the companies' headquarters during the first eighteen years of the band's existence. A note in a 1930 commemorative volume published by the club states:

Ever since our first existence, our headquarters has been located at the Chinese Six Companies building, but on August 3, we established our own headquarters at 1038 Powell Street. There had been rumors that the Chinese Six Companies had been supporting our Club all these years, but only as far as rent and lights are concerned. Nevertheless, we have reciprocated this kindness by the services our Band rendered during all those years for the Chinese Six Companies while residing in their building. The benefits in this case are mutual. However, we would like to emphasize the fact that the Chinese Six Companies has been very kind and helpful to us and as a token of our appreciation the service of our organization has and will continue to be, at the disposal of the Six Companies.[32]

A definite Western flavor has pervaded the Cathay Club's activities, musical and otherwise, throughout its existence, though its membership has been exclusively Chinese. Its bylaws, announcements, newsletters, and other printed material have always been in English, though Cantonese has predominated in speech. Its parties, anniversary banquets, and other social functions have usually been held at well-known Western-style restaurants and hotels in the Bay Area. Assimilation to American life-patterns has been a constant motif throughout the life of the club.[33]

Chick Char. If the Cathay Club of 1911 was the pioneer instrumental ensemble for purely Western music in Chinatown, the Chick Char club of 1937–1947 was its counterpart with respect to playing Chinese music on Chinese instruments. Actually a progenitor of both instrumental and Cantonese-opera clubs in the present day, Chick Char provided a training ground for many of the musicians who perform in today's music clubs.

The original impetus for the establishment of the Chick Char club was the outbreak of war between China and Japan in 1937. The club was founded by a group of youthful Chinese who wished to take an active part in promoting China's war effort. To this end, the club's one hundred or so members campaigned for aid to Chinese refugees on the Mainland and demonstrated—with picket signs and music—against ships carrying scrap metal to Japan. With

the outbreak of World War II, their activities extended to supporting the Allied war effort in the Far East in general, with special attention to the morale of American Chinese in the armed services,
through correspondence and sending gift packages to soldiers
abroad. In its various fund-raising drives and other patriotic activities, the club used music extensively, sometimes setting up loudspeakers and performing on street corners, making radio broadcasts, and taking a prominent role in the Rice-Bowl drives of the
late 1930s[34] and in the annual celebrations of "Double Ten" (10
October, the date of the founding of the Chinese Republic in 1911).
Chick Char represented Chinatown musically at the 1939 World's
Fair on Treasure Island. Music was only one of the club's activities,
though the most developed and pervasive one. Members also gave
Western-style plays, without music.

Chick Char in many respects exemplified the adaptation to Western ways that characterized Chinatown's younger generation. From
its beginning in 1937 it consisted of both men and women, the first
"coeducational" music club in the community and one of the first
mixed social clubs of any kind. About half its membership were
American-born Chinese and about one third were women. Almost
all its members were unmarried. In its heyday it was considered the
"young" music club, in contrast to Nam Chung, the "old" group.
Its relation to Nam Chung was filial in nature. Nam Chung members would coach the young ensemble; and Chick Char members
often paid visits to the more prosperous older club for meals after a
night of playing. Many of today's Nam Chung members once be-
longed to Chick Char. (Another active Cantonese-opera club in
present-day Chinatown, Que Gee, is regarded as the direct descendant of the Chick Char club.)

In general, the relationship between these clubs was a manifestation of the general friendliness that superseded intergroup rivalries
during the war years. "During the war," as one Chick Char alum-
nus told me, "everybody was a friend. During the war, we all had
one enemy."

With the end of the war, Chick Char began to dissolve, partly because promoting the war effort was the club's raison d'être, partly
because members were getting married. Unlike the community's
Cantonese-opera clubs, Chick Char did not make a transition between being a social club for young single people and being a gath-

ering place for families. With the war's conclusion, the club's work
was done, and a handful of members furnished an epilogue by publishing a commemorative volume in 1947, in which appeared
photographs of club members and their musical groups, together
with a photograph of every Chinese American serviceman that the
club could find a picture of.[35] A complimentary copy of the book
was sent to the family of every serviceman pictured in it. When the
club was formally disbanded in 1947, its remaining treasury of $400
was given to the local YMCA for the benefit of returning service-
men.

Chick Char had three musical ensembles, which could be catego-
rized as beginning, intermediate, and advanced. For music instruction, it relied largely on the teaching and advice of members of the
older music clubs, such as Nam Chung. The Chick Char repertoire
is described by former members as being "modern," as opposed to
the traditional opera music of, say, Nam Chung. The younger
group's performances would generally consist of a mix of traditional melodies together with contemporary popular songs from Southern China.

The club had no inhibitions about using Western instruments. A
picture of one of the club's performing groups in 1944 reveals that
seven instruments of the twelve-piece group are Western (*two* amplified Hawaiian steel guitars, violin, banjo, tenor saxophone,
xylophone, and vibraharp or marimba—these mixed with yang-
ch'in, two erh-hus, Ch'in-ch'in, and p'i-p'a). Other pictures from
the commemorative volume, however, show different combinations, many of which feature a majority of traditional Chinese instruments. Ubiquitous are the Western violin and the yang-ch'in
(the latter played by women, as is usual in today's Chinatown as
well). The ensembles are often shown in formal Western dress arranged in tiers, as with a swing orchestra, and graced with handsome music stands emblazoned with the club's name. The stands
were for decorative effect for the most part, as sheet music was
rarely used.

The hybrid repertoire and instrumentation of the Chick Char
club must have seemed like the wave of the future to observers in
the late 1930s and early 1940s. The "modernism" of Chick Char
was to become curiously passé, however, as Cantonese-opera clubs

(none of which had been as innovative as Chick Char) followed an opposite trend in the 1950s and actually ceased using what Western instruments they had adopted in the 1930s and 1940s, most notably in the use of the tenor saxophone, which blends effectively with Cantonese-opera sonorities and continues to be used by traveling opera companies.

Most Western instruments, as noted above, went by the wayside in the Cantonese clubs of the 1950s, with the salient exception of the Western violin, which would appear to have become just as "indigenous" to the music of South China as it is to the classical music of South India. With respect to repertoire, current popular songs from Hong Kong are occasionally heard in today's Cantonese-opera clubs, but they are incidental to the main offerings of music from opera scenes. The instrumental music clubs of today, with rare exceptions, conscientiously eschew Western instruments and customarily draw their repertoires from traditional Chinese classics, orchestrated folk songs, and, in some cases, from modern works from the People's Republic of China. Current popular music and other westernized fare from Hong Kong and Taiwan is generally avoided. In contrast with Chick Char, today's music clubs are generally almost self-consciously avoiding direct Western influences—an attitude which may paradoxically indicate a "Western" desire to preserve what is felt to be a pure musical style.

It is conceivable that Chick Char's innovations might indeed have been a wave of the future, if the future had not been subject to more powerful and influential waves, namely those of immigration. In general, the musical climate of Chinatown in the 1930s and early 1940s was a manifestation of a whole generation of American-born Chinese whose gradual westernization was not affected by the sort of fresh infusions of foreign-born Chinese that would profoundly alter the cultural milieu of Chinatown after the repeal of exclusion laws in 1943. Chinatown's youth of the 1930s were searching for an American identity, in contrast to many of today's Chinese youth who seek to rediscover or resuscitate a Chinese identity through social movements and through the arts.

Sealed off in many ways from forces that would renew specifically Chinese traits, the youth of the 1930s were perhaps the most "American" group of Chinese that Chinatown has known. In seeking compatible blends of living-patterns as well as music, the younger generation appears to have been on its way to achieving a significant synthesis of styles, and—had not demographic changes intervened—Chinatown might well have seen an evolution of style that would have followed a path similar to that of musics of other migrant groups whose music shows identifiable change from generation to generation. As it happened, this trend was rather abruptly cut off: There would be no Sino-American blend that would be more than the sum of its parts. With the superficial exception of westernized Chinese popular music, no real musical syncretism has taken place. The Chick Char club, with its remarkable "modernisms," was presaging an accultured Chinese American music that in reality would never be.

Instrumental Clubs since the 1960s. In 1961 Ho Ming-chung, a versatile musician and teacher from Taiwan, visited the United States for six months. In the course of his visit he gave Chinese-instrument lessons in San Francisco and formed a Chinese-music ensemble, which met at the Chinese Recreation Center in Chinatown. After Ho's return to Taiwan, the group continued to meet for weekly rehearsals and gave itself the name "Chinese Classical Music Club." Using sheet music from Hong Kong and also arrangements by Lawrence Lui, one of the club's founders, the group assembled a repertoire of works of both northern and southern Chinese origin. The club would perform frequently during the Chinese New Year period and was invited to perform for the Chinese Chamber of Commerce, for family-association events, for public schools, and for such institutions as Stanford University and the state universities of San Francisco and San Jose. The members also made radio and television appearances. From an original membership of seven, the group grew in size to about twenty-five members.

At the time of its optimum membership, in 1971, the club experienced a breakup of personnel, and several splinter groups were formed by former members of the original club. The group that continues to hold the title of the Chinese Classical Music Club rehearses in its rented quarters, meeting informally on weekend nights. While maintaining a repertoire of older traditional music, this group has been devoting increasing attention to current popular songs that emanate from Hong Kong and Taiwan. Several female vocalists regularly sing with the group, using the microphone and sound system that is set up in the club. In performing current, commercially popular selections, the group sometimes makes use of such Western instruments as the amplified guitar, the Hawaiian steel guitar, and Western-style trap drums. In the summer of 1973 a group of the club members, featuring a female vocalist and announcer, played weekend professional engagements in a local nightclub which offered occasional Chinese, Japanese, and Korean musical acts.[36] In their professional work at the nightclub, the players used a program comprising classical Chinese instrumental music and popular and traditional songs sung by the female vocalist.

Adhering to a more conservative repertoire is the Chinese Music Association, which was started in the early 1970s by former members of the Classical Music Club. The newer group meets for frequent rehearsals at the headquarters of a family association to which several of its players belong. Neither Western instruments nor westernized Chinese popular music is encountered with this group, whose practice sessions are characterized by a sense of concentration and intensity of purpose rarely evidenced in other Chinatown clubs. Most of the group's sheet music has been arranged by Lawrence Lui, a member of the ensemble, often as transcriptions of instrumental music recordings from Mainland China. Both the original Classical Music Club and this newer offshoot make much use of the p'i-p'a lute and the koto-like cheng, instruments rarely heard in the opera clubs. The newer group sometimes finds a use for the shrill sonorities of the hu-ch'in, the principal melodic instrument of Peking opera, in arrangements from that genre. Also notable in the newer group is the use of the ancient Chinese mouth organ, the sheng, an instrument of Northern preference which is seldom heard in Chinatown ensembles. Both the original Classical Music Club and the more recent association were founded by middle-aged musicians, but both groups include a number of younger members, some in their teens.

Still another faction that had split off from the original club turned its collective attention to the training and rehearsing of musicians to accompany the Chinese Folk Dance Association, a group of young dancers who in their previous activities had had to rely on tapes and phonograph recordings for musical accompaniment. The musicians in the accompanying ensemble meet once a week with the dancers and also hold separate rehearsals twice weekly, one of the latter meetings being devoted to the accompaniment of a choral group. The twenty-odd instrumentalists in this ensemble are carefully coached and are painstaking with regard to intonation and group coordination. It is one of Chinatown's most youthful ensembles. Most of its players are in their twenties and thirties. To a greater degree than is the case with most other groups in Chinatown, this orchestra's repertoire reflects the contemporary trends in Mainland Chinese music. Most of the repertoire has been transcribed directly from Mainland recordings.

The Flowing Stream Ensemble. The best publicized of Chinatown's instrumental groups over the past decade has been the Flowing Stream Ensemble, whose repertoire is Chinese, as are majority of its members (American-born). The group has also included black, Caucasian, and Japanese players. All of its musicians are also experienced in Western art music, and several also perform professionally in jazz.[37] The group's inception stems from an eight-week instructional session in Chinese instruments held in the summer of 1971 by David Ming-yueh Liang, then a member of the faculty of the San Francisco Conservatory of Music. Subsequently, several members of Dr. Liang's group—the sisters Betty and Shirley Wong—gathered together the musicians who would become known as the Flowing Stream Ensemble.

In the succeeding years, the ensemble has been managed by the Wong sisters and coached by Leo Lew, an experienced performer and scholar of Chinese music, who serves as the group's music director. These three individuals form the core of the ensemble, whose total membership in 1980 numbered thirteen, though not all these perform in every concert. The ensemble has performed extensively throughout the San Francisco Bay Area in concerts and in conjunction with dance presentations. Its repertoire is eclectic, reflecting both northern and southern Chinese styles, and its instrumentation is entirely Chinese, including flutes, spike fiddles, the yang-ch'in, the cheng, and the sheng. The Wong sisters and others in the group have also been actively involved in teaching classes in Chinese instruments for children and young adults, through the sponsorship of such agencies as the San Francisco Community Music Center and the East Bay Center for the Performing Arts.

One aspect of the Flowing Stream Ensemble's work which appears to characterize this group alone among local Chinese ensembles is the compositional activities of its members. Several in the group compose works for Chinese instruments, and some of these pieces have become incorporated into the ensemble's repertoire. Experiments in collective improvisation have also engaged their attention. At rehearsals, the ensemble's concentration on the work at hand is not unlike that of a Western chamber-music group. The players' precision and discipline, which contrast with the somewhat more casual approach of the older Chinese groups, particularly the Cantonese-opera societies, reflects the players' rigorous backgrounds in Western art music.

The Flowing Stream Ensemble's performances are usually for the public at large rather than for exclusively Chinese audiences. One of its players has noted that the interracial nature of the group initially caused some difficulties in its gaining acceptance by the older Chinese in the community. The musicians feel, however, that the ensemble's participation in the Chinese New Year festivities in 1973 marked its acceptance by the Chinese community in general. Several musicians from older instrumental clubs in Chinatown have assisted the group, providing both coaching and musical arrangements. Despite its new departures, the ensemble thus maintains links and continuity with more settled traditions in the musical community.

Another group, the Phoenix Spring Ensemble, was formed in the late 1970s as an experimental arm of the Flowing Stream Ensemble. Founded and directed by Betty Wong, the Phoenix Spring Ensemble presents music from a variety of traditions (including Chinese, Indian, and medieval European), together with original works by local composers, many of them Asian-American. The programs of the newer group often assume the character of multimedia events, bringing in elements of dance, poetry, and theater as well as music.[38] The group brings into sharper focus the compositional and cross-cultural interests that have characterized its parent ensemble from its beginning.

CONTINUITY OF CHINESE MUSIC TRADITIONS IN MUSIC CLUBS

Though texts for singers are written down and there is some use of musical notation by its performers, Cantonese opera is essentially an oral-tradition music, as is Peking opera. Opera styles are continued through apprenticeship training. It would appear that there is no other route to real excellence in the art than the training given during the years, from childhood on, spent in full-time apprentice practice and observation by aspirants to the profession. For amateurs, a certain amount can be learned through listening and watching, but ultimately a teacher will be necessary to impart whatever techniques can be learned by even a part-time devotee. It is possible to take Chinese-opera lessons in Chinatown without belonging to a music club. However, opera is inherently a group experience, and being in a group of like-minded individuals serves to provide a helpful milieu for the development of techniques.

As mentioned, every opera club has at least one member who has had experience on the professional stage. The teaching in the clubs is often (but not always) done by such professionals. One present-day opera club—Chung Sing—exists specifically because of the influence of a teacher who taught for a period in the Bay Area and left behind an alumni group who organized to carry on their teacher's traditions. Another club—Hoy Fung—accepts students from outside its membership, its teacher being the club's current president, who meets with his students at the club headquarters.

The largest club, Nam Chung, does not officially include lessons in its activities but is nonetheless probably the most educationally significant of the music associations, insofar as it is the most active musically: Weekend nights offer continuous singing and playing, in which guests and long-time friends of the club as well as members may participate. Here the amateur can sing with a good-sized orchestra, always presided over by a knowledgeable drummer-leader, and practice his or her art in a friendly and receptive ambience. There is of course also the opportunity to watch other, more seasoned performers in action. One can observe, for instance, the method of signaling by specific hand gestures to the drummer for a change in rhythmic patterns. One can also watch working professionals in action, as performers from Hong Kong, Singapore, and elsewhere who happen to be in San Francisco will often make it a point to sing at Nam Chung. Also, as previously mentioned, individuals who were formerly on the professional stage in China or Hong Kong and have immigrated are performing members or frequent guests of Nam Chung.

The visits of professionals and active amateurs from abroad serve to keep music-club members in current touch with trends and developments in the Cantonese opera. Such contact is also achieved through travels in the opposite direction by club members who make visits to the Far East. One such visitor, a Nam Chung member, has for years carried on a cassette-tape correspondence with a professional opera performer in Hong Kong. Through this medium they exchange ideas, with impromptu musical demonstrations, and news about musical developments in Cantonese and other regional opera styles.

In various ways, music clubs thus serve a function in keeping Cantonese-opera traditions alive and in reflecting trends from abroad. Other roles in such continuity are played by phonograph records, movies of opera (only rarely supplementing the usual fare of martial-arts movies in today's Chinatown theaters), and miscellaneous magazines and newspapers from the Far East which feature stories and pictures of Cantonese opera and its stars.

The educative role of Peking-opera clubs for their members is somewhat similar. As with the Cantonese clubs, formal and informal teaching must take the place of the apprenticeship that has been the traditional route to the professional stage. Former professionals from both Taiwan and the Mainland play important teaching roles in all the Bay Area's Peking-opera clubs.

Teaching in the instrumental music clubs is done mainly in the studios of certain members who devote their spare time to such instruction. A principal difference between these clubs and the opera groups is the use of notated music, with which the student has a basis from which to practice.[39] A certain continuity of music traditions within the community is maintained as members of older clubs serve as teachers and informal coaches for the more youthful instrumental groups, such as the Flowing Stream Ensemble and the orchestra of the Chinese Folk Dance Association.

Somewhat in a genre of its own is the music-drama that emanated from the Mainland during the Great Proletarian Cultural Revolution of the 1960s and 1970s. Such operas as *The Red Lantern*, *On the Docks*, and *Taking of Tiger Mountain by Strategy* were readily available in full score, libretto, and phonograph recordings at several of the local stores, together with scores and records for such other productions as the ballets *The White Haired*

Girl and *The Red Detachment of Women*. Although such works enjoyed a degree of local popularity, particularly among the younger Chinese, there has been no effort to date to mount a production of any of the modern music-dramas from the Mainland. Smaller-scale vocal music from the People's Republic, however, has been used by several of the groups (such as the Chinese Progressive Association and the singers in the Chinese Folk Dance group), and orchestral works from the Mainland—such as the *Yellow River Concerto* (transcribed for small orchestra)—are performed by the orchestra for the Chinese Folk Dance Association. The dissemination of modern Communist music-drama, however, is mainly through the media of records, radio, and film, not through personal participation of members of the local Chinese community.

As a rule, the learning of Chinese instruments by young people is not initially through music clubs but through private lessons and also through group classes for beginners, which are sponsored by such organizations as the Community Music Center, the Chinatown YWCA, and the Chinese Recreation Center. A degree of mutual learning is found also in the informal groups of musicians, including beginners, who simply get together for practice in varying numbers. The Chinese Library of America has for some time been a much-used gathering place for such musicians. Courses in playing Chinese instruments are also occasionally available at area colleges and universities. Among those which have sponsored such programs are the University of California, Berkeley, and the San Francisco Conservatory of Music. Lessons on Chinese instruments have also been offered by the Center for World Music in Berkeley, which opened in 1974.

SOCIAL INTEGRATION IN MUSIC CLUBS

Every type of music club in the Chinese community can be seen as socially integrative in some respects, nonintegrative in others. The Cantonese-opera clubs, for instance, appear to be decidedly nonintegrative, as they are closed, and consist of private groups of immigrants, for the most part, rarely communicating except in the

Cantonese dialect. Thus, whatever other social considerations may apply, membership is extremely unlikely for a Chinese who speaks only Mandarin or English. Yet such clubs are integrative on another level, as they bring together individuals of different family backgrounds and villages of Kwangtung whose families might lack other occasions to meet, just as do social clubs in the community that are based on, for instance, golf, photography, and chess. It should be borne in mind in any case that while such clubs do cut across family and regional lines, any prospective new member must be introduced and sponsored by at least one or two present members, and thus the base is somewhat narrowed for prospective newcomers to the clubs.

That opera-music clubs do not bring together northern and southern Chinese has been discussed above. Exceptions to this prevailing separation of styles and social functions are negligible. However, in instrumental music clubs (predominantly Cantonese in membership), one does find northern, Mandarin-speaking Chinese, even as full-fledged club members. Also, one occasionally encounters a Mandarin-speaking guest from abroad performing in one of the instrumental ensembles. The repertoire of such groups is more regionally heterogeneous than is the case in opera clubs, and notated music is used, so that language problems are minimized.

With respect to the integration of different age groups in music clubs, one finds a definite mix of generations in appreciable degree only in the instrumental music clubs, as few opera-club members are under the age of forty. In the instrumental groups, however, one may find teenagers playing alongside middle-aged and elderly musicians.

One will look in vain for non-Chinese in the music clubs, however, even as guests. Several of the basement clubs do leave their doors open during rehearsals, thus occasionally attracting a curious tourist. Such a visitor rarely stays for long, however, and his presence goes unacknowledged. It has been noted that several of the instrumental ensembles (not clubs as such) have contained non-Chinese members. Generally, however, Caucasians and other non-Chinese are simply not part of the picture in Chinatown's musical activities. Whatever limited degree of social integration is served by music clubs does not include integration outside the ethnic fold.

OUTLOOK FOR CONTINUITY AND DEVELOPMENT OF MUSIC CLUBS

It would seem a safe speculation that the same forces that gradually caused a decline of the professional Cantonese opera in San Francisco will continue to make inroads on the potentials of Cantonese-opera clubs. An argument could be made that the removal of professional opera from the scene has given, over the short term, a bit of *increased* life to clubs. One might cite the possibility that an individual's time once spent at the opera theater will be spent instead at his opera club. Additionally, the resident professional performers of Cantonese opera who are perforce in retirement might well be expected to have increased time in which to enliven the meetings of music clubs and to provide instruction for club members.

In some scattered cases it may indeed be true that the former opera-goer will now have more time for his club, but it remains that the same competitive entertainment offerings—notably television and the movies—that hastened the demise of the professional opera might reasonably be expected to monopolize the recreational hours of club members. As to whether former professionals would now channel their energies toward improving opera clubs, one may see some evidence of such activity in present-day clubs, as former professionals give the benefit of their experience to the amateur performers. Such observations apply, however, principally to those performers forced into premature retirement by the decline of the full-time theater in San Francisco. Others who have retired because of age or other factors would presumably be playing a key role in music clubs in any case. The time exigencies of the younger retirees must be taken into account: In some cases, female performers have left the stage to marry and raise a family, often moving far from the Chinatown milieu and thus the music clubs; male performers typically have taken on other work full time and, again, may have relocated far from their former professional terrain.

In a sense, Cantonese-opera clubs have been the victims of demographic trends. During the nearly one hundred years in which professional Chinese theater flourished in San Francisco, the character of Chinatown was marked by both its insular position as an ethnic enclave and by its great preponderance of males, either unattached or far from wife and family. In this "bachelor society," opera clubs thrived and the opera theater was the Chinese entertainment attraction par excellence. (As one older Chinese stated to this observer: "Where else could you go?") Only since the end of World War II has the balance of sexes—owing to immigration-law revision—changed to allow for patterns of marriage and family life denied earlier residents of Chinatown. The remaining opera clubs now serve as an adjunct to family life rather than as a substitute for it, and the continuous exodus of newly middle-class Chinese to more distant neighborhoods narrows the base of the population from which the Cantonese clubs would draw their active membership.

The destiny of the Cantonese-opera clubs is of course dependent on the tastes and attitudes of the younger Chinese. We have noted earlier that very few Chinese under the age of forty belong to such clubs or indeed show any appreciable interest in Cantonese opera. The young American-born Chinese, in addition to being affected by the cultural currents that create trends for American youth in general, have often grown up in areas outside of Chinatown, away from a milieu that gives constant exposure to Chinese speech, attitudes, and outlooks. In short, the rate of assimilation into the larger American community is accelerated. Cantonese is often no longer the language of choice. Most American-born Chinese do learn Cantonese in infancy and early childhood, but many later cease to use the language except for communicating with older relatives and retain only a limited functional vocabulary. Many Chinese youths, especially in generations beyond the second, speak no Cantonese at all. Thus American-born Chinese, to whom the language of the Cantonese opera may be in part or totally incomprehensible, cannot be expected to be attracted to this form or to the clubs that foster its existence.

Nor do youths who are recent immigrants from South China evidence significant interest in traditional opera, although the language itself is obviously no problem to them. Their dramatic tastes are generally limited to the movies, and if they show interest in Chinese music at all, it is likely to be for the present-day westernized popular music of Hong Kong and (in fewer cases) the vocal and instrumental music of the People's Republic.[40]

As has been emphasized in a previous chapter, Cantonese opera has by no means ceased to be a living dramatic form. Although this regional genre was suppressed from the middle 1960s until recent years in Communist China, there has been an ongoing, if declining, professional theatrical tradition in other areas dominated by Cantonese, most notably in Hong Kong.[41] The tenacity of this tradition, in the face of both Western and Communist Chinese competitive entertainment forms, is evidenced in San Francisco not only by the sporadic visits of Cantonese-opera troupes and the activities of music clubs but by the continuing sales of opera-music recordings and the playing of opera selections over several local radio stations which broadcast in Cantonese.

It remains, however, that the cultural and commercial interest in Cantonese opera in San Francisco is almost exclusively among the middle-aged and older. While an obituary for Cantonese-opera clubs at present would be decidedly premature, one looks in vain for an emerging constituency that would carry on the clubs' traditions twenty or thirty years from now.

The outlook for Peking-opera clubs would appear to be similarly presaged, as the lack of a present youthful membership does not bode well for these groups' ultimate future, however vigorous their activities may be in the present day. As with Cantonese opera, traditional Peking opera was a temporary victim of the Cultural Revolution on the Chinese Mainland, although its traditions were continued to some degree in Taiwan under government sponsorship. Thus the Peking-opera clubs have lacked both a living cultural counterpart on the Mainland and a generation of younger members who could be expected to keep the clubs' traditions alive in future decades.

One area in which both types of opera clubs may be expected to play an increasing role during the coming years is in explaining and demonstrating their respective musical and dramatic traditions for such institutions as universities and educational radio and television. Factors that might well precipitate increased activities in this direction include the generally increased interest in Chinese culture that has followed in the wake of improved political relations between the United States and the People's Republic of China. Also, in recent years an upsurge in interest in affirming their Chinese identity can be seen in many Chinese who are American-born and feel a desire to learn about their Chinese cultural heritage.

In line with such interests are the activities of the Chinese Cultural Foundation, established in San Francisco in 1965. The foundation has enlisted the services of music clubs in the past and intends to seek their continuing help. Members of music clubs have been invited to perform at meetings of the foundation, and Cantonese-opera selections were sung by music-club members at opening ceremonies for the foundation's auditorium in the fall of 1973. In subsequent years, Cantonese operas have been presented—with running explanations in Cantonese and English—by music-club performers in the new auditorium. From 1974 to 1979 the foundation sponsored the Chinese American Youth Orchestra, and it has also scheduled lectures and workshops in both Chinese instrumental music and Cantonese opera.

While professional Cantonese opera can still earn its way in Hong Kong, and Peking opera's traditions are continued in Taiwan (and presently are being resuscitated on the Mainland), the presentation of such performances in full scale by amateurs for a large audience in American cities can be done effectively only with the help and participation of professionals, whether active or retired. As interest has declined in traditional opera genres, however, both the demand for such entertainment and the supply of seasoned performers to provide it continue to diminish year by year. If there is no reversal of this trend, once can envisage someday the virtual impossibility of staging traditional operas except in a most superficial fashion, as neither opera type has an adequate written and notated tradition to allow for staging without the presence of professionals who have been apprenticed at an early age.

The functions served by the Cantonese-opera clubs as social gathering places have similarly declined, as we have seen, as home and family life have changed the social habits of Chinatown's former bachelor society and as families have acquired the means to move away from Chinatown. The removal of discriminatory laws against Chinese has made less necessary the protective nature of the urban ghetto while simultaneously helping to facilitate the finding of homes and jobs elsewhere. Both as musical and social institutions, the opera clubs may be viewed as a holdover from an earlier time. At present there would appear to be little reason to predict their survival beyond the lives of their present membership.

In contrast to both types of opera clubs, the instrumental music associations of Chinatown continue to attract youthful members, both immigrant and American-born, who devote much time to the rehearsal of ensemble works, both for the sheer pleasure of playing and for public performance. An aspiring player in such groups needs neither a command of Cantonese nor an ingrained knowledge of esoteric musical and dramatic customs. Thus the door is open to American-born Chinese whose working language is English and to those Chinese who speak dialects other than Cantonese. With both instruments and instruction readily available in the Chinese community, together with the interest and inspiration provided by recordings and broadcasts of high-quality instrumental music from the Mainland, Taiwan, and Hong Kong, there is both the stimulus and the means for young Chinese to become participants in ensembles. A bright and active future for such groups would seem assured, as both the music itself and the desire thus to perpetuate a proud ethnic identity find wide interest among the community's youth. In the words of one young member of the Chinese Classical Music Club:

Times have changed. Cultural involvement in this community used to be only for the older generation. The young generation had nothing to do with it. We were taught that the white culture was the "correct" culture. But now, the American-born Chinese are not afraid or . . . ashamed of their own cultural heritage. In fact they even want to participate in it.[42]

NOTES

1. Most of the information for this chapter has been gathered through interviews and conversations with individuals in the Chinese community, a number of whom I have mentioned in the Preface. For detailed information on specific areas I am indebted to Mabel L. Quon (Cantonese-opera clubs), Dr. David Huang (Peking-opera clubs), and Lawrence P.L. Lui(instrumental music clubs). Information on the Cathay Club has come largely from Thomas Lym, who was one of the club's founders in 1911. Gang C. Woo has provided most of the information about the Chick Char club, in which he was an active member. Betty Wong, one of the founders of the Flowing Stream Ensemble, has kindly supplied information on that group's history. An earlier version of this chapter appears as the article, "Music Clubs and Ensembles in San Francisco's Chinese Community," in *Eight*

Urban Musical Cultures: Tradition and Change, ed. Bruno Nettl (Urbana, University of Illinois Press, 1978), pp. 223–59.

2. A recent exception is Chun-kin Leung, "Notes on Cantonese Opera in North America," *CHINOPERL Papers* 7 (1977), pp. 9–21, in which the author concentrates on a Cantonese-opera club in Toronto.

3. In the United States, only Honolulu, with a reported 10.9 percentage of Chinese, exceeds San Francisco's officially recorded 8.2 per cent. Data derived from United States Bureau of the Census (1970 Census of Population, Subject Reports), *Japanese, Chinese, and Filipinos in the United States* (Washington, D.C., Government Printing Office, 1973).

4. Richard Springer, "The Migration to the Other Chinatown," *East-West*, 27 March 1974, p. 1; 10 April 1974, p. 1. See also Victor G. Nee and Brett de Bary Nee, *Longtime Californ'* (New York, Pantheon, 1972), p. xxiii.

5. Alien Land Acts prevented the Chinese from owning property until 1947, and restrictive covenants further served to limit their residence to Chinatown. Betty Lee Sung, *Mountain of Gold* (New York, Macmillan, 1967), pp. 238, 250.

6. The organization of American Chinese communities is detailed in Sung, pp. 134–39; Rose Hum Lee, *The Chinese in the United States of America* (Hong Kong, Hong Kong University Press, 1960), pp. 132–41; and Stanford M. Lyman, *Chinese Americans* (New York, Random House, 1974), pp. 29–53. The relationships of such organizations with the urban organization in traditional China is discussed in Lawrence W. Crissman, "The Segmentary Structure of Urban Overseas Chinese Communities," *Man* 2 (1967), pp. 185–204.

7. See, e.g., Chester, "Village Life in Old China," *East-West*, 26 March 1975, p. 6.

8. They are (with their dates of founding): Nam Chung (1925), Ngi Yeh (1937, 1938), Flying Dragon (1942), Que Gee (1942), Hoy Fung (1943), and Chung Sing (1970). Ngi Yeh represents a merger in 1948 of the Ngi Kun and Jue Yeh clubs, which had been founded respectively in 1937 and 1938.

9. "Chinese Music: The Flying Dragon Musical Club Plays the Yung-kum, the Yea Woo, the Jong and Pi-pa," *Life* 15 (15 November 1943), pp. 81–84; Alfred Frankenstein, "Flying Dragons and Sounds of Silver and Fine Wood," *This World* (*Chronicle* magazine), 7 March 1943, pp. 23, 30.

10. See above, p. 185.

11. And local amateurs, in turn, were eventually allowed to sit in with the orchestra at professional opera performances. See Frankenstein, "Flying Dragons," p. 23.

12. Nam Chung Musical Society, *Nam Chung* (in Chinese, San Francisco, 1945).

13. See Frankenstein, "Flying Dragons," p. 23.

14. Sung, p. 82.

15. See above, p. 185.

16. Him Mark Lai, "Cantonese Music," *East-West*, 26 May 1971, p. 5.

17. Rulan Chao Pian, "China," *Harvard Dictionary of Music*, 2d ed. (Cambridge, Mass., Harvard University Press, 1969), p. 153.

18. G.R. MacMinn, *Theater of the Golden Era of California* (Caldwell, Idaho, Caxton, 1941), p. 496.

19. "The Celestials at Home and Abroad," *Blackwell's Magazine* 72 (1852), pp. 98–113.

20. *Chronicle*, 29 April 1877.

21. See below, pp. 205–8.

22. Thomas W. Chinn, ed., *Historical Sketch Fiftieth Anniversary Chinese YMCA* (San Francisco, Young Men's Christian Association, 1961), p. 13.

23. Ibid., p. 14.

24. *Chronicle*, 17 June 1938.

25. Jim Walls, "Manchu Marchers on Parade," *Bonanza* (*Chronicle* magazine), 15 March 1959, pp. 8–9.

26. With the much-admired marching of the "China Boys" in 1850 and their subsequent participation in parades for holidays and civic events. H.H. Bancroft, *Retrospections, Political and Personal* (New York, The Bancroft Co., 1912), pp. 346–48; Frank Soulé, John H. Gihon, and James Nisbet, *The Annals of San Francisco* (New York, D. Appleton, 1855), p. 288.

27. *East-West*, 19 September 1973.

28. "Chamber Orchestra for San Francisco's Chinese Community," *East-West*, 5 September 1973.

29. Eliza Chan, "Oakland Concert Repeats in S.F.," *East-West*, 12 November 1975, p. 11.

30. See below, pp. 206–7.

31. *Chinese Digest*, 27 November 1937, pp. 3, 5, 14.

32. Cathay Music Club, *Cathay Chimes* (San Francisco, 1930, unpaged).

33. The first twenty-five years of the Cathay Club are surveyed by Herbert J. Haim in a four-part article, "Cathay Club of San Francisco," *Chinese Digest*, 20 March 1936 (p. 11), 27 March 1936 (p. 9), 3 April 1936 (p. 11), and 10 April 1936 (p. 11). See also "Thank You, Cathay!" (editorial), *Chinese Digest*, 15 May 1936, p. 8.

34. See above, p. 156.

35. Chick Char Musical Club, *Memoir* (in Chinese, San Francisco, 1947).

36. "Multi-purpose Theatre-restaurant Debuts," *East-West*, 13 June 1973, p. 4.

37. "Jazz, Chinese Music Featured in Concert," *East-West*, 2 May 1973, p. 4.

38. Valerie Samson, "The Phoenix Spring Ensemble," *EAR* 6:3 (May-June 1978), pp. 1-2.

39. In all cases the notation is in a system, much used in modern Chinese music, based on scale-degree numbers (in arabic numerals). Western staff notation is familiar to most of the musicians, but it is not used in the local ensembles.

40. Chinatown youth are described in Stanford M. Lyman, "Red Guard on Grant Avenue: The Rise of Youthful Rebellion in Chinatown," *Trans-Action* 7 (1970), pp. 21-34. Reprinted in Stanley Sue and Nathaniel N. Wager, eds., *Asian-Americans: Psychological Perspectives* (Palo Alto, Science & Behavior Books, 1973), pp. 20-44.

41. Manchester Fu, "Manny, Celestial," *East-West*, 12 August 1970, p. 3; Ken Wong, "The Orient Express," *East-West*, 9 August (p. 3) and 23 August (p. 3) 1972.

42. Wilma Pang, quoted in *East-West*, 21 March 1973.

Summary and Conclusion

The musical activities and tastes of San Francisco's Chinatown present an anomaly among long-established ethnic communities in American cities: The musical culture, in large measure, continues to be an imported one—in spite of the community's long history of settlement. Just as the prevailing language in Chinatown is Cantonese (or rather the dialects that are collectively referred to as that), Chinatown's tastes in music are largely geared to the music of present-day southern China and Hong Kong. Here we see not a museum-like preservation of traditions but rather a continuous sharing of musical tastes and developments from the homeland. As such, this musical insularity is part and parcel of the set-apart, "extraterritorial" character that is suggested by the very name "Chinatown" and which owes its existence in part to the singular circumstances under which Chinese have immigrated to the United States and to the treatment they have received here.

On the face of it, it would seem remarkable indeed that a settlement of over a century differs little in musical life from the areas from which its people have emigrated. But the demographic changes that would cause the dying out of musical traditions or the blending of such traditions with those of the New World have simply not existed with the American Chinese. This situation stems in large part from a lack of generational continuity. America's Chinese immigrants of the nineteenth century, with rare exceptions, did not marry or raise children in this country. Those who returned to the homeland raised their families there. Those who could not return typically lived out their days in a celibate existence. Without a continuity of generations, a hybrid musical tradition could not take root.

The insulated nature of Chinatown's musical culture is also a function of the community's own desire for separateness. As a people who carried their culture traits and social organization with them, the Chinese have traditionally sought to maintain an autonomous existence within their urban enclave, and this tendency had been strongly reinforced by the restrictions placed upon them by white society. The denial of rights as to employment, residence, and ownership of real property served to alienate the Chinese from the prevailing society in any case. The development of a regionally distinctive musical culture was prevented by circumstances both internal and external. Within Chinatown's own society, the making of music was not regarded as a proper sort of full-time activity, certainly not as a career that an ambitious sojourner might aspire to. Hence no professional class of musicians ever arose in the community. And the apartheid that existed between the Chinese and white communities effectively prevented a mixing of musical traditions.

Thus the musical culture of the Chinese community throughout the nineteenth century and much of the twentieth has been simply that of China itself, or rather that of its southern regions. The Cantonese opera that toured San Francisco and other communities in California was unchanged from China. Directly derivative from it was the singing and playing in gambling houses, restaurants, and brothels—again a direct import of the practices of singsong girls and other professional entertainers in China itself. Ritual music of funerals and celebrations was kept as intact as the ritual events themselves. Aside from the participation of some Chinese in Chinatown's Christian churches, the Chinese community had no use for Western compositions, Western instruments, or Western attitudes about music. In general there were no significant changes in musical activities of the Chinese community in the nineteenth century that were not directly due to the rise and fall of population in Chinatown.

The destruction of Chinatown by earthquake and fire in 1906 brought an abrupt end to certain facets of musical activity in the community. Certain settings for music—such as gambling halls and brothels—would simply not reappear, at least on a scale that would support professional musical entertainment. The fortunes of organized gambling and prostitution were dwindling in any case, owing both to the depletion of Chinatown's population and to the increasing condemnation of such practices by the white community. The 1906 catastrophe simply speeded up the process, wiping out in a few hours those settings which were destined to be eliminated in a few years anyway. The Chinatown that was rebuilt was more respectable in Western eyes, shorn of many of the features that had given the older neighborhood both a sinister notoriety and a setting for musical entertainment.

Chinatown's theaters were similarly removed from the scene by the destruction of 1906, but this loss was only temporary. Cantonese opera appeared almost immediately in the refugee settlement of Oakland, in which much of the displaced community took shelter as Chinatown was being rebuilt, and the Chinese theater returned to Chinatown itself as the residents returned to the rebuilt community. However, the theater was not to find permanent quarters until the mid-1920s, when two Chinese theaters were built, and the intervening years were relatively lean for the Cantonese opera. With a population sharply reduced from the heyday years of the late nineteenth century, the Chinese community was not large enough to support the kind of continuously operating theaters that had characterized the neighborhood for so many years. In the twentieth century, the theater would also have to meet the competition of motion pictures, which had made their appearance even before the new Chinatown was built. From the time of the earthquake until the completion of the Mandarin Theater in 1924, the Cantonese opera led a sort of vagabond existence, performing in various Western theaters and in tents.

With the completion of two theaters for Chinese opera in the mid-1920s, the genre experienced an upsurge of popularity and publicity. For the first time, female opera stars began to appear in significant numbers and were often the principal box-office attraction. The 1920s and 1930s were also to see the introduction of

Western instruments into Cantonese-opera orchestras and the use of Western stage properties and in some cases even modern-day costuming.

Such modernizations were indicative more of developments in China itself than of influences felt in America. However, the 1920s and 1930s did see some interesting innovations in Chinatown's musical culture, owing to the emergence of an American-born generation of Chinese. Ensembles for performing Western-style music became increasingly popular, particularly during the 1930s. The community saw the formation of many marching bands and drum-and-bugle corps, which enlivened parades for both Chinese and Western holiday occasions. Swing-era dance bands made up entirely of Chinese youths were much in demand for parties and dances through the 1930s. A fusion of Chinese and Western traditions was present in the music of the Chick Char club, whose repertoire consisted of both traditional Chinese songs and modern-day Chinese popular music, and the group made extensive use of Western instruments in conjunction with Chinese instruments. In both the marching bands and Chick Char's hybrid music, the Chinese community was finally reflecting in musical fashion a partial acculturation to American ways after many decades of near-total insularity.

The war years—which for the Chinese really began in the late 1930s—were to have much impact on Chinatown's morale, economy, and musical activities. The common adversary of Japan served to draw the community together for a common purpose, and there was much occasion for music and the cooperation of various music clubs and ensembles for such events as the Rice-Bowl parties of the late 1930s and war-bond drives in the 1940s. With the coming of World War II, many Chinese found that a larger job market was open to them, and there was an increase in money in circulation for leisure and entertainment. Western-style nightclubs sprang up in Chinatown, and there was a proliferation of private music clubs. The Chinese theater operated throughout the war years, its actors and musicians being prevented from returning to China by the war.

With the repeal of Exclusion legislation in 1943 and the steady liberalizing of immigration policies in the years to come, the Chinese community experienced a pronounced change in its social makeup. Women were becoming an important part of the picture, as war brides, other immigrants, and American-born Chinese women increasingly provided the opportunity for marriage and family life. The lifting of restrictive covenants allowed Chinese to move to residential districts of San Francisco. No longer would the theater have the captive clientele of an all-male audience that was restricted to the ghetto, and music clubs lost much of their role as a social gathering place for unattached males. By 1950 the Chinese theater, as a continuously operating enterprise, was a thing of the past, although Cantonese opera would continue to make occasional appearances as touring companies would visit for a week or two at a time.

Since the 1940s the focus of Chinatown's musical life has shifted from the professional theater to the community's amateur music-making activities. Although Cantonese-opera clubs are no longer as musically active as they were in the war years, many have adjusted to serving primarily as social clubs, the transition reflecting the growing importance of domestic life among Chinatown's residents.

The immigration of Mandarin-speaking Chinese from North China and Taiwan in the 1950s and 1960s led to the formation of Peking-opera clubs in the 1960s. That decade also saw the forming of a number of instrumental music clubs, whose membership is of both South Chinese immigrants and young American-born Chinese. The participation of Chinese youths in instrumental music clubs and dance ensembles reflects the search for ethnic identity that has characterized American minority groups in general in recent decades. The 1970s saw the introduction of Western-style chamber orchestras and concert choral groups in Chinatown, all of which have been directed by professionally trained Chinese conductors. The emergence of these groups indicates both a significant acculturation to Western art music and a sense of ethnic unity, as these groups (with rare exceptions) have been strictly Chinese in their membership, and they have featured arrangements of Chinese music, together with a Western concert repertoire.

Today's Chinatown presents a wide spectrum of musical tastes and activities. Cantonese opera, which has permeated Chinatown's musical culture since the 1850s, is still the music most widely listened to and performed, through the activities of Cantonese-opera clubs, the opera-derived pieces that form part of the repertoire of the instrumental music clubs, the radio broadcasts and record sales of Cantonese opera, and—last but not least—the professional Cantonese opera itself, as it makes its appearances in San Francisco several times a year. Peking opera has recently become part of the picture as well, through the activities of music clubs devoted to that genre. Instrumental music from China is now rehearsed by a number of ensembles, some of whom focus on recent music from the People's Republic. The westernized popular music of Hong Kong is heard in several Chinatown ensembles, and Western choral, symphonic, and chamber music is now actively pursued by a number of Chinese performers. Added to this is the purely Western fare of the community's marching bands and drum-and-bugle corps and the music of Chinatown's churches.

Such a heterogeneity of musical styles reflects a society far more diverse in its tastes and social groupings than is generally apparent to the outside observer. Although Chinatown still has a majority of foreign-born Chinese whose language and culture patterns are strongly rooted in the Kwangtung homeland, today's community also contains a significant population which has become substantially acculturated to Western ways and yet seeks to maintain a Chinese identity. The growing strength of such interests was symbolized by the establishment of the Chinese Cultural Foundation in 1965, and it has been nourished in subsequent years by the foundation's sponsorship of concerts, musical instruction, and information programs on Chinese music. A factor that has already had an impact on musical activities in the community has been the recent improved relations with the People's Republic of China, a circumstance that has been reflected in an upsurge of interest in the music, drama, and dance of the People's Republic.

In overall perspective, one may see the history of Chinese music in San Francisco to fall into two rough phases: a "monocultural" phase from 1850 to about 1930, in which virtually all the music produced in the Chinese community was Chinese, originating in the homeland; and a "bicultural" phase, from about 1930 through the present, in which the cultivation of Western traditions has coexisted with the performance and appreciation of Chinese music. The coming of the second phase coincides with the first significant generation of American-born Chinese.

One could predict still another phase—a *Western* "monocultural" one—in the distant future, basing such a prediction on the Chinese becoming assimilated into American society to the extent that
Chinese music ceases to hold their interest at all. Such a degree of
assimilation is the case for many American Chinese today, and it
will doubtless be increasingly true for future generations of American-born Chinese. However, given the continuing influx of Chinese
immigrants and the trend in American-minority thinking away
from the single-minded goal of assimilation and the awakening interest in ethnic self-identification, such a phase appears unlikely
ever to be all-encompassing. The cultivation and appreciation of
Chinese music is of vital cultural interest to Chinatown's youth today, who view it not only as a cultural heritage to be preserved but
as a source of beauty, excitement, and creative challenge.

Selected Bibliography

Ames, J.W., "A Day in Chinatown," *Lippincott's Magazine* 16 (1875), pp. 498–501.

Atherton, Gertrude, *My San Francisco*, New York, Bobbs, Merrill Co., 1946.

Bancroft, Hubert Howe, *History of California*, 7 vols., San Francisco, The History Co., 1860–1890, vol. 7 (1890).

______, *Retrospections, Political and Personal*, New York, The Bancroft Co., 1912.

Banks, Charles E., and Opie Read, *The History of the San Francisco Disaster and Mount Vesuvius Horror*, Chicago, C.E. Thomas, 1906.

Benjamin, I.J., *Three Years in America, 1859–62*, Philadelphia, Jewish Publication Society of America, 1956.

Booth, Edwina, *Edwin Booth*, New York, The Century Co., 1902.

Borthwick, J.D., *3 Years in California*, Edinburgh, William Blackford and Sons, 1857; reprinted, Oakland, Calif., Biobooks, 1948.

Brewer, William Henry, *Up and down California in 1860–1864. The Journal of William H. Brewer, Professor of Agriculture in the Sheffield Scientific School from 1864–1903*, ed. Francis P. Farquhar, New Haven, Yale University Press, 1930.

Browne, Charles Farrar, ed., *Artemus Ward, His Travels*, London, Chatto and Windus, 1890.

Capron, E.S., *History of California from Its Discovery to the Present Time . . . with a Journal of the Voyage from New York, via Nicaragua, to San Francisco, and Back, via Panama*, Boston, John. P. Jewitt & Co., 1854.

Carey, Joseph, *By the Golden Gate: or San Francisco, the Queen City of the Pacific Coast; with Scenes and Incidents Characteristic of Its Life*, Albany, N.Y., The Albany Diocesan Press, 1902.

Cathay Music Club, *Cathay Chimes*, San Francisco, 1930.

"The Celestials at Home and Abroad," *Blackwell's Magazine* 72 (1852), pp. 98–113.

Chan, Eliza, "Oakland Concert Repeats in S.F.," *East-West*, 12 November 1975, p. 11.

Chester (pseud.), "Village Life in Old China," *East-West*, 26 March 1975, p. 6.

Chick Char Musical Club, *Memoir* (in Chinese), San Francisco, 1947.

" 'China Town' in San Francisco," *Cornhill Magazine* 54 (1886), pp. 50–59.

"Chinatown, My Chinatown," *Newsweek* 30 (1947), p. 24.

"Chinese Music: The Flying Dragon Musical Club Plays the Yung-kum, the Yea Woo, the Juong, and Pi-pa," *Life* 15 (1943), pp. 81–84.

"Chinese Theatres in San Francisco," *Harper's* 27 (1883), pp. 295–96.

Chinn, Thomas W., ed., *Historical Sketch Fiftieth Anniversary Chinese YMCA*, San Francisco, Young Men's Christian Association, 1961.

_______, H. Mark Lai, and Philip P. Choy, eds., *A History of the Chinese in California*, San Francisco, Chinese Historical Society of America, 1961.

Chu, Peter, Lois M. Foster, Nadia Larova, and Steven C. Moy, "Chinese Theatres in America," Washington, D.C., Bureau of Research, Federal Theatre Project (Division of the Works Progress Administration), Region of the West, 1936. Typescript, n.p. Carbon copy in Bancroft Library, University of California, Berkeley.

Clark, Franklin S., " 'Seats Down Front!': Since Women Have Appeared on the Chinese Stage, Chinatown's Theaters Are Booming," *Sunset* 54 (1925), pp. 33, 54.

Clark, Helen F., "The Chinese of New York Contrasted with Their Foreign Neighbors," *Century* 53 (1896), pp. 105–13.

Cleaveland, Daniel, letter to J. Ross Browne, U.S. Minister to China, 27 July 1868, in G.K. Fitch Papers, Bancroft Library, University of California, Berkeley.

Cone, Mary, *Two Years in California*, Chicago, S.C. Griggs & Co., 1876.

Coolidge, Mary Roberts, *Chinese Immigration*, New York, Henry Holt and Co., 1909.

Crissman, Lawrence W., "The Segmentary Structure of Urban Overseas Chinese Communities," *Man* 2 (1967), pp. 185–204.

Culin, Stewart, *The Gambling Games of the Chinese in America. Fán t'án: the Game of Repeatedly Spreading Out. And Pák kòp piú or, the Game of White Pigeon Ticket*, Philadelphia, University of Pennsyl-

vania Press, 1891. (Publication of the University of Pennsylvania
Series in Philology, Literature, and Archaeology, vol. 1, no. 4.)

Dall, Caroline H., *My First Holiday: or Letters Home from Colorado,
Utah, and California*, Boston, Roberts Bros., 1881.

Densmore, G.B., *The Chinese in California*, San Francisco, 1880.

Derbec, Etienne, *A French Journalist in the California Gold Rush: The
Letters of Etienne Derbec*, ed. A.P. Nasitir, Georgetown, Calif.,
Talisman Press, 1964.

Dillon, Richard H., *The Hatchet Men: The Story of the Tong Wars in San
Francisco*, New York, Coward-McCann, Inc., 1961.

Dobie, Charles Caldwell, *San Francisco's Chinatown*, New York, Appleton-Century, 1936.

______, *San Francisco: A Pageant*, New York, Appleton-Century, 1934.

Drury, Clifford, *San Francisco YMCA: 100 Years by the Golden Gate*,
Glendale, Calif., Arthur H. Clark Co., 1963.

Dubs, Homer H., and Robert S. Smith, "Chinese in Mexico City in 1635,"
Far Eastern Quarterly 1 (1942), pp. 387–89.

Dyer, Francis John, "Rebuilding Chinatown," *World Today* 8 (1905), p.
554.

Earle, Anitra, "Exquisite Peking Opera," San Francisco *Chronicle*, 28 December 1963.

Eddy, Frederick W., "In the Chinese Theatres," New York *Times*, 7 April
1901, p. 16.

Ernst, Alice Henson, *Trouping in the Oregon Country: A History of Frontier Theatre*, Portland, Oregon Historical Society, 1961.

Fan Hao, *History of Communication between China and the West* (*Chung
Hsi Chiao-tung Shih*), vol. 3, Taipei, 1955 (in Chinese).

Farwell, Willard B., *The Chinese at Home and Abroad*, San Francisco,
A.L. Bancroft, 1885.

Fenn, William Purviance, *Ah Sin and His Brethren in American Literature*,
Peking, College of Chinese Studies and California College in China,
1933.

Finck, Harry T., *The Pacific Coast Scenic Tour*, New York, Charles Scribner's Sons, 1890.

Fitch, George H., "In a Chinese Theatre," *Century* 24 (1884), pp. 27–44.

"Flappers of Chinatown," *New York Times Magazine*, 27 May 1923, p.
12.

Frankenstein, Alfred, "Flying Dragons and Sounds of Silver and Fine
Wood," *This World* (magazine section of the San Francisco *Chronicle*), 7 March 1943, p. 30.

______, "An Operatic Cycle of Cathay by Benefit of Symbols and Cym-
bals," San Francisco *Chronicle*, 19 January 1936.

"From the Orient Direct," *Atlantic Monthly* 24 (1869), pp. 542–48.

Frost, John, *History of the State of California, from the Period of the Conquest by Spain, to Her Occupation by the United States of America*, Auburn, N.Y., Derby and Miller, 1850.

Fu, Manchester, "Manny, Celestial," *East-West*, 12 August 1970, p. 6.

Gagey, Edward M., *The San Francisco Stage: A History*, New York, Columbia University Press, 1950.

Gibson, Otis, *The Chinese in America*, Cincinnati, Hitchcock & Walden, 1877.

Giles, Herbert Allen, "China: Literature," *Encyclopaedia Britannica*, 11th ed., 1910, vol. 6, p. 231.

Green, Mrs. E.M., "The Chinese Theater," *Overland Monthly* 41 (1903), pp. 118-25.

Griggs, Veta, *Chinaman's Chance: The Life Story of Elmer Wok Wai*, New York, Exposition Press, 1969.

Gross, Alexander, ed., *Famous Guide to San Francisco and the World's Fair*, New York, Geographia Map Co., 1939.

Hagan, R.H., "The Opera Season Opens in Chinatown," San Francisco *Chronicle*, 29 June 1957.

Haim, Herbert J., "Cathay Club of San Francisco," *Chinese Digest*, 20 March (p. 11), 27 March (p. 9), 3 April (p. 11), 10 April (p. 11) 1936.

Halson, Elizabeth, *Peking Opera*, Hong Kong, Oxford University Press, 1966.

Hansen, Gladys, ed., *San Francisco: The Bay and Its Cities*, rev. ed., originally compiled by the Federal Writers' Project of the Works Progress Administration for Northern California; New York, Hasting House Publishers, Inc., 1973.

Harrell, Max M., "Movements for Preservation of the Chinese Temple," *Butte County Historical Society Diggin's* 14 (1970), pp. 3-10.

Hauser, Miska, *Letters of Miska Hauser, 1853*, ed. Cornel Lengyel, New York, AMS Press, 1972. Originally published by the History of Music Project, Works Progress Administration, 1939.

Helms, Ludvig Verner, *Pioneering in the Far East, and Journeys to California in 1849 and to the White Sea in 1878*, London, W.H. Allen & Co., 1882.

Hill, Katherine, "Putting on Chinese Play at Mandarin," San Francisco *Chronicle*, 25 February 1934.

Hinchliff, Thomas Woodbine, *Over the Sea and Far Away, Being a Narrative of Wanderings around the World*, London, Longmans, Green, & Co., 1876.

Hittell, John S., *A Guide Book to San Francisco*, San Francisco, The Bancroft Co., 1883.

Hudson, G.F., *Europe and China*, London, 1931.

Hyde, Stuart W., "The Chinese Stereotype in American Melodrama," *California Historical Society Quarterly* 5 (1955), pp. 357-67.

Irwin, Will, "The Drama in Chinatown," *Everybody's Magazine* 20 (1909), pp. 857-69.

______, "The Drama that Was in Chinatown," *New York Times Book Review and Magazine*, 10 April 1921, pp. 3, 17.

Jackson, Helen Hunt, *Bits of Travel at Home*, Boston, Roberts Bros., 1893.

Jones, Idwal, "Cathay on the Coast," *American Mercury* 8 (1926), pp. 460-65.

______, "The Chinese Theater Advancing," San Francisco *Chronicle*, 25 December 1934, p. 20.

Keeler, Charles, *San Francisco and Thereabout*, San Francisco, California Promotion Committee, 1902.

Kirchhoff, Theodor, *Californische Kulturbilder*, Cassel, Theodor Fischer, 1886.

Lai, Him Mark, "Cantonese Music," *East-West*, 26 May 1971, p. 5.

______, and Philip P. Choy, *Outlines History of the Chinese in America*, San Francisco, Chinese-American Studies Planning Group, 1973.

Lai, Lim, "The Talking Machine Goes East," *East-West*, 8 January 1969, p. 7.

Langley, Henry G., *The San Francisco City Directory*, San Francisco, 1863 to 1868.

Lee, C.Y., *Days of the Tong Wars*, New York, Ballantine Books, 1974.

______, *Flower-Drum Song*, New York, Farrar, Straus and Cudahy, 1957.

Lee, Lim P., Albert Lim, and H.K. Wong, co-chairmen, *Report of the San Francisco Chinese Community Citizens' Survey and Fact Finding Committee*, San Francisco, H.J. Carle & Sons, 1969.

Lee, Rose Hum, *The Chinese in the United States of America*, Hong Kong, Hong Kong University Press, 1960.

Lengyel, Cornel, ed., *Music of the Gold Rush Era*, New York, AMS Press, 1972. Originally published by the History of Music Project, Works Progress Administration, 1939.

Leung, Chun-kin, "Notes on Cantonese Opera in North America," *CHINOPERL Papers* 7 (1977), pp. 9-21.

Leung, George Kin, "The Chinese Actress: Social and Dramatic Factors in Her Slow Rise to Fame," *Pacific Affairs* 4 (1931), pp. 394-407.

Liang, Tsai-ping, *Chinese Musical Instruments & Pictures*, Taipei, Chinese Classical Music Association, 1970.

Lloyd, Benjamin E., *Lights and Shades in San Francisco*, San Francisco, A.L. Bancroft & Co., 1876.

Loomis, A.W., "Chinese 'Funeral Baked Meats'," *Overland Monthly* 3 (1869), pp. 144-53.

______, "Holiday in the Chinese Quarter," *Overland Monthly* 2 (1869), pp. 144-53.

Lowe, Pardee, *Father and Glorious Descendant*, Boston, Little, Brown & Co., 1943.

Lyman, Stanford M., *Chinese Americans*, New York, Random House, 1974.

————, "Red Guard on Grant Avenue," *Trans-Action* 7 (1970), pp. 21–34. Reprinted in Stanley Sue and Nathaniel N. Wager, eds., *Asian-Americans: Psychological Perspectives*, Palo Alto, Calif., Science & Behavior Books, 1973, pp. 20–44.

M. E. C., "The New Chinatown of the Pacific," New York *Times*, 16 September 1906.

McDowell, Henry Burden, "The Chinese Theater," *Century* 29 (1884), pp. 27–44.

MacMinn, George R., *The Theater of the Golden Era in California*, Caldwell, Idaho, Caxton Printers, 1941.

McWilliams, Carey, *Factories in the Field*, Layton, Utah, Peregrine Smith Publishers, Inc., 1971. Originally published in 1935.

Marshall, Jim, "Cathay Hey-Hey," *Colliers* 109 (1942), pp. 13, 53.

Marshall, W.G., *Through America; Or, Nine Months in the United States*, London, Sampson Low, Marston, Searle & Rivington, 1882.

Masters, Frederic J., "The Chinese Drama," *Chautauquan* 21 (1895), pp. 434–42.

Moritz, Frederic A., "Chinese Opera for Americans," *Christian Science Monitor*, 21 March 1975.

Moy, Ernest K., ed., *The Pacific Coast Tour of Mei Lan-fang*, San Francisco, The Chinese Dramatic Club, 1930.

Nam Chung Musical Society, *Nam Chung* (in Chinese), San Francisco, 1945.

"Nee, Nee, Nee," *New Yorker* 28 (1952), pp. 29–30.

Nee, Victor G., and Brett de Bary Nee, *Longtime Californ': A Documentary Study of an American Chinatown*, New York, Pantheon Books, 1972.

Nettl, Bruno, ed., *Eight Urban Musical Cultures: Tradition and Change*, Urbana, University of Illinois Press, 1978.

Nordoff, Charles, *California: For Health, Pleasure and Residence*, New York, Harper & Bros., 1873.

Odell, George Clinton Densmore, *Annals of the New York Stage*, 15 vols., New York, Columbia University Press, 1927–49.

O'Flaherty, Terence, "The Golden Voice of Chinatown," *This World* (magazine section of San Francisco *Chronicle*), 11 May 1951, p. 31.

Palmer, Julius A., Jr., "Ah Ying and His Contemporaries," *Old and New* 2 (1870), pp. 692–97.

Pfeiffer, Ida, *A Lady's Visit to California*, Oakland, Calif., Biobooks, 1950. Reprinted from idem, *A Lady's Second Journey Round the*

World: from London to . . . California . . . , London, Longmans, Brown, Green, & Longmans, 1855; New York, Harper & Bros., 1856.

Pian, Rulan Chao, "China," *Harvard Dictionary of Music*, 2d ed., ed. Willi Apel, Cambridge, Mass., Harvard University Press, 1969, pp. 153–54.

Rae, W.F., *Westward by Rail*, London, Longmans, Green, and Co., 1870.

Reinhardt, Richard, *Out West on the Overland Train; Across the Continent Excursion with Leslie's Magazine in 1877, and the Overland Trip in 1967*, Palo Alto, Calif., American West Publishing Co., 1967.

Riddle, Ronald, "Music Clubs and Ensembles in San Francisco's Chinese Community," *Eight Urban Musical Cultures: Tradition and Change*, ed. Bruno Nettl, Urbana, University of Illinois Press, 1976, pp. 223–59.

Rodecape, Lois, "Celestial Drama in the Golden Hills: Chinese Theatre in California, 1849–1869," *California Historical Quarterly* 23 (1944), pp. 97–116.

Rosskam, Edwin, *San Francisco: West Coast Metropolis*, New York, Longmans, Green and Co., 1939.

Rusling, James F., *The Great West and Pacific Coast*, New York, Sheldon & Co., 1877.

Sala, George Augustus Henry, *America Revisited*, London, Vizetelly & Co., 1882.

Samson, Valerie, "The Phoenix Spring Ensemble," *EAR* 6:3 (1978), pp. 1–2.

Sandmeyer, Elmer C., *The Anti-Chinese Movement in California*, Urbana, University of Illinois Press, 1939.

San Francisco's Chinatown: An Aid to Tourists and Others in Visiting China Town, San Francisco, Portola Editions, 1909.

San Francisco Standard Guide, San Francisco, North American Press Association, 1913.

Saxton, Alexander, *The Indispensable Enemy: Labor and the Anti-Chinese Movement in California*, Berkeley, University of California Press, 1971.

Scott, A.C., *Mei Lan-fang*, Hong Kong, Hong Kong University Press, 1959.

Scott, Barbara E., "We Bow to Mei Lan-fang," *North American Review* 229 (1930), pp. 572–75.

Soulé, Frank, John H. Gihon, and James Nisbet, *The Annals of San Francisco*, New York, D. Appleton, 1855.

Sung, Betty Lee, *Mountain of Gold: The Story of the Chinese in America*, New York, Macmillan, 1967.

Taylor, Frank J., "San Francisco's New Chinese City," *Travel* 52 (1929), pp. 18–21, 54.

Tory, Alan, "A Visit Behind Scenes at the Chinese Theater," *This World* (magazine section of San Francisco *Chronicle*), 20 July 1952, p. 12.

Whitaker's Almanack, London, 1882.

Williams, Albert, *A Pioneer Pastorate and Times, Embodying Contemporary Local Transactions and Events*, San Francisco, Wallace & Hassett, 1879.

Wong, Jade Snow, *Fifth Chinese Daughter*, New York, Harper & Bros., 1945.

Wong, Ken, "The Orient Express," *East-West*, 9 August 1972, p. 3.

Wood, Ellen Rawson, "California and the Chinese: The First Decade," M.A. thesis, University of California, Berkeley, 1961.

Wood, Ruth Kedzie, *The Tourist's California*, New York, Dodd, Mead & Co., 1914.

Woon, Basil, *San Francisco and the Golden Empire*, New York, Harrison Smith and Robert Haas, 1935.

World Almanac, 1962, New York, New York World-Telegram Corporation, 1962.

Yang, C.K., *Religion in Chinese Society*, Berkeley, University of California Press, 1961.

Yee, Richard, "Staging a Chinese Opera," *California Living* (magazine section of San Francisco *Chronicle*), 24 February 1974, pp. 12–15.

Yung, Bell, "The Music of Cantonese Opera," Ph.D. dissertation, Harvard University, 1976.

————, "A Trip to Sok Gu Wan with a Cantonese Opera Troupe," *CHINOPERL Papers* 7 (1977), pp. 49–57.

Index

CPSIA information can be obtained
at www.ICGtesting.com
Printed in the USA
BVHW030124011220
594560BV00004B/21